Industrial Economics

Industrial Economics

An Applied Approach

W. Stewart Howe

First edition 1978
Reprinted 1978, 1982

Published by
THE MACMILLAN PRESS LTD
London and Basingstoke
Companies and representatives throughout the World

Typeset by
SANTYPE INTERNATIONAL LTD
(Coldtype Division)
Salisbury, Wiltshire

Printed and bound in Great Britain by
UNWIN BROTHERS LTD
The Gresham Press, Old Woking, Surrey

British Library Cataloguing in Publication Data

Howe, William Stewart
Industrial economics.
1. Microeconomics
I. Title
338.5 HB171.5

ISBN 0-333-21411-0
ISBN 0-333-21412-9 Pbk

for Kerrie

‘Political Economy . . . is an abstract science which labours under a special hardship. Those who are conversant with its abstractions are usually without a true contact with its facts; those who are in contact with its facts have usually little sympathy with and little cognisance of its abstractions . . . And so the “theory of business” leads a life of obstruction, because theorists do not see the business, and the men of business will not reason out the theories. Far from wondering that such a science is not completely perfect, we should rather wonder that it exists at all.’

Walter Bagehot, *Economic Studies*

Contents

Acknowledgements

A very pleasant part of the total work of writing a book is to acknowledge the help of others. The task is not difficult in comparison with other aspects of authorship; but it is salutarily humbling to realise one's debt to others in the context of what to many readers may otherwise appear a solo effort.

As with all labourers in this particular vineyard of economics, I owe a debt to all whose works I have read and whose writing and conversation has stimulated me. I am particularly grateful for the period of three years from 1969 to 1972 which I spent pursuing research in industrial economics under Professor Dennis Swann at Loughborough University.

As regards particular help with this text I am very happy to be able publicly to express my sincere thanks to Dundee College of Technology library for helping me to secure various material, and to other researchers in the field for access to unpublished papers and direction to lesser-known publications. A number of people kindly read various chapters of the book in draft form: Peter Maunder, Mike Fleming, and Keith Blois of Loughborough University, and Dr. Douglas Garbutt, my Head of Department. But for their help and constructive criticism there might have been further blemishes in the final product. They should not, however, be held responsible for any errors of analysis or fact which readers may discover. These really are mine alone.

Finally, some acknowledgements are due to the ladies. First, to my wife Kerrie for her patience and support during the writing of this book. Second, to our secretarial staff – Pat Sawers, Liz Middleton, Maggie Galloway and Anne Campbell – who, in addition to their other Faculty duties, have been responsible for the efficient progress of the text from uncertain pen and ink sketches to typed manuscript.

Dundee, 1977 W.S.H.

Introduction

The purpose of this text is to offer a survey of the world of industrial economics. Briefly, this is the world of the business firm – large or small: the enterprise as it is referred to in economic statistics. Industrial economics cannot exist within the broad discipline of economic analysis as a separate watertight compartment. But as a separate perspective within the area of microeconomics it exists apart from, but alongside, business finance and managerial economics. Chapter I is devoted to a more detailed enquiry into the scope, perspective and methodology of industrial economics.

Broadly, the course adopted in this text is to show the student the environment in which the modern business corporation operates, and to consider in more detail some of the most significant aspects of this world. Thus, Chapter I is followed by an analysis of the theory of the firm. This is an area of economics which has changed fairly rapidly over the past decade or so; and Chapter II deals in particular with the more recent developments in the theory of the firm along managerial and behavioural lines. In Chapters III and IV a more detailed treatment is given of the market structure, conduct and performance model which is the basis of an increasing number of industrial economics studies. Included in this treatment is some reference to the growing volume of statistical work in this area which is helping economists to develop some of the earlier purely *a priori* analysis.

The first three chapters deal with the environment of industrial economics at the more general level. As a contrast they are followed by four somewhat more specialist chapters on economic phenomena which are crucial to an understanding of the modern business firm. These are the tendency, on the one hand, for businesses to bring within one organisation a number of successive stages in the production of any commodity, and on the other hand the increasing desire for businesses to make more than one product –

indeed in some cases a range of quite diverse products. Chapter VII looks in some detail at why and how firms set about acquiring other businesses as a means of expanding output; while in Chapter VIII an analysis is offered of the relevant economic aspects of the pricing decision in business.

Finally an examination is made of the influence of the State in industrial economics. In other contexts – such as the provision of goods and services, or the location of industry – the U.K. economy is characterised by considerable government intervention. Likewise in the area of industrial economics few firms are free of some form of State control. Decisions on pricing methods, mergers, market dominance, or even entry into particular markets are all areas within which government policies impinge upon the private decision-taking of business.

Two points need to be made about the content of this text. First, some topics have had to be omitted: partly because of the space constraint, but more importantly because they have been dealt with satisfactorily in separate texts. These include the retail trade, and the role of the small firm in the economy. Second, some topics are dealt with here in a wider context and may thus appear either to have been omitted altogether or to have been given insufficient emphasis. These include cost conditions (including the extent of economies of scale), the role of research and development, and the quite new concept of X-efficiency. These have been dealt with in the context of market structure and (in the case of X-efficiency) the theory of the firm. Wherever possible U.K. data have been used throughout the text, and U.S. figures are only used where no U.K. data are available and there is reason to assume a close correspondence between the situation concerning a phenomenon on both sides of the Atlantic.

Finally, two points may be made. First, only a limited knowledge of formal economic analysis or of mathematics is required to understand the text. (This latter aspect will no doubt come as a relief to many readers; and indeed to the author also!) With regard to the former, students are assumed only to have a knowledge of basic supply and demand curves (including elasticities) and also to have a basic understanding of cost conditions.

Second, there may appear to some to be an excessive number of footnotes or references for a text of this level (first or second year undergraduate). The explanation for this is not academic pendantry, but a desire to allow the reader to follow up the references to the management and economics literature, i.e. to show that industrial economics is a living discipline; and also the need to emphasise the controversial nature of much of industrial economics, i.e. to remind the student that on a number of issues in this field there is no unique answer. In an obituary notice to him the story is told of the reaction of the late Professor P. W. S. Andrews to the news that the son of a friend of his was going up to a prestigious university to study economics. Andrews is said to have remarked rather sadly that the young man would not now be likely to be encouraged to read the really great books in economics. But without having read such texts – including Andrews' own *Manufacturing Business*, published in 1949 – no one can be said to be really educated in industrial economics. The reader is encouraged to use the references in this text to turn from the brief treatment of a number of issues to read some of the original books, and to discover for himself the painful origins from which some of the now fully accepted ideas in industrial economics sprang. This experience will undoubtedly lead to a greater understanding of the current conflicts in the field.

Chapter I

What is Industrial Economics?

Overview

The purpose of this chapter is to define the subject area of this text, to discuss the approach and methodology of industrial economics in dealing with these matters, and to highlight some of the major topics in the field.

A. Definition and Scope

When trying to define the scope of economics to first-year students I often find myself falling back upon suggesting that economics is, amongst other things, about what economists do. With no apology for tautology, then, we could at least begin by saying that industrial economics is about economic aspects of industry – of markets and firms. Thus 'the broad objective of industrial economics', it has been suggested, 'is the development of satisfactory explanations of the ways in which economic forces operate within the industrial sector'.[1] The more aggregated world of macroeconomics is, therefore, left behind (although no person studying industrial economics can afford to be ignorant of macroeconomic factors and their impact on the environment of the business world), and analysis in industrial economics is carried out within the general framework of microeconomics. But although traditional microeconomics and industrial economics have a common field of reference, a number of differences has arisen in the evolution of the latter subject which have resulted in its adoption of a rather separate approach to broadly the same issues.[2]

B. The Approach of Industrial Economics

Three features in particular distinguish the approach of industrial economics to the analysis of economic aspects of industry from that of microeconomics. First, microeconomics has traditionally been concerned with the establishment of an equilibrium position in the firm and in economic markets. Only in its later and more complex stages of development have the forces of disequilibrium and the possibility of independent action on the part of individual firms been examined. Firms have largely been treated as automata operating as the agents of 'market forces'. The analysis which established market equilibrium was particularly satisfactory when the conditions of 'perfect competition' in the market could be assumed to exist. However, the close correspondence between supply and demand forces at the industry and the firm level was destroyed by the recognition of downward-sloping demand curves for individual firms, and the possibility of persistent increasing returns to scale. The individual firm's supply curve could no longer be given by the marginal cost curve above average variable cost; the relationship between the slope and position of the firm's demand curve and that of the market as a whole became complex; and the concept of an equilibrium level of output for the individual business under production conditions of increasing returns to scale was made more difficult. It was the early empirical studies in what would now be called industrial economics which encouraged the revisions in microeconomic theory associated with Chamberlin and Robinson and at the institutional level by Berle and Means.[3] Yet even the new theoretical microeconomic writings were geared towards the analysis of equilibrium conditions for firms and markets, and not to the actual processes of adjustment themselves or an analysis of the business policy decisions involved. Nor was there any place in these theories for discretionary behaviour on the part of individual firms. The point of departure for industrial economics studies was to place much more emphasis on the behaviour of individual firms and markets along the dimensions of growth, concentration, merger and diversification.

A second difference between microeconomics and industrial economics lies in the level of detail of the analysis of business behaviour considered to be appropriate. The microeconomist seems to be happier with a more abstract 'model' of firm behaviour; the industrial economist conceives the need to know more of the institutional details of a situation before arriving at an explanation of the present conditions or putting forward recommendations for policy. The former, then, prefers the potentially quantitative rigour of a few variables; the latter may be frustrated at what 'would seem to be the penchant of economists to study essentially theoretical issues . . . rather than grappling with empirical matter or current policy issues'.[4] Thus, contrasting the perspectives of industrial organisation and microeconomic theory, Scherer emphasises

> 'They differ mainly in the richness of the independent variables they attempt to subsume, and in their concern for applying predictions and explanations to concrete real-world cases. The pure microeconomic theorist thrives on simplicity and rigor; he is happiest when he can strip his model to the barest few essential assumptions and variables. The industrial organization economist is more inclined toward explanations rich in both quantitative and institutional detail'.[5]

C. Methodology

The real cause of this second contrast lies, however, in the third and most important: the very real differences in methodology between the two approaches. The explanation is largely historical. Microeconomics stems from the so-called

English school of economic analysis which was established in the 19th and early 20th centuries. The basis of this school has been summarised as follows:

> 'It has been characterised by the acceptance of certain behavioural assumptions about individual consumers and firms, which were believed to be of widespread applicability, economic analysis taking the form of searching out the logical implications of these behaviour patterns when confronted by resource scarcity. This form of analysis readily lent itself to generalised theorising and the use of mathematical tools in relatively long and complex chains of reasoning. It also necessarily involved a high degree of abstraction from the events of the real world to enable this degree of generalisation to be achieved'.[6]

Industrial economics, by contrast, derived from the Historical and Institutional schools which had their origins in Germany and the United States. As a result of this background industrial economics inherited a tradition which placed considerable emphasis, in coming to an understanding of the economic behaviour of industry, upon empirical examination of the institutional framework, upon placing such findings in their historical context, and upon the importance of economic forces which bring about changes in existing institutional arrangements. The English school achieved its status, and enhanced the status of economics as a 'science', by virtue of its deductive powers; whereas industrial economics is largely an inductive discipline. It follows from this contrast that industrial economics stands out as being empirical rather than offering a great deal of scope for abstract theory.

But therein lies the problem for further development in industrial economics. Even those well disposed towards the discipline have recognised its 'tenuous and uneasy relationship with neo-classical, microeconomic theory';[7] and a stern warning has come from one eminent industrial economist that 'Industrial economics only too frequently is treated as a descriptive, institutional, even anti-theoretical discipline to which the lesser able and the under-motivated students of economics are directed as a substitute for a vocational course in business studies'.[8]

A former President of the Royal Economic Society, recognising that to many people business economists, among others, were working 'in what, considered academically, is a twilight of near-economics' offered a social explanation for the apparently low status of industrial economics and its failure to develop a *modus operandi* of its own.

> 'In every science the ascending scale of intellectual status tends to be one of rarification: the more abstract, the more rigorous, the more general, so much the more distinguished. This is natural, because distinction is conferred by rarity, and few of us are capable of soaring into the empyrean of abstraction, whereas there is a saying that no man is so short that his feet do not touch the ground. In economics at least those who devote themselves to the direct observation of attitudes and behaviour have commonly been regarded as playing in the 2nd XI. I have heard them called the hewers of wood and drawers of water'.[9]

It has never been felt, however, by those working in industrial economics that their task was solely to describe what 'is' is the area of their enquiry, or to offer a large amount of institutional detail for its own sake. Thus Professor P. W. S. Andrews, writing at the time of the beginnings of industrial economics as a separate approach, and recognising that a real understanding of price formation and business behaviour in general would only come from 'empirical work on actual businesses', nonetheless went on to stress the purpose of such empirical work.

> 'To get the theory we need we cannot continue to tinker "realistically" with what was originally a derivative of theorising at a difficult level (i.e. microeconomic market analysis). We need to approach the matter in a more truly scientific manner. *If we wish to theorise fruitfully about individual businesses, we must find out what are the facts of their behaviour and then construct a general theory especially in order to take account of these facts.*'[10] (Emphasis added.)

This point was emphasised a decade later by Professor P. Sargent Florence when he pointed out that in taking a 'realistic' approach in analysing the behaviour of firms he implied 'an approach based on observation and records of real facts, *but proceeding beyond mere description and empiricism to comprehensive measurement and causal interpretation and a hunt for some possible underlying logic*'.[11] (Emphasis added.) Once again – and in the context of a path-breaking empirical study of business behaviour – the need for a combination of a sound theoretical base and the collection of accurate data has been stressed.

> 'It is essential to combine economic facts and economic theory, first for the purpose of testing theoretical relationships between economic variables, secondly for estimating the form and the parameters of such relationships, and thirdly for predicting the future behaviour of the dependent economic variables. Such a combination is also useful for a fourth purpose – the specification of new economic theories.'[12]

Even here, however, there is a gap between the work of some industrial economists seeking an 'explanation' for certain behaviour or analysing the 'effects' of, for example, a particular piece of legislation affecting business conduct, and those who operate within a more narrowly defined framework of positive economics. Perhaps the most powerful statement of the latter case has come from the Chicago economist Milton Friedman. His view is that the task of positive economics is 'to provide a system of generalisations that can be used to make correct predictions about the consequences of any change in circumstances', and that 'the only relevant test of the *validity* of a hypothesis is comparison of its predictions with experience'.[13] Friedman's view is that the value of a theory in industrial economics as elsewhere lies in its predictive validity. What is important about such a theory are the implications which it throws up for certain courses of action. What *assumptions* the theory embodies, and how 'realistic' these are in comparison with real events are not criteria by which any theory in positive economics should be judged.

There are, however, a number of problems thrown up by this approach – some of which are recognised by Friedman himself. One of these is that two quite different 'theories' may predict the same outcome under certain circumstances, so that the observation of that particular behaviour may be consistent with either theory. For example, at a simple level, both profit maximisation and sales revenue maximisation as business goals involve no change in the level of optimum output level given an increase in *fixed* costs.[14] Such behaviour is consistent, therefore, with either theory; and the proof of the correctness of one or other of the hypotheses would involve their being tested under other circumstances. A second misgiving of some in this area concerns the use, or abuse, of correlation analysis. Correlation (multiple or single variable) is merely a statistical tool which measures the degree of association between changes in two or more variables; and it may be concluded that a certain proportion of the observed change in one variable (the dependent) may be accounted for by changes in the independent variable(s). Again at a simple level, profitability is a common dependent variable in correlation analysis; and associated independent variables may be firm size, market concentration, or rate of growth or acquisition activity over a preceding period of time. Now while the correlation coefficient may be a useful statistical weapon, its use is also open to potential danger. Thus, speaking of the craze for correlation analysis in the U.S., the Chicago economist Viner depicted those who 'began correlating furiously and indiscriminately and with an inverse correlation between zeal and discretion which . . . approached . . . perfection'.[15] Too many people fail to resist the temptation of assuming that correlation presumes a *causal* relationship; and the question of the *direction* of the causal relationship is again often approached in a superficial manner. To go back to the instance cited above. For example, if it could be established that large firms, or firms in concentrated markets, achieved significantly higher levels of profitability than smaller firms or firms in unconcentrated sectors, could we conclude that size or concentration *bring about* increased profits? Or, to take a slightly more complex set of circumstances, if a statistical relationship were established between the degree of concentration in a market and the level of advertising and promotional expenditure, would we conclude that the advertising created a patronage barrier to the entry of new firms and so created (or at least preserved) the existence of an oligopoly group, or that the high level of advertising expenditure was the *outcome* of oligopoly and the avoidance of direct price competition, with associated product differentiation? As a final example, a relationship which has generated a considerable volume of academic discussion is that between firm size or market concentration and technological progress. The problem is, firstly, that on purely *a priori* grounds it is possible to argue that *either* small firms and unconcentrated markets[16] *or* large, oligopolistic firms[17] are more conducive to technological progress. Secondly, there are enormous problems of definition and identification involved in measuring 'technological progress'. Finally, even when a statistical relationship (usually a correlation coefficient between two or more variables) has been established associating company size or industry concentration with technological advance, can one necessarily claim that the latter is a product of either of the two former conditions? It may also be the case that the increasing costs of research and development exclude small firms from participating in this activity, that this trend encourages merger activity, with the result that we could claim that technological advance encourages oligopoly, and not *vice versa* as could be suggested from similar data.

A final issue here is that there may be circumstances in which for public policy reasons it is necessary to have an 'explanation' for certain behaviour rather than a set of variables with a good record of predictive performance. In these cases more detailed, qualitative empirical research is necessary, and the realism of the hypothesis is of considerable importance.

Industrial economics, therefore, differs in its approach, scope and methodology from both other broad areas of economics and its ancestor microeconomics. Whether one approach or another is appropriate to a particular issue probably depends greatly upon the question one is asking and upon the purpose to which the answer is going to be applied. Not only may the answers in industrial economics be less precise than in the case of microeconomic analysis, but the industrial economist may find himself agreeing with Professor Shackle that 'clear and definite questions cannot be asked about a vague, richly detailed, fluid and living world'.[18]

D. In Conclusion

To many people the study of industrial economics may be unsatisfying. Even to the most enthusiastic there are moments of frustration! Few of the data required are available in an ideal form: it was not until the 1967 Companies Act that limited companies were obliged to publish their annual turnover figures. Many of the data used by industrial economists were neither collected nor published with their use of them in mind. Classifications of such data may not suit our purpose: the Census of Production data fall into this category through using a definition of industry based upon common technology or inputs in contrast to the economist's concept of a market as a chain of substitute products measured by reference to price cross elasticities. The industrial economist has to accept these difficulties as part of the price to be paid for working in a field characterised by rapid institutional change, and where analysis, to be meaningful, has to be based upon what is actually happening in the business world.

What this text is concerned to do is to indicate a framework within which the issues raised in this field may be systematically studied. What is offered is a group of techniques which will allow us to study and understand the behaviour of business firms in their markets.

References

1. P. J. Devine, R. H. Jones, N. Lee and W. J. Tyson, *An Introduction to Industrial Economics*, Allen and Unwin, London, (1974), p. 23
2. See R. T. Nelson, An Outline of Industrial Economics, *Economics*, Vol. X, (1974), 211–26
3. One of the early studies which still deserves reading today is A. A. Berle and G. C. Means, *The Modern Corporation and Private Property*, Harcourt, Brace and World, New York (1932), rev. ed. (1967)

4. W. P. J. Maunder, U.K. Competition Policy Legislation: The Sanitary Ware Industry as a Case Study, *Business Education Review*, Vol. I, (1974), 23
5. F. M. Scherer, *Industrial Market Structure and Economic Performance*, Rand McNally, Chicago (1970), p. 2
6. P. J. Devine *et al.*, Ref. 1, p. 14
7. *Ibid.*, p. 7
8. C. K. Rowley in the preface to his *Readings in Industrial Economics*, Vol. II, Macmillan, London (1972)
9. E. H. Phelps Brown, The Underdevelopment of Economics, *Economic Journal*, Vol. LXXXII (1972), 2 and 9
10. P. W. S. Andrews, Industrial Economics as a Specialist Subject, *Journal of Industrial Economics*, Vol. I (1952), 75
11. P. S. Florence, *Economics and Sociology of Industry: A Realistic Analysis of Development*, C. A. Watts, London, Preface (1964)
12. P. E. Hart, *Studies in Profit, Business Saving and Investment in the United Kingdom, 1920–1962*, Allen and Unwin, London (1965), pp. 12–13
13. M. Friedman, *Essays in Positive Economics*, University of Chicago Press, Chicago (1953) pp. 4 and 8–9
14. In this case the turning point of the total revenue function is not affected (i.e. the point where marginal revenue is zero and so total revenue is maximised). Likewise the gradient of the total cost curve at any level of output is unaffected, so that the profit-maximising level of output where the gradients of the total cost and total revenue curves are equal (i.e. MC = MR) is unchanged
15. Quoted in D. P. O'Brien, *Whither Economics?*, Durham University, Durham (1974), p. 9
16. See J. Jewkes, D. Sawers and R. Stillerman, *The Sources of Invention*, Macmillan, London, 2nd ed. (1969)
17. See J. K. Galbraith, *American Capitalism: The Concept of Countervailing Power*, Hamish Hamilton, Boston (1952), Ch. VII
18. G. L. S. Shackle, *The Years of High Theory*, CUP, Cambridge (1967), p. 47

Chapter II

Theory of the Firm

Overview

This chapter is divided into four sections. In the first we consider the meaning and scope of theories of the firm, and the role of a theory of the firm in economic analysis. The second section highlights the principal difficulties involved in formulating theories of the firm at the present time. In the third, and principal, section a review is offered of some of the newer managerial and behavioural theories of the firm, and a contrast is drawn between these and what is regarded as the neo-classical theory of the firm. The final section offers some conclusions on what has gone before, and suggestions as to the direction of future developments.

A. Theory of the Firm

The theory of the firm is a vast area of economics dealing with almost every aspect of the behaviour of firms in their markets. As such it is concerned with trying to throw light on why businesses act in particular ways: why they merge, diversify, etc.; how particular market structures come about – how barriers to entry arise and their impact upon business behaviour; and how efficient management strives to be – whether or not new forms of business have blunted management's enthusiasm for earning maximum profits.

The discipline of economics has always had some broad concept of a business firm, if only to act as an agent in determining market prices and outputs in the theory of value. The role of the firm in traditional economic analysis can be gauged from the following summary:

> 'The firm in the theory of the firm has no precise legal or organizational significance: it is an abstraction, an idealized business form, a rational but bloodless entity which exists for the purely economic purpose of satisfying a want by providing a good or service at a price. This firm is assumed to operate in a given environment and normally makes only one product. The dominant, indeed the sole, motive guiding its operations from the theoretical point of view is the desire to maximize profit, or minimize loss. It is taken to have full knowledge of its costs on the basis of their relevance to pricing decisions in the long and the short run. It is also assumed to know the critical portion of the demand schedule for its product, which shows the prices that consumers are ready to pay for different quantities of the good. . . .
>
> The theory has been exposed to considerable criticism, but despite this, and the lack of unanimity on its content, it retains a central place in orthodox economic doctrine. If it were to be cast out it would leave a void which no alternative theory can at present satisfactorily fill, and it continues to appeal to many people on this score and on two other important counts as well. These are, first, that the theory is susceptible of very sophisticated treatment while also being suitable for presentation in a basically simple, yet logically satisfying, way; and, second, that given the assumptions on which it rests the theory is a tool for predicting the precise outcome of a particular course of action in specified conditions, which makes it attractive to those who assert that economics is a positive science.'[1]

However, a continuing reassessment of the relative merits of logical sophistication and the need to reflect the reality of the business world has created a powerful voice in favour of recasting the theory of the firm in a more 'institutional' mould. It is the diverse form of these revisions which makes a study of the theory of the firm such a rewarding experience at the present time.

In order to limit our discussion to reasonable proportions we must define more closely our view of the extent of the theory of the firm. The possible extent of the topic may be gained from the following:

> 'A survey of the literature reveals that "theory of the firm" has been used in four different ways. First of all, it can mean an analysis of how objectives are determined in a business organisation. Because great stress is laid in this kind of analysis on the organisational aspects of business and the hierarchical relationships that exist within business, this approach is also known as the *organisational* or *behavioural approach* to the theory of the firm. Secondly, one may refer to the development of techniques that are used by business in an attempt to achieve particular objectives. Examples of such techniques are decision theory, operational research, and programming. Thirdly, "theory of the firm" may describe the analysis of the reaction of firms to changes in their environment. Finally, it can also be understood to mean a combination of the approaches to firms' behaviour just described.'[2]

The discussion in this text is limited to the first and third of these four aspects of the theory of the firm. No attempt is made to assess the quantitative techniques which may be used by businesses to achieve the corporate objectives which we discuss. We shall, however, have occasion to refer to the impact upon business behaviour of the knowledge (or lack of knowledge) of these techniques on the part of business managers; and this discussion will extend to the availability or otherwise of the information necessary for the use of such techniques.

In order to understand why, how and on what basis firms in the contemporary economy operate we must have some clear idea of the forces which motivate firms, and of the resulting corporate goals. Only then can we set about explaining the existing behaviour of firms or predicting future conduct. It will also be necessary in this context to bear in mind the conditions relating to market structure (seller and buyer concentration, product substitutability and entry conditions), and cost and demand conditions. As a starting point we should consider the main groups which may be in a position to influence the goals of the firm, and the aims which each of these groups may have.

Influence group	Possible goals
Shareholders:	
private	profit maximisation – long- or short-term, capital appreciation
institutional	earnings stability, capital appreciation
Management	maximisation of managerial objective function
Employees	increased (real) wage income, stability of employment

From a fuller consideration of these goals it is possible to draw up a list of corporate objectives. It may be noted that many of these cannot be defined in operational terms, and that a number of the goals may be in conflict with each other. When we come to examine individual theories of the firm we shall find that at some stage or another all of these goals have been associated with corporate behaviour.

Corporate goals
Profit maximisation: long- or short-term
Capital appreciation on equity investment
Earnings (or dividend) stability
Sales maximisation
Corporate growth maximisation
Market share maximisation
Price stability
Output stability
Multiple goals
'Satisficing' goals
Ethical corporate goals

It is only from a recognition of corporate goals that we can move on to an understanding of the behaviour of the modern business firm. *It is the understanding of this behaviour which is the contribution of the theory of the firm to economic analysis*. Unless we have this understanding then we may class as 'irrational' a large part of contemporary management behaviour and corporate policy: for example, on business growth and diversification. We may also fail to understand how *macroeconomic* policies operate in practice if we assume, for example, that businesses seek to maximise profits and not sales revenue. The appropriateness or otherwise of such assumptions may significantly alter the result of certain tax policies.

B. Methodological Difficulties

There are three characteristics of this area of economic enquiry which peculiarly add to other difficulties. These are the changing nature of our principal object of enquiry – the business firm; the increasing need to make use of other behavioural disciplines in this enquiry; and the wider question of the appropriate method of study – including the use of statistical analysis.

(*a*) *The business firm in economics*

The business firm is a changing organisation. As rapidly as the analytical techniques available to economics for studying the firm are developed (for example, increased mathematical expertise, or improved methods of data processing such as computers) the firm itself changes its form, and analysis has in some respects to begin again at Square One. This change in corporate form is most obvious with respect to the *size* of the typical modern business, and the *position of the salaried management vis-à-vis* the shareholders. The former characteristic has also obviously helped to bring about significant changes in the structural characteristics of most product markets: for example, the predominance of oligopoly as a market form. The pace of these changes has meant the increased need to recognise the scope for a significant updating of the theory of the firm. Indeed, as one more recent author has pointed out, 'it would be doing Adam Smith an injustice to imagine that he would not have wanted to think again when confronted with I.C.I. and General Motors'.[3] Galbraith has particularly emphasised with reference to this area that 'the shortcomings of economics are not original error but uncorrected obsolescence'.[4]

In many respects the history of the development of the theory of the firm as a body of economic knowledge is that of a theory constantly having to change in order to accommodate itself to reality. It is possible, for instance, to trace a number of revisions of the theory of the firm to changes in firm size and market structure, and to the changed composition and power of equity shareholders. For example, with the increased popularity and acceptability of limited liability as a corporate form at the end of the last century, the possibility arose of a permanent business firm which would outlive and have a separate existence from its entrepreneurial founder. That this development was appreciated by contemporary observers may be gathered from the changes which Alfred Marshall made in the various editions of his *Principles of Economics*. In drawing his analogy between the trees in the forest and the birth, growth and inevitable decline of the typical business firm Marshall concluded in each edition up to and including the 5th (1907):

> 'And as with the growth of trees, so it is with the growth of businesses. As each kind of tree has its normal life in which it attains its normal height, so the length of life during which a business of any kind is likely to retain its full vigour is limited by the laws of nature combined with the circumstances of place and time, and the character and stage of development of the particular trade in which it lies.'

In the 6th edition (1910), however, this was changed to:

> 'And as with the growth of trees, so it *was* with the growth of businesses as a general rule *before the great recent*

> *development of vast joint-stock companies* which often stagnate but do not readily die.'[5]

The growth of large firms and increased market concentration has been of even more significance in causing revisions of theories of the firm.[6] Large firms, exempt from the traditional discipline of the market place, have more freedom to pursue goals other than profit maximisation. It is this freedom and the use made of it which is at the core of some managerial theories of the firm.

These changes in firm size and market structure outlined briefly above were accompanied by a growing loss of power of control over the business on the part of its legal owners – the equity shareholders. This control, it was contended, had passed into the hands of the salaried management; and this trend had been analysed in respect of the U.S. by the 1930s.[7] There was thus born an accepted divorce between ownership and control in the large business firm. It has always been assumed that the shareholders would want their business to achieve maximum profitability, and that it is their impotence *vis-à-vis* salaried management which has led to profit maximisation being sacrificed to the satisfaction of managerial corporate objectives. There are, however, doubts as to whether the average shareholder of today is avidly concerned with maximising his dividend income – at least in the short term. For most personal equity shareholders dividend income is not likely to be a large proportion of their total earnings. These people are likely to have a well-distributed portfolio of shares from which they expect to derive a regular income and some capital appreciation. Current dividend maximisation is thus an imperfect approximation of their objective. For some, and this was surely especially true for those shareholders with high marginal rates of personal taxation and prior to the introduction of a long-term Capital Gains Tax in 1965, capital appreciation may have been preferable to high distributions. We cannot conclude, therefore, that personal shareholders will stimulate businesses to unqualified short-run profit maximisation. A further point to note (see table I below) is the growth in importance of the institutional shareholder. Again there are no grounds for supposing that insurance companies, pension funds, etc., invest for profit maximisation. Dividend stability and regular modest capital gain are more likely to be their objectives.

TABLE I

*Beneficial Owners of Ordinary Shares in the U.K.**

Category of owner	Percentages 1957	1963	1970	1973
Persons, executors and trustees	65.8	54.0	47.4	42.0
Insurance	8.8	10.0	12.2	16.2
Pension funds	3.4	6.4	9.0	12.2
Investment trusts	5.2	7.4	7.6	6.5
Unit trusts	0.5	1.3	2.9	3.4
Banks	0.9	1.3	1.7	3.3
Stock Exchange	0.9	1.4	1.4	..
Other finance	1.6	2.6	1.1	..
Non-profit	1.9	2.1	2.1	4.4
Non-financial companies	2.7	5.1	5.4	4.3
Public sector	3.9	1.5	2.6	2.5
Overseas	4.4	7.0	6.6	5.2

* Beneficial owners are different from registered holders because the latter contain a large number of nominees and trustees who hold shares on behalf of persons and companies.

Source: J. Moyle, *The Pattern of Ordinary Share Ownership 1957–1970* (Cambridge, 1971) p. 18. 1973 data (not strictly comparable with earlier years) taken from *Royal Commission on the Distribution of Income & Wealth* Report No. 2 (H.M.S.O., Cmnd. 6172, 1975), Tables 1 and 6.

Having commented upon the goals of personal and institutional investors, we must ask how far those in control of businesses are likely to follow a path of profit maximisation. The point is that, certain notable exceptions apart, shareholders are in no position to take part in management. These exceptions would include Mr. Maxwell Joseph in Grand Metropolitan Hotels, Sir John Cohen and his two sons-in-law in Tesco Stores, the Burton, Showering and Wolfson families respectively in Montague Burton, Allied Breweries and G.U.S.. the Clark brothers in Plessey, and Mr. Garfield

Weston in Asssociated British Foods.[8] In most cases, however, corporate controllers do not own the business concerned (i.e. they are not significant shareholders), and the owners exert their control only to a minimal extent. The more typical situation in the U.K. can be seen in terms of the data in table II.

TABLE II

Nominal Value of Average Director's Holdings in 6 U.K. Companies with Assets of Over £120m in 1971

Company	Assets (£m)	Ordinary share capital (£m)	Ordinary shares held by board (%)	Nominal value of average director's holding (£)	Market value of average director's holding (£)
Unilever	825.8	45.8	0.01	216	1,565
Imperial Tobacco	400.2	141.9	0.04	3,400	14,864
Courtaulds	231.4	67.4	0.16	8,508	53,308
British American Tobacco	576.1	59.4	0.01	461	5,996
Imperial Chemical Industries	974.5	468.7	0.02	4,500	11,665
Dunlop Holdings	128.5	48.0	0.04	1,074	5,981

Source: J. R. Wildsmith, *Managerial Theories of the Firm* (London, 1973) p. 4.

A recent survey relating to attendance at the 1969 A.G.M.'s of 49 companies drawn from the top 200 U.K. businesses found that the average attendance was 26 shareholders per 10,000 on the register (0.26%), that seldom is more than 1% of the equity capital represented at the meeting, and that the average length of meeting was 23 minutes.[9] It is small wonder that the author felt that more attention should be devoted to this 'procedural facade of company control, which is hallowed more by tradition than by use and effectiveness'.[10]

Without unduly anticipating subsequent analysis it may not be out of place to highlight some of the implications of what we have said in this sub-section. The two phenomena discussed above are normally found together: the largest companies tend to be most characterised by the divorce between control and ownership. Moreover the effect upon business behaviour of these two phenomena is reinforcing. This aspect has been particularly emphasised by Monsen and Downs.[11] These authors – whose central theme is that 'the behaviour of each firm with respect to profits depends upon certain elements of its internal structure' – point out that the tendency of firms to maximise profits will be reduced as management is taken out of the hands of owners. Top management, Monsen and Downs suggest, act to maximise their own lifetime incomes: 'income' being taken to include all aspects of managerial utility, such as corporate sales or asset growth. In this situation shareholders are normally in a poor position to assess management performance, and thus become satisficers rather than maximisers with regard to corporate performance as a result of reduced capability rather than intention. Increased firm size is considered to reduce the likelihood of profit maximisation in the context of technical inefficiency (e.g. loss of control and co-ordination), and divergence of goals both between management and owners, and *within* the total management structure. This would lead one to conclude that even if a firm is owner managed (in the sense of top management comprising large shareholders), if the business is large, profit maximisation is unlikely to be achieved. Thus,

> 'even if we agreed with traditional theory that the owners of a firm wish to maximize profits, we would contend that the difference between *owner* motivation and *managerial* motivation (even in the case of firms which are in the accepted sense owner-controlled) will cause systematic deviations from profit maximizing behaviour as long as the firm is large enough so that the owners themselves cannot supervise all facets of its activities.'[12]

(*b*) *A multidisciplinary approach?*

A further point which is now being recognised is that economic analysis alone cannot fully explain the workings of modern business even in terms of a firm's 'economic' behaviour. This need for the use of other behavioural disciplines in developing a theory of the firm which is to have any value for economic analysis has increased with both the growing complexity of market relationships under conditions of oligopoly and the increasing complexity of business forms such as multinational conglomerates. As long ago as 1947 K. W. Rothschild ventured to suggest that a study of the technique of operation of Alexander the Great rather than of the technique of analysis of Adam Smith might lead to a greater understanding of the workings of oligopoly.[13] More recently other behavioural disciplines have offered to come to the aid of economics in this area.

> 'All those matters that from the aspect of pure economics were seen as interference, friction, extra-economic factors, data, special problems and exceptions may from the sociological point of view acquire systematic relevance. Thus it is rather interesting to note that *especially in the case of oligopoly, where the social phenomenon of competition was brought out even by the theorists of the neo-classical tradition*, the confines of purely economic, static thinking are most clearly and visibly exploded, thereby evoking strong doubts about the usability of the neo-classical concept. *All that is most essential to a sociological interpretation of the economic complex comes most conspicuously to the fore in an analysis of the problem of oligopoly*: we realize that a purely decision-logical treatment in the old style cannot get us anywhere; that any claim to methodological autonomy must remain most questionable; that in the face of conspicuous analogies in other sectors of social life (e.g. in political and military fields) any pretence to logical autonomy must fall; and that finally, as no closed domain of economics can be constituted in fact, theoretical autonomy cannot justifiably be proclaimed if we aim truly at an explanation of market phenomena.'[14] (Emphasis added.)

We shall find as we progress further in this area that there can be no pure economic theory of oligopoly, and that phenomena such as price leadership and other competitive or uncompetitive practices cannot be fully 'explained' by economic analysis alone. Similar reservations have been voiced regarding the analysis of management behaviour within complex business organisations.

> 'The conglomerate issue arises in large measure, however, out of the alleged inadequacies of the theory of the firm as a basis for public policy toward conglomerate enterprise. The modern corporation, and especially the modern conglomerate, is far too complex an organization to be cast in the procrustean mold of marginal revenue-marginal cost nexuses. The utility surfaces, or horizons, to which corporate management react are in large measure shaped by long-range strategic considerations, at least some of which are divorced from the interests of those who in legal theory represent ownership, i.e. the stockholders.'[15]

We have really implied the need for two developments in the future for the theory of the firm: the need for more work at the institutional level, and the recognition of the value of the potential contribution of other disciplines. The one development cannot come without the other. The more we investigate in detail the behaviour of individual markets and firms the more we should realise the limitations of trying to understand and interpret the encountered behaviour in terms of traditional economic analysis. Is it any wonder that a president of the Royal Economic Society should have emphasised that the need for a greater accommodation of empirical material concerning traditionally 'economic' phenomena 'implies the removal of the traditional boundary between the subject-matters of economics and other social sciences'?[16]

(*c*) *Realism and the theory of the firm*

One of the main criticisms which students make of the theory of the firm – and it is at times as much a questioning of the need for studying the theory at all as a criticism simply of that theory's methodology – is that the theory is 'unreal'. The assumption of profit maximisation as the single goal of corporate behaviour, the use of Marshall's 'trees in the forest' analogy of the growth and decline of business firms, and the comparative failure in many cases to discuss or explain the existence of conglomerate or multi-national businesses have bred a certain disillusionment among students. To some students, on the other hand, it must seem that the theory of the firm is merely an arena for more or less acrimonious academic discussion and pedantic argumentation. Thus, while one author, discussing the current model of oligopoly and its assumptions regarding firm's conjectural variations and reaction functions, has concluded that 'not to put too fine a point on it, the model works only if firms are run by mental defectives',[17] and J. K. Galbraith has pointed out that 'the theory of the firm makes little distinction between a Wisconsin dairy farm and General Motors Corporation except to the extent that the latter may be thought more likely to have some of the technical aspects of monopoly';[18] it has had to be pointed out that 'in fact, one writer or another has questioned the methodological relevance, the factual premises, or the theoretical utility of virtually all of the proposed revisions',[19] and that 'there is not enough evidence as yet to draw any definite conclusions about the relative merits of any of the alternative theories'.[20]

The principal counterargument to these criticisms of the lack of 'realism' in the theory of firm is that the theory is not supposed to be 'realistic' in the narrow sense with regard to its descriptive content or detailed assumptions. Thus, speaking of the use of economic models in the theory of the firm one author highlights two possible approaches.

> 'Some of the tests made on these models were direct in the sense of actually observing firms and businessmen in action over a period of time, and then comparing their behaviour and expressed motives to those assumed by the theory. Other tests involved a comparison of the predictions made by these models with respect to prices, output, profits, etc., and the actual behaviour of firms. Economists in general tend to prefer the second type of test, because, *even if the assumptions underlying a theory might be very general, as long as the theory predicts accurately then the simplicity of the assumptions does not matter.* This, however, is a somewhat dangerous approach to the empirical testing of propositions because we are not provided

with a plausible explanation of why firms behave in a particular way.'[21] (Emphasis added.)

This last difficulty poses problems so long as two theories (each embodying different assumptions) each correctly predict the outcome in terms of business behaviour (e.g. changes in price or output) of a change in a firm's environment (e.g. an increase in the rate of V.A.T.). Despite this problem, however, predictive reliability remains the principal criterion of the usefulness of theories of the firm. Thus:

> 'To criticise the validity of the assumptions of a model, although easy enough, is a futile undertaking: it is in the very nature of a model that it requires abstraction and simplification! Clearly a more interesting question to ask is whether with the aid of a model we can predict correctly how a firm will react, in terms of the choice of its strategic variables such as price, output, advertising, staff expenditure, etc., when experiencing a change in, for example, profits taxation . . .
>
> The reader is warned that for the validation of our models of business behaviour it is not necessary that businessmen actually and literally use the models we develop when reaching their decisions. The economic agents whose behaviour we want to explain may behave in the way our models predict without consciously using any model. Clearly, such models would still be useful.'[22]

The latter part of this last quotation raises a further criticism of the theory of the firm. If business men do not understand marginal analysis, can a theory of the firm be said to be realistic if it is based upon such analysis? Again some theorists would argue that it is not necessary for managers to understand the 'theory' of profit maximisation (i.e. that the level of output should be determined by marginal cost and revenue calculations) in order to be said to be profit maximisers. Quite apart from the reply that many managers probably now do have a knowledge of the appropriate economic concepts, those who defend traditional theory – or the need for any theory – would argue along the lines of

Machlup's 'theory of overtaking'.[23] Few motorists wishing to overtake a heavy lorry but faced with an oncoming vehicle have a knowledge of their own speed and potential acceleration, the existing speed and likely reaction of the other vehicles involved, or the distances initially separating the vehicles. And yet bearing in mind the road conditions and other possible hazards such as the entry upon the scene of a fourth vehicle, the average motorist will decide whether or not to overtake the lorry without much hesitation. The 'theory' of such a situation probably never enters our motorist's head.

There is, however, one fundamental criticism of the theory of the firm which Machlup's telling analogy raises. We may accept that business men strive to maximise profits (or any other function) without fully understanding the *principles* or rules involved. But can they be said to be doing so in the absence of the necessary *information*? This seems to the author to be a much more valid criticism of the theory of the firm than any of those dealt with above. If managers do not possess the necessary information to pursue a policy of maximising profits or sales revenue or corporate growth, how can they be said to have profit or sales revenue or growth maximisation as an objective? Equally important from the standpoint of research by economists into the theory of the firm, is the fact that if researchers cannot observe changes in business behaviour because they lack the necessary data then there is no possibility of proving or disproving otherwise purely *a priori* speculation as to how firms behave and the motivating forces which cause such behaviour. Lack of information is a problem in almost all areas of research in economics. Some appear to feel that it militates against any sophisticated theory of the firm. Thus one researcher accepted as being at the forefront as far as studies of business behaviour are concerned emphasised at the outset of one study:

> 'Finally, it should be emphasised that the subsequent analysis contains no attempt to estimate a single integrated model of the economic behaviour of the firm. The main reason for this is that the author has been unable to

discover, in the current theoretical literature, any such model which is testable within the confines of the available accounting data. This partly reflects serious gaps in the data, such as absence of annual sales figures or share prices, but it also reflects a lack of concern by theorists for deriving empirically testable propositions.'[24]

C. The New Theories of the Firm

The new theories can be divided into two groups, reflecting the main strands of criticism of the neo-classical or traditional theory of the firm. The two main sources of discontent with the traditional theory have centred around the motivation assumptions and the analysis of the decision-making processes involved. Traditional theory has assumed that the goal of the firm in economics is profit maximisation; and that decisions within the firm on prices and production levels are made by a single entrepreneur who is in possession of all the necessary information to arrive at the correct 'rational' decision. The new theories which substitute other goals for profit maximisation are generally referred to as 'managerial' on account of the dominant role in decision-taking in this area which they give to management as opposed to shareholders. Those theories which concentrate upon the need to revise traditional theory in favour of greater realism of the conflict resolution and concensus or compromise involved in group decision-taking within large businesses are known as 'behavioural'. This section is divided into two parts to deal with these two broad approaches, using Oliver Williamson's terminology of Realism in Motivation and Realism in Process to distinguish between the two approaches.[25]

(*a*) *Realism in motivation*

If we assume that the divorce of ownership from control frees management from its stewardship obligation to accept profit maximisation as a single goal, what are we to assume that management does with this freedom? If management is, by implication, free to operate the firm in its own interests, what policy goals will be pursued? A number of possible managerial goals has been put forward. One of the most persistently canvassed of these has been growth.

> 'Growth is a source of prestige and a means of satisfying managerial ambitions, and the increases in the firm's income which it generates provide the financial fuel for still more investment and growth in progressively rising sequence.'[26]

This has been refined by some into the goal of sales revenue maximisation, normally achieved subject to the earning of a minimum acceptable level of profits, and is usually associated with the American economist W. J. Baumol.[27] Of course it is usually pointed out in this type of analysis that, apart from considerations of prestige, it is not necessarily sales maximisation for its own sake which is being pursued. In some cases management bonuses may be related to sales achievement as being a fairly obvious index of management performance. But sales maximisation may be of more direct economic significance as a business goal. Sales maximisation (if this implies a more rapid rate of growth than a firm's market in aggregate, and assuming that the growth is not entirely gained through diversification) may lead to an increased market share and market dominance. It is generally found that increased firm size and market dominance are statistically associated with a reduced variability of corporate earnings. It is a reasonable assumption from basic economic analysis that a dominant firm will achieve monopsony and monopoly gains in the respective areas of input purchases and sales. These will be most obvious in the case of lower prices charged by suppliers and higher prices realised in product markets. A dominant firm may also have the opportunity to affect the industry price structure to its own advantage by adopting the role of price leader; and quite apart from the issue of market dominance as such it should also be remembered that size alone may bring advantages to a firm in terms of cheaper finance and general standing in the world of industry. To this extent sales revenue maximisation through diversification may be attractive to a business. What must be stressed, therefore, is that sales revenue maximisation should not be seen as a totally 'irrational' business goal. It is even possible to demonstrate mathematically (and most business people realise it intuitively) that under conditions of a high volume of fixed production costs, sales maximisation with prices set on the basis of a fixed markup on costs produces the same approximate output decision as profit maximisation.[28] Detailed analysis has been undertaken of the fuller implications of this model of firm behaviour for oligopoly pricing and the use of advertising to stimulate sales.[29] What is important about the basic Baumol model is that it suggests *why* firms should seek to maximise sales revenue, *how* the maximising position is reached, and the *possible implications* of the imposition of a minimum profits parameter.

Baumol's diagram (figure 1) contains the normal assumptions as to cost and demand conditions. The sales revenue maximising output is OQ_s: at this point MR = 0 and thus η (the price elasticity of demand) = 1. By comparison, profit maximisation (MC = MR) would dictate the output OQ_p. Minimum profit constraints, $OP_1 - OP_3$, are introduced.

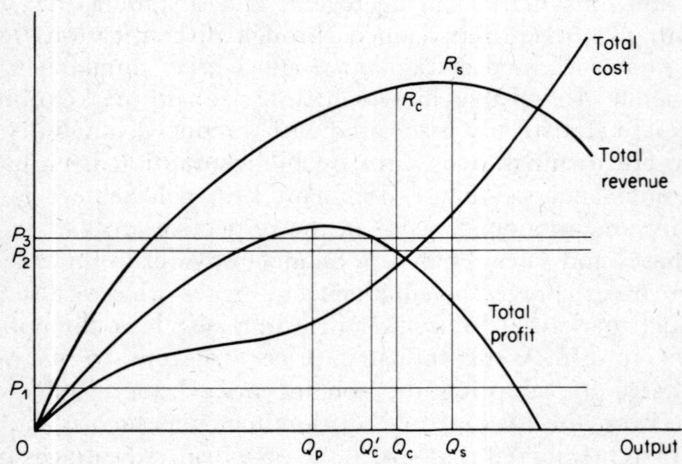

FIGURE 1 (Source: Baumol, W. J., *Economic Theory and Operations Analysis*, Prentice-Hall, New Jersey, (1965) pp. 295–303, 2nd edn.)

Since OQ_s will always be greater than OQ_p (MR will be zero in the former case but always positive in the latter) the profit constraints will dictate levels of output between OQ_p and OQ_s. In his own more detailed analysis of sales revenue maximising behaviour Baumol confirms that in his view 'this hypothesis . . . is at best only an approximation to a set of complex and variegated facts', and that his evidence for suggesting that particularly under oligopoly conditions management seek to maximise sales revenue rather than profits is 'again highly impressionistic; but . . . quite strong'.[30] In supporting his sales revenue maximisation hypothesis Baumol suggests that *falling* business turnover will: further turn consumers from a firm's products if they feel that these are of diminishing popularity (a sort of reverse 'bandwagon' effect); leave banks unimpressed and thus make temporary funds harder to secure; cause wholesale and retail distributors to become less interested in handling the firm's goods, and so jeopardise further final consumer purchase; result in loss of personnel and so make employment relations difficult and unpleasant; and finally bring about a reduction in business monopoly power. If one adds to these rather negative inducements the more positive effects of increased turnover on managerial incomes and (rather more questionably) shareholder satisfaction, then one may conclude with Baumol that 'the volume (in money terms) of sales approaches the status of a prime business objective'.[31]

Baumol stresses, however, that there will always be a profit floor which management will be constrained by in maximising sales revenue: see figure 1 above. This minimum level of profits is set because sales revenue maximisation is a long-term as much as a short-term objective. Long-term maximisation requires funds for fixed-capital expansion; and profits influence directly and indirectly the availability of these funds. Directly, they influence the volume of internal funds available through retentions. Indirectly, they influence the cost and availability of external funds – bank loans, new share issues, rights issues – as the providers of these funds will need to have some assurance on earnings and dividends before committing themselves. Management must therefore balance unconstrained short-run sales revenue maximisation against long-term sales growth. It is this which induces management to accept a profits floor.

Robin Marris' exposition of this theory of 'managerial' capitalism is much more all-embracing than Baumol's sales revenue maximisation hypothesis. Also, in comparison with Williamson's approach (which we shall examine shortly), Marris' book is more daunting because the mathematical modelling is built into the text rather than left to an appendix.[32] The main contention in this text is that with the demise of shareholder power, and the growing significance of undistributed business profits in company finance, the assets of a business no longer belong to the equity shareholders but to management. Hence, the growth of managerial capitalism. Having established that management of the large business organisation is free from shareholder control, and thus from an immediate requirement to maximise profits, Marris suggests that growth of gross assets becomes the business goal. This objective will be maximised within the constraint established by the wish to avoid loss of office, i.e. the need to avoid being taken over. As a proxy for the likelihood of takeover Marris uses the ratio of the stock-market value of the firm to the book (i.e. accounting) value of its net assets (total assets less current liabilities). This is known as the valuation ratio (V). The valuation ratio may be taken as some indication of the likelihood of a firm's acquisition by another business insofar as if the ratio falls below unity the stock-market value of the firm (some indication of the figure for which it could be bought on the market) must be less than the accounting value of the underlying assets. Conversely a valuation ratio of more than one would (within the simplifications involved in the use of these data) tend to ensure the survival of the business as an independent organisation. Thus Marris sums up his analysis of the various financial and behavioural assumptions underlying his theory: 'The main concluding theorem is that the various pressures mentioned above lead managers to maximise the rate of growth of the firm they are employed in subject to a constraint imposed by the security motive'.[33]

Just as in the case of Baumol's analysis of the managerial utility attaching to sales revenue maximisation, Marris is able to suggest on a number of grounds why management seek, within the security parameter, to maximise the growth rate of corporate assets. Apart from the supposed correlation between management salaries or other forms of income and corporate growth (as opposed to profitability), Marris sees business growth as providing a number of forms of management utility. One additional point to notice is that this growth tends to be self-sustaining in financial terms, as any increased revenue produces funds for more growth. Thus,

> 'If sales can be made to expand, the resulting revenue is sufficient justification and means for hiring new personnel, and the necessary capital can be obtained directly or indirectly from the profits of previous successes. But all expansion requires organisation and planning, and if not carefully organised and planned may be halted by various failures expressed economically in reduced profitability. Well-planned and well-executed expansion, on the other hand, is both stimulating and self-sustaining, and may thus represent to the executive a challenge similar to the challenge of difficult climbs in mountaineering. But both in mountaineering and in business there is little sympathy for those who overreach themselves. Here then, perhaps, we have the beginning of a theory. It is difficult to award the accolade of professional ability to a chief executive who competently maintains a constant output, with constant profits, constant product mix, and constant methods of production in a constant market! In order to demonstrate ability he must develop new markets, increase his share of old ones, develop new methods of production, organise a merger or at least do *something* . . .
> When a man takes decisions leading to successful expansion, he not only creates new openings but also recommends himself and his colleagues as particularly suitable candidates to fill them (and the colleagues, recognising this, will be glad to allow him a generous share of the utility-proceeds). He has demonstrated his powers as a manager and deserves his reward. So personal ability also becomes judged by achieved growth, and the encouragement of growth becomes a motive for not only collective

but also individual advancement, thus reinforcing the basic connection.'[34]

As mentioned before, management's desire to maximise corporate growth is tempered only by the obvious desire for survival. Thus *V*, both as a proxy for the latter and possibly also as a reflection of the more direct utility to management of an attractive stock-exchange quotation, can be seen as being traded off by management against growth. As a result of examining the relationship between the asset growth rate (as the independent variable) and profitability, and rate of return on capital (as the independent variable) and the permissible asset growth rate (with *V* held constant), Marris is able to show the relationship between *V* and any asset growth rate as below; the tangency between the curve representing this relationship and an indifference curve indicating management's trade-off between growth and security giving the optimal combination of the two variables (figure 2).

Again we should stress that it has only been possible to offer here a summary of Marris' views. His is essentially a managerial revision of the traditional theory of the firm. Management freedom from profit maximisation is assumed to lead to growth maximisation with a security constraint.

The most wide-ranging managerial revision of the theory of the firm is that embodied in Williamson's model of managerial discretionary behaviour.[35] His thesis is original but essentially simple. We have to accept three broad propositions. *First*, that shareholders (both personal and institutional) are relatively powerless when it comes to having any significant influence in directing corporate behaviour. This is simply an acceptance of the 'divorce of ownership from control' characteristic of modern business. The formal conclusion from this premise is that there is no reason to suppose that the corporate objective function will be dominated by profit maximisation. *Second*, Williamson stresses the diminished impact of competition in product markets – economic natural selection – in forcing businesses to operate with maximum efficiency and increase profits. As most product markets are characterised by elements of monopoly

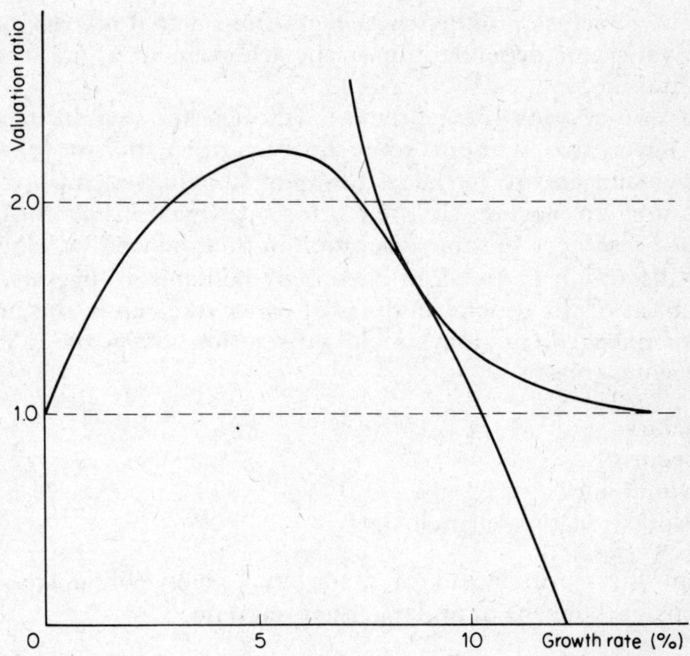

FIGURE 2 (Source: Marris, R., *The Economic Theory of 'Managerial' Capitalism*, Macmillan, London, (1964) p. 255)

or oligopoly, by barriers to competitive entry, and by product differentiation there is no reason to suppose that those firms which do not strive to maximise profits will be driven to the wall. Again, management is not forced to pursue profit maximisation to ensure its own survival. *Third*, it is held that the corporate takeover process – competition in the capital market – will not ensure that even in a world of imperfect product markets firms failing to earn maximum profits (or, in financial language, maximising the long-run sum of their discounted earnings) will be acquired by the more efficient, with the consequent elimination of the management of the former. In other words, poor firms survive takeover by the more efficient. This failure of the market in corporate control may be due to lack of information on takeover potentials, or the financial difficulties involved in taking over large businesses. Again, therefore, the formal conclusion under these conditions is that management survival is not dependent upon the achievement of maximum profitability.

If one accepts these premises (though few would accept the latter two without some qualification) then it follows that management in large businesses, being exempt from pressures to devote all their efforts to maximising profits, must be subject to some discretion in their behaviour. How is this discretion or freedom exercised? Williamson suggests, on the basis of the general findings of wider research in this area, that management may seek satisfaction of goals in the following areas:

Salary
Security
Dominance
Professional excellence

From this formulation of managerial goals Williamson develops his concept of an 'expense preference'.

> 'By expense preference I mean that managers do not have a neutral attitude toward all classes of expenses. Instead, some types of expenses have positive values attached to them: they are incurred not merely for their contributions to productivity (if any) but, in addition, for the manner in which they enhance the individual and collective objectives of managers. Conventional economic theory treats all expenses symmetrically: individuals are indifferent toward costs of all types. Expense preference replaces this attitude of indifference by positive tastes for certain classes of expenses. Asymmetry thus develops in the attitude toward costs.'[36]

The particular forms of expense thus chosen can be classified into Staff, Emoluments and Discretionary Profit. Spending in each of these areas satisfies one or more of the managerial goals listed above. Thus, if management is free from the constraints of shareholder control, product-market competition or takeover one would expect profitability to be sacrificed to one or more of these goals.

What Williamson is essentially suggesting is that because *external* pressures upon management in large firms (i.e. shareholders, product competitors or management of more aggressive firms) are dormant, ineffective or face institutional friction in operating, then management is freed from the basic obligation to operate at greatest efficiency to maximise profits. The managerial discretion which is thereby created is used to satisfy more individual or personal managerial objectives. These, Williamson contends, find expression in the recruitment of otherwise excessive numbers of staff, in unnecessarily high management salaries (i.e. where the element of economic rent is a significant component), or the earning of some discretionary level of profit above the minimum level required by shareholders or creditors so as to finance these other discretionary expenditures internally.

What is of some significance about Williamson's thesis is that he has himself gone some way towards suggesting more recently that changes in organisational structure within firms may eliminate managerial discretion and the consequent pursuit of non-profit goals. This almost 'behavioural' revision on Williamson's part may suggest that a neo-classical analysis of firm behaviour may not be as inappropriate as many suggest. Speaking of the modern large business firm, Williamson suggests that 'its vitality is attributable in large part to organisational innovations that have permitted the corporation to limit the degree of control loss and subgoal pursuit that, without innovation, were predictable consequences of large size. Rather than be overcome by what otherwise would have been serious bureaucratic disabilities, the corporation has responded with a demonstrated capacity for self-renewal'.[37]

The organisational innovation upon which Williamson concentrates is the change in organisation structure from a functional or unitary (U-form) basis to a multidivisional (M-form) basis. That is, to a business divided into autonomous product operating units such as Motor Cars, Diesel Engines, Domestic Appliances, etc., as opposed to the more traditional establishment of functional units – for example, Purchasing, Sales, Finance or Personnel. This change is held to eliminate interfunctional dispute and co-ordination failure, both of which lead to either a loss of efficiency and reduced profits or a more conscious pursuit of non-profit managerial objectives. Businesses organised on an M-form basis create smaller, more operationally accountable and more easily managed operating units. Multidivisionalisation may be carried out on the basis of product or geographical area. A central co-ordination and control staff ensures that profit targets in each division are achieved, and may adjust top divisional management salaries and the availability or otherwise of expansion capital in the light of profit performance.[33] Williamson summarises his own conclusions as follows:

> 'The transformation of a large business firm for which divisionalization is feasible from a unitary to a multidivision form organization contributes to (but does not assure) an attenuation of both the control loss experience and subgoal pursuit (mainly staff-biased expansion) that are characteristic of the unitary form. Realization of these attenuation effects, however, requires that the general office be aggressively constituted to perform its strategic planning, resource allocation, and control functions. Both the form and substance of multidivision organization are required for this transformation to be effective. Expressed in conventional goal pursuit and efficiency terms, the argument comes down to this: *the organization and operation of the large enterprise along the lines of the M-form favours goal pursuit and least-cost behaviour more nearly associated with the neo-classical profit maximization hypothesis than does the U-form organizational alternative.*'[39] (Original emphasis.)

(*b*) *Realism in process*

The new managerial theories discussed above have been concerned with revising the traditional theory of the firm in the light of corporate management's relative freedom to pursue goals other than that of profit maximisation. This is the freedom of managerial discretion held to derive from the divorce between corporate ownership and management. The managerial theories see businesses as being free to *maximise* some function other than profits, e.g. sales revenue or business growth, albeit subject to the maintenance of a minimum value of some parameter such as profit or the valuation ratio. The real advantage of these theories is that given the value of the parameters and a knowledge of the cost and revenue functions, we can trace the implications of the adoption of any of these newer objective functions in terms of pricing and output decisions, and compare this situation with that which would exist under conditions of profit maximisation. For example we know that output will be greater if the firm is seeking to maximise sales revenue than it will be if profit maximisation is the goal. We can therefore conclude that sales maximisation generally leads to greater outputs and lower prices in imperfect markets than profit maximisation.

An additional advantage of these theories is that changes in the business environment (such as an increase in the business's fixed costs, or a rise in the rate of V.A.T.) can be incorporated into the 'model'. Again this enables us to distinguish between the reactions, in terms of changes in price and output, of profit or sales revenue or growth maximisers. Figures 3 and 4 illustrate the impact upon profit

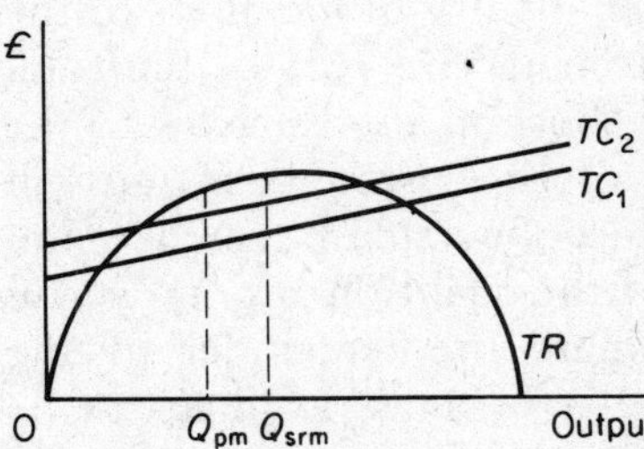

FIGURE 3 The rise in fixed costs is shown by a parallel upward shift in *TC*. In this case neither Q_{pm} nor Q_{srm} changes: so far as the former is concerned the *gradient* of *TC* is unchanged, and thus also the level of output where the gradients of *TR* and *TC* are equal

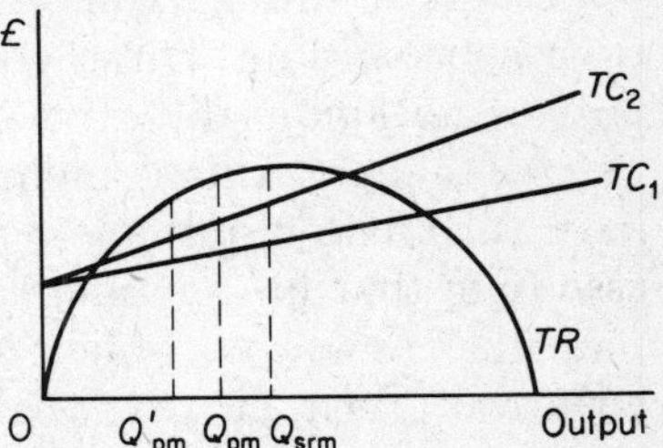

FIGURE 4 The increase in the rate of V.A.T. is reflected in a change in the gradient of *TC*. Thus Q_{srm} remains unchanged, but Q'_{pm} lies below Q_{pm} – firms reducing output and raising price following the tax change

and sales revenue maximisers respectively of increased fixed costs and a rise in V.A.T. A knowledge of such likely reactions is obviously essential in forecasting the effect of macroeconomic fiscal policies.

These characteristics of the managerial theories of the firm have been highlighted as a contrast to the *behaviour* revisions to existing theory. The behavioural theories of the firm do not start with a preconceived idea of corporate goals, but devote a considerable part of their analysis to the *process* by which corporate goals are arrived at. For example Cyert and March – the leading proponents of behavioural theories of the firm – stress the need to look at any business as a coalition: a coalition of managers, employees, shareholders, bank lenders, etc. The goals (and one should emphasise their plurality) of the organisation will arise from interaction within the coalition.[40] We can no longer assume that a business will have a single goal either as a result of the dominance of the corporate hierarchy by a single owner-manager entrepreneur, or through a happy concensus within the coalition. Rather in order that the coalition may continue to operate each member will be able to demand not only fairly obviously his monetary income but also what Cyert and March term policy commitment side payments. These involve policy objectives which the business will undertake in order to maintain the loyalty of members of the existing coalition. These commitments are part of the total cost of obtaining the services of those members. Now to the extent that individual members of an existing coalition will have different requirements as to policy side payments, and assuming that no one member of the coalition is so powerful that his views on policy dominate the remainder of the coalition, then at any one time a business is likely to be trying to pursue a policy which is in fact composed of a number of frequently contradictory sub-goals. Cyert and March suggest that the areas of these sub-goals can be identified as: production, inventory, sales, market share, and profit. Obvious areas of potential conflict in these categories are the desire for long production runs of standard commodities in order to achieve economies of scale (Production) combined with minimum stockholding costs achieved by low finished-goods stock (Inventory), in contrast to customer's demands for immediate delivery from stock of a wide selection of goods incorporating customer-specified extras (Sales, Market Share).

Even more 'organisational' characteristics tend to be built into behavioural theories of the firm. Not only do such theories reject the idea of maximising a single function; they reject the concept of maximising or minimising anything. Instead a business is seen as striving to achieve *satisfactory* performance in a number of areas as suggested above. This behaviour can thus be termed 'satisficing' rather than maximising. Performance is judged to be satisfactory or otherwise in comparison with aspiration levels incorporated into budgets which are based upon past achievement modified as necessary in the light of forecast changes in the firm's external environment.

A novel feature which Cyert and March build into their behavioural theory is the phenomenon of organisational slack. This comprises 'payments to members of the coalition in excess of what is required to maintain the organisation'.[41] This 'slack', which has the characteristics of economic rent, can accrue to any persons supplying an input to a business: shop-floor employees, shareholders, material input suppliers or senior management. Each of these may under certain conditions receive wages, dividends, prices or salaries above those for which they would otherwise be willing to offer their goods or services. However, it is obvious that senior management will be in the best position to receive the benefits of slack in the form of additional remuneration or perquisites or reduced effort. Slack most obviously arises in boom times when sales volume and prices are moving up *ahead of expectations*. Such unanticipated gains are absorbed by slack in the forms suggested above. As the reverse process will occur during a downturn in business conditions, i.e. businesses will 'tighten up' their organisation, and senior management will accept reductions in holidays, perquisites or even salaries, slack will act as a cushion between changes in the business environment and actual movements in corporate profitability. The latter will not, therefore, be of the same timing or amplitude as the former.[42] A very similar concept has been evolved by the American economist Leibenstein, using the term X-inefficiency to indicate the gap between actual and potential output with a given allocation of resources.[43]

The behavioural theories of the firm lie very much on a borderline between economics and organisation theory. Cyert and March recognise this fact at the outset of their analysis in claiming that 'in order to understand contemporary economic decision making, we need to supplement the study of market factors with an examination of the internal operation of the firm'.[44] The authors explicitly include within this an analysis of organisation structure and 'conventional practice' as being essential to an understanding of the process of goal formation in modern business. Dissatisfaction may, however, be felt with this approach: either because it is 'not economics', or because such a theory does not conform to the main criteria of economic models of business behaviour – it cannot predict how businesses will behave. Thus:

> 'Non-maximising models may offer useful insights but they will be ultimately unsatisfactory if they fail to yield identifiable equilibrium conditions. Satisficing, mark-up pricing, adaptive systems, all run the risk of being no more than descriptions of business behaviour masquerading as economic analysis. Realism may in the end be destructive of logic and of understanding alike.'[45]

But what the behavioural theorists are essentially seeking is a model of business behaviour which, while concerning itself with 'economic' variables such as pricing and output and advertising expenditure, and also being capable of aggregation so that market as well as firm behaviour may be predicted, will nonetheless place appropriate emphasis on the business decision-making process. At the present moment none can say whether this has been achieved. But the whole approach deserves the support of all concerned that the economic theory of the firm should, within the bounds of economic analysis, take account of business reality.

D. Conclusions

The business firm in economics has only in the past half century been treated as a phenomenon deserving special analysis. Until the early decades of this century economic analysis was chiefly concerned with aggregated market behaviour or with national economic phenomena. Thus, of the classical economists, Smith was concerned with national economic wellbeing – 'the wealth of nations' – while Ricardo traced the inexorable rise in material prosperity of the landowner. The later economists of the 19th century – most obviously Karl Marx – were concerned with rises and falls in national economic prosperity (the problem of the trade cycle) and with the distribution of national income between wages and profits. In all of these writings the firm appears to be a mere agent of macroeconomic analysis. It is one participant in the rounds of the circular flow of income.

Had the business firm not become a more complex organism (a sequence discussed in Section B above) there might have been no need to develop a 'theory of the firm'. It may also be true to say that as the status of industrial or business or managerial economics within the whole profession is low compared with, say, quantitative macroeconomics, progress was likely to be slower in this branch. To some it has appeared that it is the macroeconomic function of the firm which has retarded the development of a separate micro approach to the theory of the firm. The behavioural theorists put the issue as follows:

> 'The theory of the firm, which is primarily a theory of markets, purports to explain at a general level the way resources are allocated by a price system. To the extent to which the model does this successfully, its gross assumptions will be justified. However, there are a number of important and interesting questions relating specifically to firm behavior that the theory cannot answer and was never developed to answer, especially with regard to the internal allocation of resources and the process of setting prices and outputs.'[46]

Their approach is to develop separate theories for macro and micro purposes.

> 'Ultimately, a new theory of firm decision-making behavior might be used as a basis for a theory of markets, but at least in the short run *we should distinguish between a theory of microbehavior, on the one hand, and the microassumptions appropriate to a theory of aggregate economic behavior on the other.*'[47] (Emphasis added.)

Nonetheless, it is in the field of macroeconomics that some of the benefits of advances in the theory of the firm may be gained. We have mentioned this above in pointing out the implications for fiscal policy of distinguishing between profit and sales-revenue maximisation as corporate goals. The need for this feedback from the newer micro theories to macro policy has been stressed by Marris who criticises 'the rather common idea that macro-economic growth theories can validly be formulated without benefit of explicitly associated micro theories'. The same author again placed the theory of the firm in a wider context:

> 'It must always be the case that the analysis of a decentralised economic system will depend on a specific theory of the behaviour of the units to which decisions are delegated, in other words on some kind of theory of the firm.'[48]

It is, indeed, the failure of some macroeconomists to understand fully the behaviour of the large modern business which, in the opinion of Galbraith and others, has led these people to exaggerate the efficacy of the traditional techniques of monetary and fiscal policy. In particular, the differential effect of the same policies on large and small businesses appears to have been almost entirely ignored.[49]

It will not be surprising if we also claim that a further benefit of greater study and recognition of the value of the newer economic theories of the firm should be a multidisciplinary approach to this particular field of analysis. It might also encourage economists to recognise the value of neighbouring disciplines in other areas of enquiry, e.g. labour economics. Economists must recognise the complexity of the modern business firm. A study of economics alone will not enable us to analyse its market behaviour and performance. And yet this latter is the heart of industrial economics.

A considerable problem even with the newer approaches to this topic is that there is no longer a single general theory of the firm. We have now had to discard the idea of each individual firm in an atomistic market maximising profit by increasing output of its single product until $MC = MR$. If we had a single alternative replacement of general validity then the problem for students would simply be to understand the nature of the data required and master the necessary mathematics. But instead the alternative to the neo-classical theory appears, in the words of one author, to be 'a seemingly endless array of theories, individually persuasive but often mutually contradictory'.[50] This particular author, while pointing out that realism in the face of the enormous diversity and complexity of the everyday industrial scene might dictate the co-existence of quite diverse theories of the firm, does almost reach the point of asking whether the whole exercise of attempting to generate theories of the firm of even limited generality is worthwhile.[51] Shubik is less affected by these qualms. In his view 'logical consistency between one theory in microeconomics and another is a luxury and not a necessity'.[52] Each theory is of value in its own right if it contributes to answering a particular limited set of questions, or if it gives a useful emphasis to one issue in business behaviour. In this sense the managerial and behavioural theories have each a contribution to make in the field. It is in the light of these numerous, and sometimes conflicting, theories of the modern business firm that this text examines the structure of different product markets, the performance of firms in specific policy areas such as pricing, merger, integration and diversification, and the financial performance of businesses.

References

1. O. S. Hiner, *Business Administration*, London (1969), pp. 11–12
2. K. Heidensohn and N. Robinson, *Business Behaviour*, Philip Allan, Oxford (1974), p. 2
3. C. J. Hawkins, *Theory of the Firm*, Macmillan, London (1973), p. 9
4. J. K. Galbraith, *The Affluent Society*, Hamish Hamilton, London, 2nd ed. (1969), p. 33
5. This interesting change is highlighted, and emphasis in the original text added, in S. J. Prais, A New Look at the Growth of Industrial Concentration, *Oxford Economic Papers*, Vol. XXVI (1974), 274
6. See K. W. Rothschild, Price Theory and Oligopoly, *Economic Journal*, Vol. LVII (1947), 299–320. For data on aggregate and market concentration see S. J. Prais, Ref. 5, p. 283; and J. F. Pickering, *Industrial Structure and Market Conduct*, Martin Robertson, London (1974) pp. 15 and 17
7. A. A. Berle and G. C. Means, *The Modern Corporation and Private Property*, Harcourt, Brace and World, New York (1933)
8. For further data on large personal holdings in large firms see A. F. Freris, Profit or Sales Maximising or 'Managerial'? Some Recent Evidence on the Theory of the Firm in the U.K., *Business Education Review*, Vol. I (1974), 117
9. K. Midgley, How Much Control do Shareholders Exercise?, *Lloyds Bank Review*, No. 114 (1974), 24–37
10. *Ibid.*, 37
11. R. J. Monsen and A. Downs, A Theory of Large Managerial Firms, *Journal of Political Economy*, Vol. LXXIII (1965), 221–36
12. *Ibid.*, p. 230. The full implications of these phenomena are by no means established. It has yet to be established if it would be in the shareholders' best interests to attempt to force management to conform to profit maximising behaviour. Statistical evidence on the relative profit and growth performance of 'management controlled' and 'owner-controlled' firms is inconclusive. See K. J. Blois, Profit Maximisation by Whom?, *Loughborough Journal of Social Studies*, Vol. II (1967), 10–16; and H. K. Radice, Control Type, Profitability and Growth in Large Firms: An Empirical Study, *Economic Journal*, 1971, Vol. LXXXI (1971), 547–62
13. See K. W. Rothschild, Ref. 6, 305
14. H. Albert, The Neglect of Sociology in Economic Science in K. W. Rothschild (ed.), *Power in Economics*, Penguin, Harmondsworth (1971), p. 27
15. J. W. Markham, *Conglomerate Enterprise and Public Policy*, Harvard Business School, Boston (1973), p. 165

16. E. H. Phelps Brown, The Underdevelopment of Economics, *Economic Journal*, Vol. LXXXII (1972), 7
17. C. J. Hawkins, Ref. 3 (1973), p. 28
18. J. K. Galbraith, *A Contemporary Guide to Economics, Peace and Laughter*, Deutsch, London (1971), p. 9
19. R. M. Cyert and J. G. March, *A Behavioral Theory of the Firm*, Prentice Hall, New Jersey (1963), p. 13
20. K. Heidensohn and N. Robinson, Ref. 2, p. 133
21. A. F. Freris, Ref. 8, 103
22. K. Heidensohn and N. Robinson, Ref. 2, pp. 3 and 6
23. See F. Machlup, Theories of the Firm: Marginalist, Behavioral, Managerial, *American Economic Review*, Vol. LVII (1967), 1–33
24. G. Whittington, *The Prediction of Profitability*, CUP, Cambridge (1971), p. 2
25. See O. E. Williamson, *The Economics of Discretionary Behaviour: Managerial Objectives in a Theory of the Firm*, Kershaw, London (1974), p. 11
26. O. S. Hiner, Ref. 1, p. 15
27. See W. J. Baumol, *Economic Theory and Operations Analysis*, Prentice Hall, New Jersey, 2nd ed. (1965), pp. 295–303
28. Given that profit is maximised when MC = MR, and sales revenue is maximised when MR = 0, then the nearer MC is to zero the more closely will profit maximising and sales revenue maximising outputs and prices coincide.
29. See C. J. Hawkins, On the Sales Revenue Maximization Hypothesis, *Journal of Industrial Economics*, Vol. XVIII (1970), 129–40
30. W. J. Baumol, *Business Behaviour, Value and Growth*, Harcourt Brace, New York, rev. ed (1966), pp. 14 and 47
31. The question of the relationship between directors' remuneration and firm size, and the relative incentive which directors appear to have to pursue either growth or profitability is attracting increased empirical research. Differences in firm size certainly appear to go a long way in explaining differences in managerial incomes. Some doubts, however, remain as to the role of profitability and growth in explaining differences in the level of executive remuneration; although it would appear that the pattern within quoted companies differs from unquoted. See G. Meeks and G. Whittington, Directors' Pay, Growth and Profitability, *Journal of Industrial Economics*, Vol. XXIV (1975), 1–14; and A. Coch, The Remuneration of Chief Executives in the United Kingdom, *Economic Journal*, Vol. LXXXV (1975), 75–94
32. R. Marris, *The Economic Theory of 'Managerial' Capitalism*, Macmillan, London, (1964)

33. *Ibid.*, p. 47
34. *Ibid.*, pp. 58–9 and 102
35. See O. E. Williamson, Ref. 25
36. *Ibid.*, p. 33
37. O. E. Williamson, *Corporate Control and Business Behaviour*, Prentice Hall, New Jersey (1970), p. vii
38. A recent case of the anticipated benefits of the change from a functional to a multidivisional organisation structure is that of Dormer Ltd., formerly known as Sheffield Twist Drill & Steel. Under the previous functional organisation, according to one business correspondent, 'the sales and production sides . . . were gradually growing apart . . . individual directors, moreover, found themselves facing several different directions at once. The final solution was to break the whole organisation down into smaller units with their own boards under a four-man holding company board at the very top . . . The subsidiaries were now separate, identifiable profit-centres with a system of transfer-pricing which has given middle management through the company impetus and responsibility'. See S. Caulkin, The Drill at Sheffield Twist, *Management Today* (April 1975), 45–6
39. O. E. Williamson, Ref. 37, (1970), pp. 133–34
40. R. M. Cyert and J. G. March, Ref. 19, Ch. III
41. *Ibid.*, p. 36
42. An interesting practical example of this can be seen in the working of Cadbury Schweppes' Operations Profitability Committee established in the light of the merged food giant's failure to achieve anticipated profits in 1970. By the end of that year the Committee had cut executive main board director salaries by 10%, limited directors to four weeks holiday in the following twelve months, limited directors' overseas travel, and sought reductions in 'peripheral expenditure'. The company chairman further ordered, 'We must not subsidise the meals in directors' dining rooms'! See A. Vice, Blending Cadbury-Schweppes in *The Strategy of Takeovers*, McGraw Hill, Maidenhead (1971), p. 79
43. See H. Leibenstein, Allocative Efficiency vs. 'X-Efficiency', *American Economic Review*, Vol. LVI (1966), 392–415. J. K. Galbraith looks at the other side of the coin. Thus not only can one see 'slack' as arising when non-profit-maximising firms pay excessive prices for inputs (costs which are reduced in times of poor business conditions). Slack may also be seen in businesses setting output prices lower than could be achieved; increases being implemented only when it becomes necessary to cover unforeseen cost increases such as a major wage settlement. In the light of the drive on the

part of large business firms for corporate growth and management security, Galbraith claims 'the prices that are so set . . . will almost always be lower, and on occasion much lower, than those that would maximise profits over some period relevant to managerial calculation', *Economics and the Public Purpose*, Deutsch, London (1974), pp. 115–6

44. R. M. Cyert and J. G. March, Ref. 19, p. 1
45. J. R. Wildsmith, *Managerial Theories of the Firm*, Martin Robertson, London (1973), p. 30
46. R. M. Cyert and J. G. March, Ref. 19, p. 15
47. *Ibid.*, pp. 15–16
48. R. L. Marris, Why Economics Needs a Theory of the Firm, *Economic Journal*, Vol. LXXXII (1972), 321
49. See J. K. Galbraith, *The Liberal Hour*, Hamish Hamilton, New York (1960), Ch. IV
50. C. J. Hawkins, Ref. 3 (1973), p. 8
51. *Ibid.*, pp. 81–3
52. M. Shubik, A Curmudgeon's Guide to Microeconomics, *Journal of Economic Literature*, Vol. VIII (1970), 412

Chapter III

Industrial Market Structure and Conduct

Overview

This chapter introduces the concepts of market structure, conduct and performance. It is this approach to the analysis of economic markets which particularly distinguishes industrial organisation studies from more formal microeconomics. The purpose of this chapter is to consider in more detail the dimensions of market structure and conduct, with emphasis on the conceptual analysis and data problems involved. Consideration of market performance and of the interrelationships between structure, conduct and performance is deferred until the following chapter.

A. Structure, Conduct and Performance

One of the characteristics which distinguishes industrial economics or industrial organisation from more formal microeconomics is a particular framework within which economic markets are examined. This is embodied in the market structure, conduct and performance model.

This framework or approach can be said to have three particular advantages. First, it is a means of highlighting, from the midst of a wealth of institutional detail, the salient features of any economic market. Second, on the firm basis of microeconomic theory we would expect there to be significant relationships between aspects of market structure and conduct and performance, such that performance may be predicted from structure, or, as a feature of public policy, that legislative intervention in structure may bring about desirable reforms in conduct or performance. Third, it may be possible to move 'backwards' from certain desirable, acceptable or 'workable' patterns of market performance to market structures which, although highly 'imperfect' in terms of traditional microeconomics, may be acceptable in the light of the market conduct and performance with which they are associated.

B. The Dimensions of Structure, Conduct and Performance

Bain defines market structure as 'those characteristics of the organization of a market that seem to exercise a strategic influence on the nature of competition and pricing within the market'.[1] On the basis of the writings of Bain and others the following dimensions of structure are considered to be the most significant.[2]

Market Structure

Dimensions	Characteristics
(i) Seller concentration	Atomism, oligopoly, monopoly
(ii) Buyer concentration	Atomism, oligopsony, monopsony
(iii) Product substitution	Product homogeneity or differentiation
(iv) Entry conditions	Freedom of entry, impeded entry or blockaded entry

Correspondingly Bain identifies market conduct as 'patterns of behaviour that enterprises follow in adapting or adjusting to the markets in which they sell (or buy)'.[3]

Market Conduct

Dimensions	Characteristics
(i) Price policies:	
(a) objectives	Profit, sales revenue, growth, etc.
(b) bases	Cost plus, marginal cost
(c) tactics	Price discrimination, etc.
(d) co-ordination	Price leadership, collusion, etc.
(ii) Product and sales policies:	
(a) product policies	Technological progressiveness in product design and production processes
(b) sales policies	Advertising and promotional techniques and expenditure

Finally Bain classifies as performance 'the composite of end results which firms in any market arrive at by pursuing whatever lines of conduct they espouse'.[4]

Market Performance

Dimensions	Characteristics
(i) Profitability	Rate of return on capital employed, etc.
(ii) Efficiency	Technical efficiency – plant size, production methods, etc. (including technological progressiveness and rate of response to changes in demand)
(iii) Product	Design, quality and variety
(iv) Promotion	Advertising/sales ratio

It must be emphasised that schema such as the above will always remain tentative and open to discussion. One problem is that of steering a path between the Scylla of a set of titles which will describe every aspect of any industry, and the Charybdis of a skeletal paradigm on which one can build a flesh of R^2's without necessarily making the schema intelligible to someone interested in how a market fundamentally operates. A second difficulty, probably not wholly avoided above, is that of distinguishing between those phenomena which are structure or conduct or performance. Integration and diversification are immediate examples. But what of concentration and product differentiation? Technological progressiveness can be a dimension of conduct and of performance; but it also affects structure through the cost function – often by increasing the ratio of fixed to variable costs in the production process. A third problem is that of measuring many of the variables, and in particular of establishing criteria for performance dimensions. This latter aspect is dealt with in the following chapter under the heading of workable competition.

(*a*) *Buyer and seller concentration*

This is one of the most popular measures of market structure. It is an attempt to measure the amount of market power possessed by the most significant firms (buyers or sellers) in any market. As such there are really two issues to discuss: the measure of power to be adopted, and the definition of the market to be accepted.

Leaving aside for the moment the issue of defining the market, the measure of relative power normally chosen is that of the size of the largest n firms relative to the total market.[5] Size may be measured in terms of inputs (capital or labour) or outputs (sales). None of these three possible measures of firm size (assets, employment or sales) will necessarily produce the same rank order of firms in a market. In particular as firms grow larger (by any measure) their use of capital tends to rise faster against output relative to the use of labour: large firms have higher capital–output ratios than smaller ones.[6] For this reason and others (there is, for example, no reason to suppose that all firms in the same industry measure their constituents of capital employed on a comparable basis) sales are normally adopted as the measure of firm and industry size.

In order to measure concentration or market power, the total sales of the *n* largest (by sales) firms are expressed as a ratio of the total sales of the firms in the market. So far as U.K. data are concerned *n* is usually three; and the ratio is thus called a three-firm sales concentration ratio.

Some dissatisfaction has been felt with this measure however. It is too partial a view of the degree of power in any market: a single snapshot rather than a total panoramic view. For example the ratio discussed above could have a value of 60%, and comprise one seller with 57% of the market, one with 2% and one with 1%. Unlikely, perhaps; but considerable differences in the spread of concentration between industries can be obscured by this measure. The solution, provided the necessary data are available, is to know the share of any market held by each firm – or at least each significant firm. These may then be presented on a cumulative frequency basis as below.

Sales of Garden Shrubs (£'000 per annum)

		%
Firm A	946	26
B	630	17
C	435	12
D	274	7
E	195	5
F	105	3
14 firms each with less than 100	1,076	30
	3,661	100%

Apart from noting that the three-firm sales concentration ratio is 55%, one can plot the data on a simple cumulative frequency curve, measuring market share on the vertical axis. As a further advance on this, the horizontal axis can be used to measure not the number of firms but the cumulative proportion of firms. The curve indicating this is known as a Lorenz curve, and is valuable in that it can be used to give a measure of the inequality of firm size: the Gini coefficient. On the axes used to plot the Lorenz curve a 45° line would indicate an equal distribution of sales throughout the market. By comparing the actual Lorenz curve in respect of any market with the 45° line a measure of deviation from equality can be gained. The Gini coefficient is the ratio of the area between the Lorenz curve and the 45° line to the triangle AOC in figure 5. The greater the equality, the nearer the ratio will approach zero. Increased inequality will result in the ratio approaching one.

A more sophisticated measure of market concentration involves a knowledge of the size distribution of all firms in the market. These are plotted on the usual axes: firm size on the horizontal axis, and frequency on the vertical axis. This measure would in the case of most markets give a highly skewed distribution: brought about by the large number of small firms and small number of giants. In fact the size distribution of firms in most markets is lognormal, i.e.

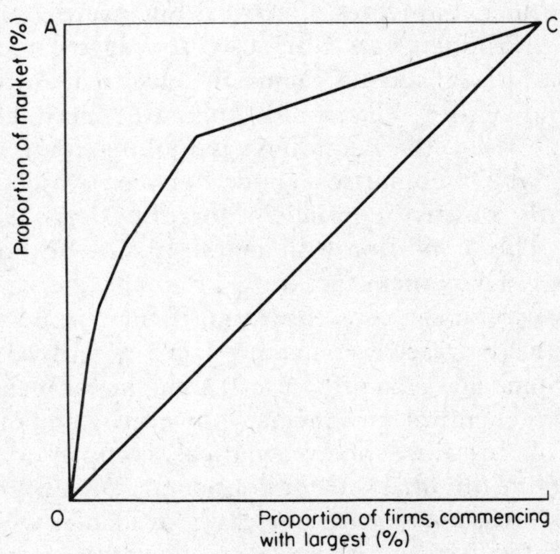

FIGURE 5

plotting the logarithm of firm size on the horizontal axis produces a 'normal' or bell-shaped curve. Once this population of logarithms has been plotted against frequency, inequality of firm size within the group, as a measure of concentration, can be obtained by calculating the standard deviation of this population around the mean. The higher the standard deviation, the less homogeneous the population, and therefore the greater the inequality of firm size.[7]

However, as with so many issues in industrial economics, statistical sophistication can easily march ahead of the availability of meaningful data. Data from Government sources on industry structure are usually based upon the Standard Industrial Classification. This system, originating in 1948 and most recently revised in 1968, classifies firms into industries, where the latter are drawn up on the basis of the use of common raw materials, or a common manufacturing process. The data are given at two levels of aggregation: Orders and Minimum List Headings (M.L.H.). The 1968 S.I.C. comprises 27 Orders and 181 Minimum List Headings; and, although data are sometimes given at a greater level of disaggregation called Product Groups, the economist may find some difficulty in identifying meaningful 'markets'. Orders (e.g. Chemicals and Allied Industries, Electrical Engineering, or Coal and Petroleum Products) are obviously too aggregated. Even an individual M.L.H. such as Domestic Electrical Appliances, or Radio and Other Electronic Apparatus may be too all-inclusive.[8] What the economist is looking for is a product grouping which comprises goods between which there is a significantly positive coefficient for price cross elasticity of demand. This condition will certainly not be bounded by technology. Glass manufacturers are not in the same market, so far as economists use the term, if their respective plants are specifically geared to making jam jars and vehicle windscreens. Some glass manufacturers, some metal manufacturers and some chemical producers, however, compete for the custom of brewers, pharmaceutical companies and food processors in the 'market' for containers. Data to match such a concept of a market are not easily available. On the other hand, if disaggregation is carried to an extreme it may lose its purpose. Consider the concentration ratios for food processing given in Appendix I (this chapter). So long as one is not dealing with a vital necessity the high ratios for baked beans, potato crisps, tinned fruit or frozen vegetables should not arouse too much concern. There are available immediate substitutes (spaghetti and other cold food snacks). Thus the market is being too narrowly defined, and should include fresh fruit or fresh and tinned vegetables.[9] Undoubtedly the proper definition of a market and obtaining the necessary data are among the greatest problems in measuring industrial concentration and using concentration ratios as a meaningful tool in describing market structure or as a guideline for public policy. Even the apparently rather mundane issue of the appropriate geographical market to consider is not a straightforward matter. What is monopoly at the municipal level may be atomism in E.E.C. or world-wide terms. Some Governments may tolerate, or even encourage, national monopoly for the sake of international competitiveness.

As mentioned above, concentration data are available at a number of levels. Although it does not concern us directly here, aggregated concentration data show that between 1949 and 1970 the proportion of total net output accounted for by the 100 largest manufacturing firms in the U.K. rose from 21% to about 45%.[10] The data in Appendix II (this chapter) show that oligopoly is a very common form of market structure in important individual markets in the U.K. More generally it was reported in Hansard in April 1970 that there were 156 products for which *one* producer accounted for over 50% of the U.K. supplies.[11] So far as trends are concerned, Pickering's analysis of movements of five-firm concentration ratios between the 1963 and 1968 Censuses of Production showed 77 cases where the ratio had risen 'markedly' and only 22 where it had fallen to a like extent.[12]

Seller concentration in terms of a concentration ratio does not, however, tell us everything about the competitive power of the largest firms. On the one hand the concentration ratio will understate this market power if the firms are also parties to a restrictive trading agreement (of either a formal or informal type), if price leadership is practised, or if there are any other institutional factors which encourage 'common policy' in the industry.[13] Among these last would be an influential trade association, interlocking directorates, or the need for other common meeting grounds brought about by Government legislation on wages and prices. The harmful competitive effects of high concentration ratios may, however, be less significant in rapidly growing markets; and may be significantly offset by the existence of either imports or countervailing power. It is normally assumed that high levels of concentration have a less harmful effect upon competition in expanding markets as these create new opportunities for competing sellers; and the total market may expand more rapidly than the largest suppliers can increase their output. As most measures of market concentration use total sales by U.K. enterprises as a denominator they overstate the real degree of market power to the extent that imports comprise a significant part of the market. The converse is, of course, the case in respect of exports. Consider the case of the large car assembly firms. Here British Leyland holds about 35% of the market, if this is defined as its share of U.K. production. But with some 40% of the U.K. market taken up by imports, Leyland's share of total market sales falls to around 20%.

The power of large producers in the market, as revealed by high levels of concentration, may also be limited by a degree of power on the other side of the market. Monopolists may sell to monopsonists; oligopolists to oligopsonists. To this competitive force from the other side of the market, as opposed to traditional competition from fellow producers, Galbraith has given the name countervailing power.[14] Galbraith argues that the emergence of monopoly or oligopoly in any market is bound to induce the development of countervailing power. Buyers have a dual incentive to amalgamate when faced with concentrated selling power: they can thereby protect themselves from further exploitation by monopolists, and may also hope to participate in the monopoly gains currently enjoyed by the sellers. Furthermore, these buyers may not be averse to the prospect of monopoly gains in the markets in which they in turn are sellers. Sofar as market power and competition are concerned, Galbraith appears to see some form of natural equilibrium emerging: 'In this way the existence of market power creates an incentive to the organization of another position of power that neutralizes it'.[15] Certainly there are a number of statistical examples of countervailing power in the U.K. economy. Some of these stem from the operation of nationalised industries: the Post Office in respect of telecommunications equipment, the Electricity Board as a predominant buyer of water-tube boilers, certain sizes of transformers and switchgear, and the N.C.B. as a monopoly buyer of certain types of wire rope.[16] In the private sector of the economy high concentration in motor component supplies (tyres, batteries, clutches, etc.) is matched by the buying power of British Leyland, Ford and Chrysler; and concentration in many areas of food processing is offset by the buying power of the large retail grocery chains (Tesco, Sainsbury, Allied Suppliers and Fine Fare). In each of these cases a monopoly group of sellers has its power severely curtailed by a single large buyer or a small group of large customers. Apart from the fact that, as Galbraith himself stressed, countervailing power does not operate during a period of inflation, the analysis is not wholly satisfactory. It may tell us something about the redistribution of power in economic markets; but there is no indication of the net effect upon welfare.[17] Countervailing power among a group of intermediate buyers is almost certain to put these in an oligopoly position at a subsequent market stage. As one economist put it in the context of the food processing and distribution market: 'If chain stores buy advantageously as oligopsonists, are they not also oligopolistic resellers who would retain those gains for themselves?'[18] The concept should not, however, be ignored as an explanation of certain trends in market structure, a tempering force in monopoly conditions, or an indirect means of controlling monopoly without recourse to direct Government intervention.[19]

(*b*) *Product substitution*

Product differentiation refers to the ability on the part of producers to differentiate (on a physical or psychological basis) products one from another, so that although the goods may be broadly speaking competing in the same market they are no longer perfect substitutes in the eyes of consumers. To this extent product differentiation constitutes another form of departure from the conditions of perfectly competitive markets.

The effect of this departure is to create downward sloping demand curves for the products concerned. Thus, even assuming complete freedom of entry – and hence the absence in the long run of monopoly profits – markets will not operate in a completely efficient manner. Given a demand curve other than a horizontal line, then in the long run at output MR = MC, AR will equal AC, but price will be above MC and 'excess capacity' will exist: the optimum level of output will be less than minimum average cost. It may even be suggested in these circumstances that a smaller number of producers for a given size of market would constitute greater efficiency insofar as some excess capacity would be eliminated. The danger here, however, is that a reduction in the number of producers might produce oligopoly or monopoly conditions such that even with excess capacity eliminated AR persists above AC in the long run, thus raising price and restricting output compared with the outcome of a more competitive market structure.

So far as producers are concerned, the objective of the various forms of product differentiation (of which advertising is only the most obvious) is to decrease the degree of product substitutability in the market. The purpose is to lower the price elasticity of demand, and also to shift the product demand curve to the right. The firm's decision on the optimal amount of, say, advertising will be based upon a comparison of AR and AC conditions given different levels of advertising expenditure: increased levels of advertising will raise AC and shift AR to the right. The problem is likely to be more complex, obviously, as promotional expenses take on the characteristic of an investment decision: funds being spent now in the expectation of increased, although uncertain, returns in the future. This approach, which is certainly appropriate in respect of research and development expenditure, is obviously more realistic than others but does raise the usual issues of the treatment of uncertainty and the choice of discount rate.

Finally, it should be mentioned that the possible rewards

from product differentiation will vary between markets according to the nature both of the product and of the buying process. There is obviously less scope for differentiation in the case of industrial goods markets (i.e. where the product is being bought as a material input into a further manufacturing process) than in the case of consumer goods (where the product is being bought for end use by the final consumer). The existence of detailed technical specifications or British Standards, the degree of technical expertise or time spent making the purchasing decision by the buyer, and other conditions will all have an impact upon how much product differentiation a seller finds it profitable to devote resources to.

(*c*) *Entry conditions*

Competitive entry into and exit from a market is an essential part of microeconomic analysis. It is the possibility of new entry into perfectly and monopolistically competitive markets which eliminates long-run monopoly profits. Correspondingly, it is the absence of such entry into 'monopoly' markets which allows long-run supernormal profits to be sustained.

Entry conditions define a relationship between firms already established in a market and potential entrant firms into that market. So far as entry barriers are concerned they are a measure of the advantage possessed by established firms over potential entrants. The assumption is that behind entry barriers established firms have a degree of freedom of economic behaviour (e.g. pricing) which can be exercised so long as actual entry is not induced.[20] The height of the entry barrier can thus be expressed by measuring the maximum degree of latitude open to existing firms which does *not* induce entry. This is most easily seen in terms of existing firms being able to sell in the long run at prices above minimum average cost. Thus,

> 'The highest selling price that established sellers in an industry can persistently charge without attracting new entry may be referred to as the maximum entry-

forestalling price. Then *the condition of entry is measured numerically as the percentage by which the maximum entry-forestalling price exceeds the minimum attainable average costs of established firms.*'[21] (Original emphasis.)

One of the factors which makes computation of the likelihood of entry difficult is the output reaction of existing producers to new entry. This decision will of course affect the post-entry market price; and the potential entrant's decision on actual entry must obviously be based upon a comparison of his existing cost conditions and the *post-entry* level of prices. It may be that the simplest assumption to make is that existing producers hold their output levels constant following entry (the so-called Sylos postulate) in which case, aggregate supply having risen, the market price will fall. The precise extent of the fall will be dictated by the slope of the industry demand curve, that is, the price elasticity of demand for the product. The less elastic is demand for the product the greater will have to be the fall in the market price to absorb a given increase in supply. Thus all of the formal analyses of the impact of the entry of new firms into a market (which require extended graphical treatment to aid exposition) require to make assumptions as to: (i) the goals of the businesses involved – particularly the time horizon adopted; (ii) the respective cost functions of existing producers and entrants; (iii) the price and output reaction of existing firms to the advent of entry; and (iv) the price elasticity of demand for the product faced by each party.[22]

Barriers to entry are normally thought of as stemming from one or more of three sources: (1) product differentiation advantages for existing firms, (2) absolute cost advantages possessed by existing firms *vis à vis* potential entrants, (3) advantages of economies of scale accruing to existing firms and not enjoyed by potential entrants.[23] It is also normally recognised that the necessity for a high initial capital investment in a market may create a barrier to entry.

A product differentiation barrier may exist because current producers in the market enjoy goodwill (or simply inertia) on the part of consumers which makes customers unwilling to try something different. Potential entrants face a choice of overcoming this inertia either by offering a similar product (with similar average cost conditions) at a lower price, and therefore at a loss or lower profit to the entrant, or spending additional resources on product promotion, etc., in order to conquer existing consumer habits. Either of these two alternatives involves potential entrants in additional costs or reduced revenue; and it is the extent of these costs or the reduced revenue which creates the barrier behind which existing firms can raise their selling prices above average cost.

Existing firms in a market may have lower levels of average cost than potential entrants at all levels of output. In this case existing firms are said to enjoy absolute cost advantages. In this case again, therefore, existing firms may enjoy supernormal profits in relation to *their* average costs without inducing competitive entry. Bain suggests that the advantages under this heading may accrue to existing firms by virtue of their use of superior production, etc., techniques (maintained by patent protection); possession of superior resources – raw materials or management – or their acquisition on more favourable terms than those applying to entrants; or, as a particular example, that potential entrants face a higher cost of finance or a general lack of availability of such funds.

The most frequently discussed barrier to entry, however, is that arising from scale economies possessed by large existing firms which are held to prevent competitive entry into oligopolistic industries by smaller competitors. Economies of scale arise when long-run average costs decline as output expands.[24] The sources of such economies are varied, and quantification of their impact is complex. Basically, they arise due to the existence of non-proportional inputs: costs which rise less than proportionately with output. This may occur for certain fairly straightforward reasons, as when the volume of a tank (its usefulness) increases as the cube of its dimensions whereas the cost is likely to be a function of the square of the dimensions; or for more complex reasons relating to the availability and cost of finance and other scarce resources to small firms as opposed to large. All of these factors will be reflected in the shape of the long-run average cost curve. The rate of decline of average cost will depend upon the achievement and exhaustion of scale economy potential; and the lowest output at which full scale economies are achieved is known as the point of minimum efficient scale (m.e.s.) (figure 6).

The most important issues concerning economies of scale are: (1) Are the major economies realised at plant or firm level? (2) Within any industry what proportion of the total market is it necessary for a firm to acquire in order to operate at m.e.s.? (3) How less efficient does a firm become (in terms of a rise in average costs) by operating at, say, 75% of m.e.s.? The answers to these questions suggest that some element of monopoly may have to be accepted in return for scale efficiency, but that scale economies are often related to plant rather than to firm size. That is, the achievement of lower average costs is dependent upon the size of plant (establishment) operated by the firm rather than upon the size of the firm (enterprise) itself. This suggests that there may be very few cost advantages available to large multi-plant firms.

The difficulty for the potential entrant in this case where there are only scale economies and no absolute cost differences is twofold. First, for the potential entrant to enter the market at the level of output for m.e.s. or beyond may considerably 'rock the boat' so far as market supply is concerned, and may, depending upon the price and output reaction of existing firms, considerably lower the market

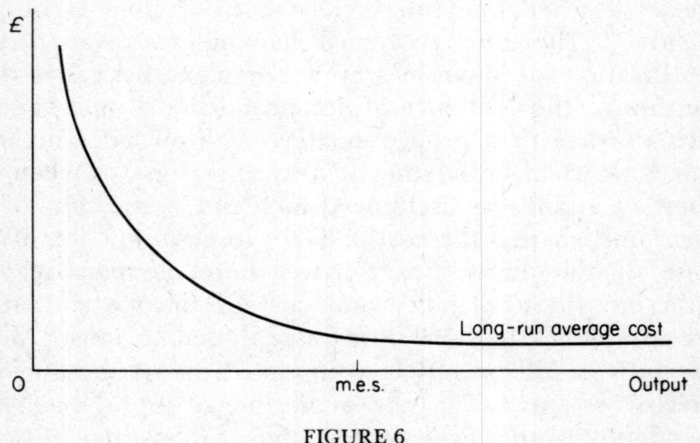

FIGURE 6

price. The comparison to be made by the potential entrant is, therefore, between his average costs at various levels of output and the post-entry market price. Second, if the potential entrant decides to produce for the market at a level of output below m.e.s., by what proportion will his average costs rise?

In fact, as Pickering points out in his analysis, Bain appears to neglect the complications introduced into the whole question by the possibility of entry into new markets by firms established in other market areas. Such firms may be induced to enter new markets by their awareness of profit opportunities, as part of a general strategy of diversification, or as a result of marketing a by-product. Firms may also be directly encouraged to enter a market by dissatisfied customers of existing suppliers. The point is that 'established' businesses do not face the same entry costs in moving into a new market as enterprises which are, so to speak, starting from scratch. These established businesses may have considerable financial resources, management ability, market power, and possibly even technical commonality which can be used in the new market area. All of this means not only that there is probably no way of measuring unique barriers to entry in respect of any single market, but also that barriers to entry of 'established' businesses are much lower than for entirely new enterprises.[25]

A well-documented case of this type of new entry is the U.K. potato crisp market. Smith's market dominance in the early 1960s (65% of the market in 1961) was disturbed by the entry of Imperial Tobacco's subsidiary Golden Wonder. By 1972 the new entrant had a market share of 39%, while Smith's was reduced to 32%. New entry was successful here despite a change in technology by the early 1960s which necessitated considerable initial capital investment and offered scope for production economies of scale. Golden Wonder's success was in fact built upon considerable further investment in advertising, which both consolidated its own market position and helped to expand the total market. The possibility of this new and powerful entry was obviously related to the financial strength and other market advantages of Golden Wonder's parent, Imperial Tobacco.[26] Other studies of the impact of new entry competition have stressed the role of existing firms moving into new markets (in petrol retailing), and the role of new entrants in reflecting the balance of supply and demand in the market. It was excess supply of world petroleum in the mid 1950s which allowed small non-integrated wholesalers to enter the market with cut-price petrol. Similarly, John Bloom's firm, Rolls Razor, took advantage of an expanding washing machine market in the early 1960s to introduce innovations through door-to-door selling, reduced prices and high levels of national advertising. It is interesting to note that in neither of these two markets did existing firms in the market behave in a particularly sophisticated manner in repelling entry. Response was rather slow, and in both cases the powerful competitive effects were swamped by further changes in demand conditions. Shortages of petroleum by the late 1950s put an end to price competition; and Bloom himself (largely because of a lack of financial control) failed to survive the period of poor demand for appliances of the mid 1960s.[27]

Finally, while there may be considerable difficulties involved in distinguishing between 'natural' barriers to entry (for example the need for large initial sums of finance where plant is of a large minimum size) and artificial barriers created by monopolists or oligopoly groups to preserve their existing market power, it is necessary to be aware of such a distinction. Some of the changes in technology at the current time make large minimum plant size inevitable. There are, however, some monopolistic practices which are operated solely to preserve existing positions of market power. Monopolists, for example, may use 'fighting companies': subsidiaries (perhaps undisclosed) which undercut rivals on a regional basis by charging very low prices. In this case entry forestalling pricing really becomes a form of uncompetitive predatory pricing. A variant of this practice is to sell at low prices in one sector of the market in order to secure custom in another.[28] Certain distribution policies may also create artificial barriers to entry. Ownership of retail outlets by producers, loyalty rebates or graduated discount scales (especially if aggregated among a group of suppliers) may undoubtedly act in this manner. Many of these may be quite unnecessary so far as distributive efficiency is concerned, and may add significantly to the difficulties of competitive entry into the market.

C. Business Behaviour

So far as this analysis is concerned market conduct has been broken down into two major areas: pricing, and promotional policies. Because a separate chapter is devoted to pricing in this text it is proposed to deal here only with the issue of the competitiveness of the making of pricing decisions, leaving the remainder of the issues on pricing to a separate chapter. This section also examines the role of advertising in market conduct.

(*a*) *Pricing*

In formal microeconomic analysis the overall pricing decision for producers in competition with each other, or for monopolists, is fairly straightforward. In between, however, is the area of oligopoly. Here, in the absence of formal restrictive trading agreements, the interdependence brought about by the fewness of suppliers produces a mutual respect for each other's reaction to individual pricing and output decisions. Although some discussion of oligopoly pricing has centred around the possibility that each firm would, at least initially, make some contribution towards maximising aggregate group profits (the qualified joint profit maximisation hypothesis),[29] more attention has recently been paid to thinking largely in terms of a kinked oligopoly demand curve facing individual producers. The existence of this kinked demand curve is held to account for two aspects of business pricing behaviour: the tendency for individual oligopolists to hold their selling prices constant despite changes in cost and/or demand conditions; and the corresponding tendency for all producers within an oligopoly to change their selling prices at the same time and in line with each other. As part of their examination of pricing behaviour the Oxford economists Hall and Hitch drew attention to a number of reasons for which firms operated on a full-cost (as opposed to a marginal cost and revenue) basis, and in particular why price-level changes should be infrequent. These centred upon inadequate knowledge of consumers' preferences (including the price elasticity of demand facing the producers as a group), and the uncertainty of the reaction of rivals (including potential entrants) felt by individual producers under conditions of oligopoly.[30] Basically, each oligopoly producer fears that his competitors will not follow him if he raises his own price from the existing level, while such individuals conversely fear that their rivals will, however, follow them in respect of price reductions.

It was the American economist George Stigler who first classified price leadership into two distinct types: dominant and barometric. Having carried out a number of tests using empirical data, however, Stigler actually found that price rigidity (indicating the existence of a kink in the imagined demand curve of individual producers) was *greater* under monopoly than under oligopoly, and that (again contrary to the established theory) price rigidity increased in those markets characterised by explicit collusion. On the basis of his findings Stigler distinguished between dominant price leadership and barometric leadership. Dominant price leaders have no kink in their demand curve – their market domination eliminates the wish or need for rival producers to sell at any price other than that established by the dominant firm. On the other hand the barometric price leader is only a price leader at all to the extent that his price 'reflects market conditions with tolerable promptness'. This type of price leadership also, in the opinion of Stigler, eliminates the kink in the demand curve in respect of significant changes in cost or demand conditions.[31] Again it was an American economist, Markham, who took Stigler's basic ideas further. Having regard to the public policy implications of this type of pricing behaviour, Markham concluded that price leadership as analysed to date was either inevitable and part of the monopoly problem in its 'dominant' form, or mainly a useful formulation of competitive price adjustments in the case of 'barometric' price leadership.[32] The only occasion upon which Markham saw a less-than-completely-dominant form of price leadership as having undesirable (and avoidable?) effects was where it was either openly associated with other restrictive trading agreements (Markham instanced trade-association activity, zone pricing, basing-point agreements, etc.) or (in terms of Markham's own tripartite division of price leadership) in those cases where price leadership operated in lieu of an overt agreement. Markham envisaged this occurring where a market comprised a small number of large-sized firms, where entry barriers were high, where there was reasonable product homogeneity in the market, where the aggregate market price elasticity of demand was not much greater than unity, and where cost conditions among firms were fairly similar. One may criticise the restrictive definition of this form of price leadership; but it is obviously necessary to have this additional category if the phenomenon is to be regarded as a special case in market conduct analysis and worthy of Government policy measures. Neither of these could be warranted in respect of dominant or barometric price leadership of themselves.

A limited amount of empirical work has been carried out in this area in the U.K. J. B. Heath investigated the area of potential price leadership in lieu of an overt agreement insofar as a question on price leadership was included in his questionnaire and interview follow-up of restrictive pricing agreements registered with the Registrar of Restrictive Trading Agreements under the terms of the 1956 Restrictive Trade Practices Act but subsequently abandoned. He found that in 37–41% of the cases examined a price leader was recognised.[33] More general comment on the existence of price leadership in this country has come from authors of business economics texts. These refer to the existence of price leadership in the synthetic fibres and motor car markets.[34] Further suggestions have also come from *The Economist*, which considered that it was 'no mysterious instinct' which allowed the electric light bulb manufacturers to institute parallel price increases in 1963, and which commented on the 'apparently telepathic simultaneity' with which the major gramophone record manufacturers changed their prices in the same year.[35]

The most recent empirical work in this field has been

carried out by Maunder in the context of a much broader study of restrictive trade practices in this country.[36] In an attempt to establish examples of the practice Maunder took three cases of apparent dominant price leadership (B.I.C.C. in electrical cables, British Ropes in wire ropes, and Hepworth Ceramic Holdings in clay pipes), and three areas where barometric price leadership could be considered to have occurred – plant-baked bread, glass bottle manufacture, and sanitary ware industries. Maunder found no evidence to suggest the existence of legitimate dominant price leadership in the first three industries above; and, on the basis of the latter three industries studied, concluded that barometric price leadership must be 'a somewhat fluid concept',[37] particularly when analysed in the context of information agreements (which obtained in respect of the glass bottle and bread industries discussed) and the operation of the Labour Government's 'early warning system' for price and wage settlements: both of which would tend to underpin any attempt at parallel price movement in the industry.

As part of the research related to its Parallel Pricing Report, the Monopolies Commission carried out a series of case studies covering bread, electric lamps, gramophone records, petrol and tyres.[38] While admitting the limitations involved in dealing with such a small sample, including the other instances of price leadership to which the Commission's attention has been drawn, it nonetheless felt able to conclude that 'we think it reasonable to infer from the evidence available that parallel pricing is a fairly widespread phenomenon in industry as a whole'.[39] Despite this, however, the Report was unable to present any *a fortiori* conclusions as to the impact of parallel pricing on consumer welfare. The Commission found no direct or causal relationship between parallel pricing and excessive profits or costs, impaired technological progressiveness or aggravated inflationary tendency in the economy. Too many other factors were involved in predictions under any of these headings for the Commission to come to any firm conclusions; and it might well be that parallel pricing is merely an additional characteristic *outcome* of more fundamental underlying market imperfections, e.g. oligopoly with significant barriers to entry. The

Commission was, therefore, led to conclude that a remedy for the possible defects arising from price leadership must include changes in market structure or direct Government supervision of prices in the industries concerned.[40] The issue of price leadership is a complex one – deriving largely from the oligopolistic structure of many markets in the U.K. economy. The task for anyone interested in analysing business behaviour is to distinguish between genuine dominant price leadership, an inevitable degree of barometric leadership encouraged by large common cost elements, etc., and a desire within a market to exist quietly under the umbrella of the largest (but not necessarily most efficient) firm free from the rigours of competitive market behaviour.

(*b*) *Promotional policies*

To judge from the space devoted to the topic in the business press (and the salaries paid to successful practitioners) advertising and promotional activities are a vital part of business conduct. Little, however, appears to be known about the impact of advertising upon demand for specific products, or about the wider effects of advertising upon market performance. Advertising as such, of course, is only the most obvious form of promotional activity by firms. Other expenditures in this area include 'below-the-line' payments to certain retailers for promotional facilities within stores, etc.

Total expenditure on advertising appears large to those outside the industry: £1.26m in 1976, or 1.6% of total consumer spending; and this figure is dominated by certain industries such as food, drink and tobacco, household and leisure goods, and toiletries and medical products.[41] Since 1922 when Alfred Marshall distinguished between 'constructive' and 'combative' advertising it has been assumed that economists were by and large critical of the impact of advertising.[42] This is perhaps an overstatement of the position; but a number of issues is certainly raised by the practice. Doyle highlighted three major issues. First, expenditure on advertising 'unnecessarily' raises costs and, under imperfect market conditions, prices. The epithet unnecessary would appear to be appropriate if one can conclude that much of advertising falls into Marshall's combative category, i.e. expenditure designed merely to combat advertising by one's competitors. Second, it is argued that the bulk of advertising is misleading, and therefore reduces the element of consumer sovereignty in markets. Third, it is contended that advertising tends to increase concentration in markets, and also acts as a barrier to entry. This would tend to occur when advertising expenditure was characterised by certain minimum threshold levels before it was effective or if there were significant economies of scale in such expenditure. High levels of advertising would also have the effect of creating patronage barriers to entry.[43] To set against these, Doyle argues that advertising may encourage technological progressiveness, and produce competition in terms of increased quality of goods.

In order to evaluate promotional conduct it would seem necessary to examine all of the above factors at the level of the individual market. As some of the data above suggested, the incidence of advertising varies from one market to another. Sofar as market structure is concerned, the pioneering study of Kaldor and Silverman found that advertising was particularly associated with oligopoly (as opposed to situations either of monopoly or of competition);[44] although Doyle points out that concentration alone does not explain high or low advertising/sales ratios: he points to the low figures in consumer durables (largely oligopolistic markets) and industrial goods (where other forms of conveying product information are used).[45] Similarly, an earlier study using variables to take account of the costs of supplying information (in terms of the total value of sales and the number of products being advertised) as well as concentration in the market established no clear relationship among the variables.[46]

Government investigative agencies have not, however, always been critical of high levels of advertising. In the case of confectionery the N.B.P.I. encountered an increasingly oligopolistic group facing a fairly static aggregate market in volume terms. Advertising expenditure was high: indeed for the confectionery market as a whole in 1967 it was higher in total expenditure terms than either beer, wines and spirits, or cigarettes and tobacco; and for some confectionery lines advertising and promotions accounted for almost 10% of selling prices. The Board, however, felt that the industry was competitive at both the manufacturing and retailing level; and that a high level of promotional spending was the price paid by the four largest firms for expanding their share of the market.[47] In the case of cigarettes and tobacco the Monopolies Commission, although it was not unduly critical of Imperial Tobacco's general conduct, recognised that the large advertising and promotional expenditure by Imperial did mean that smaller firms would find it difficult to enter the market and compete against Imperial's established brands.[48]

The most serious reservations on the role of advertising have been reserved, so far as Government reports are concerned, for the market for detergents. In this duopolistic market (in the Monopolies Commission's reference market the respective market shares of Unilever and Procter & Gamble were 45% and 43%) combined advertising and promotional expenditures as a proportion of net selling prices were found to vary from 12% to 25%, and were in some cases as high as 30%.[49] Each of the two Reports recognised that benefits to the public could arise from advertising: both in terms of information, the achievement of economies of scale, and, for example, reduced retail margins. It was felt, nonetheless, that advertising expenditure by those two firms went well beyond the level necessary to keep consumers informed. The Commission concluded on this point:

> 'Our principal criticism is that competition in advertising and promotion has tended to displace price competition. The effects of this are not only to increase prices to the extent that the additional expenditure in this field is wasteful, but also (except perhaps in the field of washing-up liquids) to keep new entrants out of the market, to weaken other competitive restraints on prices and profits, and to create a situation in which even the less successful of the two principal competitors can earn extremely comfortable profits while those of the more successful are outstandingly high.'[51]

The recommendations of the two bodies included an invitation to the two firms to consider areas in which they could compete on the basis of price, and a suggestion that they should restrain promotional and advertising expenditure;[51] and the Commission recommended an immediate reduction of 20% in the companies' selling prices accompanied by a 40% reduction in selling expenses.[52]

D. Conclusions

This chapter has highlighted the major variables within the structure–conduct–performance framework. It is in terms of this model that the more specialist chapters of the book should be read. In particular, the following chapter examines the problems of the measurement of market performance, and the statistical relationships which have been established between structure, conduct and performance variables.

Appendix I: Three-Firm Sales Concentration Ratios – U.K. Food Processing

Market	Ratio (%)	Comment	
Cereals	87	Kellog	56%
Bread and flour	64		
Cakes	66	Own labels	16%
Biscuits	63*	Associated Biscuits	42%
		United Biscuits	21%
		Own labels	27%
Corned beef	78*	Brooke Bond Liebig	60%
Chocolate and sugar confectionery	60		
Baked beans	100	Heinz	69%
Tea	74	Brooke Bond Liebig	40%
Instant coffee	80*		
Sugar	96	Tate & Lyle	60%
Tinned fruit	69*	Del Monte	36%
		Libby	33%
Canned potatoes	45	Mars (Yeoman)	17%
		Imperial Tobacco (Smedleys)	14%
		Cadbury Schweppes (Hartleys)	14%
Lager	65	Bass Charrington (Carling, Black Label and Tennants)	30%
Beer	49		
Frozen meat/poultry	81	Unilever (Birds Eye)	40%
Frozen fish	88	Unilever (Birds Eye)	63%
Frozen vegetables	94*	Unilever (Birds Eye)	74%
		Nestlé (Findus)	20%
Potato crisps	79	Imperial Tobacco (Golden Wonder, Chipmunk)	38%
Packaged cakes	44	Own labels	27%
Cider	96	H. P. Bulmers (Woodpecker, Strongbow, etc.)	60%

* Indicates two-firm ratio.
Source: *Trade Statistics*

Appendix II: Numbers of companies in the 22 main industrial classifications which held 50 per cent or more of the net assets in their classifications at end-1957 and end-1967*

Classification	End-1957 number	End-1967* number
Food	7	4
Drink	12	4
Tobacco	1	1
Chemicals and allied industries	2	2
Metal manufacture	6	4
Non-electrical engineering	23	19
Electrical engineering	5	3
Shipbuilding and marine engineering	4	3
Vehicles	5	2
Metal goods n.e.s.	2	2
Textiles	8	3
Leather, leather goods and fur	3	3
Clothing and footwear	3	1
Bricks, pottery, glass, cement, etc.	6	6
Timber, furniture, etc.	5	6
Paper, printing and publishing	6	3
Other manufacturing	2	1
Construction	7	5
Transport and communication (excl. shipping)	4	3
Wholesale distribution	21	14
Retail distribution	6	6
Miscellaneous services	4	5

* Adjusted for mergers which took place in 1968.

Source: Monopolies Commission, *A Survey of Mergers 1958–1968* (London, H.M.S.O., 1970) Appendix 10.

References

1. J. S. Bain, *Industrial Organization*, Wiley, New York, 2nd ed. (1968), p. 7
2. See, for example, F. M. Scherer, *Industrial Market Structure and Economic Performance*, Rand McNally, Chicago (1970), Ch. 1; and R. T. Nelson, An Outline of Industrial Economics, *Economics*, Vol. X (1974), 211–26. These authors both include the extent of diversification and integration as dimensions of market structure. These have not been included in the schema in this text because the author is unsure whether these can be considered as structure divorced from conduct, and because a separate chapter is devoted to each of these phenomena later in this text
3. J. S. Bain, Ref. 1, p. 9
4. *Ibid.*, p. 10
5. Strictly speaking the sales of the *n* largest firms relative to all firms classified as being in the market. This raises a problem over imports and exports, which will be dealt with below in the text
6. In general it might be assumed that there is a high degree of correspondence between various measures of firm size, and there has been shown to be a high correlation between these various measures. Bates, therefore, concluded that for purely 'statistical' purposes the choice of a particular size parameter was immaterial. However, the implication that a high degree of correlation between measures of firm size means that they are 'interchangeable', in the sense that studies of profitability against firm size (for example) will yield the same results irrespective of the measures of firm size and the denominator of the profits ratio, has been challenged on both theoretical and empirical grounds. See J. A. Bates, Alternative Measures of the Size of Firms in P. E. Hart, *Studies in Profit, Business Saving and Investment in the United Kingdom, 1920–62*, Allen and Unwin, London, (1965) Vol. I, Ch. 8; and D. J. Smyth, W. J. Boyes and D. E. Peseau, *Size, Growth, Profits and Executive Compensation in the Large Corporation*, Macmillan, London, (1975) Chaps. 2, 3 and 6
7. A more detailed statistical discussion of concentration measures is to be found in P. E. Hart and S. J. Prais, The Analysis of Business Concentration: A Statistical Approach, *Journal of the Royal Statistical Society*, Ser. A., Vol. CXIX (1956), 150–190. A further concentration measure involving the use of data on the market shares of all firms is the Herfindahl index (H). This is the sum of the squares of individual market shares. H will equal 1 in the case of pure monopoly, lower values indicating less concentration

8. A good discussion of this is contained in P. J. Devine *et al.*, *An Introduction to Industrial Economics*, Allen and Unwin, London (1974), pp. 55–63
9. This was certainly the view taken by the frozen food processors following a Monopolies Commission reference in June 1974. The processors argued that frozen foods were in competition with tinned and fresh vegetables, etc., and that frozen fish, for example, was also in competition with sausages, etc. See Why the Finger Points at Frozen Foods, *Financial Times*, 15th June (1974)
10. See S. J. Prais, A New Look at the Growth of Industrial Concentration, *Oxford Economic Papers*, Vol. XXVI (1974), 283. Figures relating to aggregate concentration by net assets show the top 100 firms moving from 60.1% of the total to 74.9% between 1957 and 1969. See L. Hannah, *The Rise of the Corporate Economy*, Methuen, London (1976), p. 166. As well as being a trend worth examining in its own right, there is obviously likely to be a relationship between economy-wide aggregate concentration data and individual market concentration. The trend of the former is generally recognised as moving ahead of the latter due to the diversified nature of the largest firms in the economy. It has been clearly shown, however, that those firms which are responsible for the high degree of aggregate concentration also play a predominant part in creating high levels of market concentration. See S. J. Prais, *The Evolution of Giant Firms in Britain*, CUP, Cambridge (1976), p. 21; and M. A. Utton, Aggregate versus Market Concentration, *Economic Journal*, Vol. LXXXIV (1974), 150–53
11. These are listed in G. Walshe, *Recent Trends in Monopoly in Great Britain*, CUP, Cambridge (1974), Appendix A
12. J. F. Pickering, *Industrial Structure and Market Conduct*, Martin Robertson, London (1974), p. 15. 'Markedly' was taken, broadly, to mean a movement of 20% in the concentration ratio over the period 1963–68
13. As this draft is written in 1976 readers may enjoy being reminded of Smith's observation that 'people of the same trade seldom meet together even for merriment and diversion, but the conversation ends in a conspiracy against the public, or in some contrivance to raise prices'.
14. See J. K. Galbraith, *American Capitalism*, Hamish Hamilton, London (1957), Ch. 9
15. *Ibid.*, pp. 125–6
16. For example the manufacturers of water-tube boilers held that a restrictive trading agreement which they operated would be justified by the need to counteract the buying power of the Electricity

Board which over the period 1952–58 placed 83% of total home orders for this product. See P. W. S. Andrews and E. Brunner, *Studies in Pricing*, Macmillan, London (1975), p. 50

17. See M. E. Sharpe, *John Kenneth Galbraith and the Lower Economics*, Macmillan, London (1973), pp. 15–21
18. R. B. Heflebower, Mass Distribution: A Phase of Bilateral Oligopoly or of Competition?, *American Economic Review*, Vol. XVIII (1956), 282
19. I myself have argued that the desire to achieve countervailing power might be a part of the explanation for the growth of supermarket chains in the U.K. in the late 1950s and early 1960s (in the face of food processor dominance), and for the corollorous merger movement among food processors in the late 1960s (to counteract the buying power of the multiple supermarkets). See W. S. Howe, Bilateral Oligopoly and Competition in the U.K. Food Trades, *Business Economist*, Vol. V (1973), 77–87. For reservations in respect of this industry see A. Hunter, Notes on Countervailing Power, *Economic Journal*, Vol. LXVIII (1958), 89–103
20. For a brief econometric analysis of the impact of barriers to entry see K. D. George, Concentration, Barriers to Entry and Rates of Return, *Review of Economics and Statistics*, Vol. L (1968), 273–5. George concludes that an examination of the height of barriers to entry should be a central part of any competition-policy enquiry
21. J. S. Bain, Ref. 1, p. 253. An extended treatment of this issue is contained in the same author's *Barriers to New Competition*, Harvard University Press, Cambridge, Massachusetts (1956)
22. For a more rigorous discussion of these issues see D. Needham, *Economic Analysis and Industrial Structure*, Holt Reinhart, London (1970), Ch. 7; K. D. George, *Industrial Organization*, Allen and Unwin, London (1971), pp. 92–98; and J. S. Bain, *ibid.* (1968), Ch. 8
23. J. S. Bain, Ref. 1 (1968), pp. 260–1
24. One of the most interesting accounts of economies of scale is still R. S. Edwards and H. Townsend, *Business Enterprise*, Macmillan, London (1958), Ch. 6. For research in the field see C. F. Pratten, *Economies of Scale in Manufacturing Industry*, CUP, Cambridge (1971); and for a survey of the major issues see A. Silberston, Economies of Scale in Theory and Practice, *Economic Journal*, LXXXII (1972), 369–91
25. See J. F. Pickering, Ref. 12, 70–73
26. See A. Bevan, The U.K. Potato Crisp Industry, 1960–72: A Study

of New Entry Competition, *Journal of Industrial Economics*, Vol. XXII (1974), 281–97

27. For further details see the case studies in R. W. Shaw and C. J. Sutton, *Industry and Competition*, Macmillan, London (1976), Ch. 2. Sometimes entry may come from an indirect source, as in the case of the packaged cakes market. In the early 1960s J. Lyon was the market leader; but during that decade the position was challenged by firms from the bread (Rank–Hovis–McDougall), confectionery (Cadbury), and biscuit (McVitie & Price) markets. See P. J. Barker *et al.*, *Studies in the Competitive Process*, Heinemann, London (1976), pp. 17–18
28. Further discussion of these practices, together with specific examples, is given in Chapter 8
29. See R. G. Lipsey, *Introduction to Positive Economics*, Weidenfeld and Nicolson, London, 3rd ed. (1971), pp. 271–3 for details of this
30. See R. L. Hall and C. J. Hitch, Price Theory and Business Behaviour, *Oxford Economic Papers*, Vol. II (1939), 22–23
31. See G. J. Stigler, The Kinky Oligopoly Demand Curve and Rigid Prices, *Journal of Political Economy*, Vol. LV (1947), 432–49
32. See J. W. Markham, The Nature and Significance of Price Leadership, *American Economic Review*, Vol. XLI (1951), 895
33. J. B. Heath, Restrictive Practices and After, *Manchester School*, Vol. XXIX (1961), 184
34. G. Bannock, *The Juggernauts*, Weidenfeld and Nicolson, London (1971), pp. 54–5 and 283
35. *The Economist* (9th February 1963), 528; and (29th June), 1408
36. W. P. J. Maunder, Price Leadership: An Appraisal of its Character in some British Industries, *Business Economist*, Vol. IV (1972), 132–40
37. *Ibid.*, p. 139
38. See Monopolies Commission, *Parallel Pricing*, H.M.S.O. (1973), Cmnd. 5330, Ch. 2
39. *Ibid.*, para. 40
40. A good critique of the Commission's Report is G. and P. Polanyi, Parallel Pricing: A Harmful Practice?, *Moorgate and Wall Street* (Spring 1974), 39–62
41. See J. F. Pickering, Ref. 12, 212–13. Pickering reports an even greater concentration of advertising expenditure within these groups in respect of television advertising. See N.B.P.I., *Costs and Revenues of Independent Television Companies* No. 156, H.M.S.O. (1970), Cmnd. 4524
42. See C. Gilligan and G. Crowther, *Advertising Management*, Philip Allan, Deddington (1976), Ch. 3

43. See P. Doyle, Economic Aspects of Advertising: A Survey, *Economic Journal*, Vol. LXXVIII (1968), 570 and 578
44. N. Kaldor and R. Silverman, *A Statistical Analysis of Advertising Expenditure and of Revenue of the Press*, CUP, Cambridge (1948)
45. P. Doyle, Ref. 43, p. 586. A good example of this is bread, where again an oligopolistic market structure is accompanied by relatively low levels of promotional expenditure. In this case the nature of the product and of demand for it limit the effectiveness of brand advertising. See W. P. J. Maunder, *The Bread Industry in the United Kingdom*, Loughborough University, Loughborough (1969), pp. 67–9 and 95–6
46. See P. K. Else, The Incidence of Advertising in Manufacturing Industries, *Oxford Economic Papers*, Vol. XVIII (1969), 88–110
47. See N.B.P.I., *Chocolate and Sugar Confectionery* No. 75, H.M.S.O. (1968), Cmnd. 3694, paras. 24–25 and Appendix L
48. See Monopolies Commission, *Cigarettes and Tobacco and Cigarette and Tobacco Machinery*, H.M.S.O. (1961), H.C.P. 218, para. 515
49. See Monopolies Commission, *Household Detergents*, H.M.S.O. (1966), H.C.P. 105, para. 32; and N.B.P.I., *Household and Toilet Soap Powders, etc.* No. 4, H.M.S.O. (1965), Cmnd. 2791, para. 39
50. Monopolies Commission, Ref. 49 (1966), para. 116
51. N.B.P.I., Ref. 49 (1965), paras. 48 and 61
52. Monopolies Commission, Ref. 49 (1966), para. 127

Chapter IV

Market Performance

Overview

This chapter is concerned with examining in more detail the measurement of market performance. Having outlined the basic approach and some of the difficulties involved in measuring performance, a number of studies is examined which involve establishing relationships between structure, conduct and performance dimensions. The chapter concludes with a brief introduction to the concept of workable competition.

A. Market Performance

As was outlined in the previous chapter, market performance is considered in terms of dimensions of Profitability, Efficiency, Product and Promotion. At a simple level performance is seen as being the 'outcome' of structure and conduct, with intervention in market structure and business conduct being justified as indirect means of bringing about desired changes in performance. Insofar as such intervention occurs to correct 'bad' performance it is very necessary to have a clear idea of how performance is measured, and of the statistical relationships between structure, conduct and performance dimensions.

B. Measuring Market Performance

The purpose of this section is to highlight some of the issues which arise in appraising market performance. These issues resolve themselves into three categories. (1) The lack of correspondence between certain concepts or phenomena in microeconomics and in the language of business people or Government statistics. (2) Allied to (1), the absence of data on many phenomena, and the problems of inconsistency and non-comparability of data between firms or industries and over time. (3) The problem of interpreting data in the context of performance measurement.

So far as the first of the above problems is concerned, the microeconomist's concepts of market, profit and firm are all imperfectly reflected in the available data. Some 'markets' such as cement or bricks are probably quite accurately reflected in trade statistics. Others such as containers, floor-coverings or industrial fasteners are not. These markets are often spread across quite different technologies (as in the case of containers) and even the largest producers of the goods concerned may be subsidiaries of large multi-product firms.[1] These circumstances make meaningful market analysis in some cases almost impossible. Profit is also a concept where microeconomists and practising accountants reflect different approaches. This applies both to asset valuation and income measurement, where the concepts of opportunity cost and discounting over an infinite time period are not applied by accountants. The ubiquitous diversified 'holding' company probably accords only to a limited extent with the economist's concept of the firm.

The second problem, that of inconsistency and non-comparability of data, is probably as significant as the first. The danger lies in the fact that this latter source of error is less well recognised than the former. Company accounting data present some of the greatest difficulties in the context of performance analysis: Oscar Morganstern described them as belonging to 'the category of functionally false statistics, of which they are probably the most significant illustration'.[2] This is more than a question of accountants failing to measure Hicksian income. Periodic revaluation of assets by companies would, one would anticipate, bring these more into line with the economist's concept of asset value. However, it appears that large companies have a significantly greater propensity to revalue their assets than smaller ones.[3] This will obviously overstate the asset growth rate of large companies *vis à vis* smaller ones; and will also understate the profitability ratio of larger firms. So far as small, unquoted companies are concerned it has to be recognised in their profit calculation that the deduction for directors' fees probably contains elements of both salary and profit. The final profit figure subject to tax is thereby understated; and to this extent surveys of the relative profits of large and small firms probably understate the earnings of the latter.[4] These and similar problems in the measurement of a number of important economic variables mean that the results of correlation analysis using company performance indicators over different industries and time periods should be treated with some caution. As in so many areas of investigation, the economics researcher may also find a complete absence of vital data. Turnover, i.e. sales, data were not required to be published by companies prior to the 1967 Companies Act. That Act also required the directors of a company to give a breakdown of turnover and profits (but not assets) by product group (see sections 17(1) and (2)). The breakdown, however, is seldom carried to a sufficiently disaggregated level to permit a meaningful market-by-market analysis of individual company performance.

The third problem, which must again be viewed in the context of those issues already discussed, is that of interpreting company performance data – particularly if this is being done with a view to implementing Government policy on industrial behaviour or performance. Take, for example, the question of expenditure on advertising and promotion – raised particularly by the Monopolies Commission in respect of detergents. One commentator raised a number of queries.

> 'The first difficulty, therefore, in establishing and justifying the Commission's diagnosis was the inadequacy of the available data for comparing selling costs in detergents with those of other industries. The second and more decisive weakness of the analysis was the lack of criteria by which to assess whether advertising or distribution costs as a whole were "excessive". Even if complete data made it possible to establish that the supply of household detergents entails a relatively high proportion of all forms of

advertising expenditure (not only press and TV) as a proportion of turnover (which is so in the U.S.A. for the 'soaps' group of industries) or, plainer still, to show that total distribution expenses (including other selling costs and retailers' margins) are relatively high as a proportion of retail price in this industry, the critic would still be left with the unresolved problem of whether the proportion is "excessive" and should be reduced in the interests of better use of resources and a lower price to the consumer.'[5]

Similar difficulties apply, perhaps more surprisingly, in respect of profit measurement. Not only are there the measurement problems discussed above; the interpretation of profit levels is not unambiguous.

'(One) implication of perfect competition is the absence (in long-run equilibrium) of unusually high rates of return on capital. For this reason, a high rate of return on capital is one of the traditional indicators of the existence of market power. Unfortunately, the test is ambiguous for a variety of reasons. In the first place, competitive markets are rarely, if ever, in equilibrium, and high rates of return on capital may reflect the presence not of market power but of competitive disequilibrium; alternatively, high rates of return earned by surviving firms may reflect high-risk activity and not market power, and even in perfect competition the perfect knowledge assumption is restricted to the present and does not encompass the future. In the second place, the existence of market power does not imply necessarily that rates of return on capital will be high. The market for the product may be subject to secular decline, and monopoly can offer only limited protection in such circumstances; alternatively, available high profits may be squandered in one way or another by management and/or workers in the privileged firm. At best, therefore, rates of return on capital provide an ambiguous measure of market power even when the inevitable problems of measurement themselves have been accounted for.'[6]

The issues highlighted in this section should serve to emphasise some of the problems confronting those involved in statistical analysis of market performance. They also suggest reasons why there is often little unanimity among researchers on many of the issues in this area. Furthermore, it should remind those involved in research and policy making that the concept, measurement and interpretation of profit is a particularly difficult task. This even applies to periods of stable money value, let alone to those of inflation.

C. Relationships Within the Basic Model

As was mentioned above, one of the attractions of the structure, conduct and performance model is the possibility of establishing some form of relationship – hopefully a causal relationship – between, for example, aspects of structure and conduct, and performance. This is in fact the assumed direction of cause and effect, based upon standard microeconomic analysis. Some of these relationships are suggested by arrows in the diagram below.

Structure	Conduct	Performance
Buyer concentration	Price policies	Profitability
Seller concentration	Product policies	Efficiency
Product substitutability	Sales policies	Product design, etc.
Entry conditions		Promotion

1. High levels of concentration may lead to a reduction in the degree of price competition and to the earning of monopoly profits.
2. Concentration may also lead to significant attempts to differentiate products and to high advertising/sales ratios.
3. Difficulties of competitive entry may sustain long-run monopoly profits.
4. Seller concentration may, with the avoidance of direct price competition, lead to greater emphasis on product

competition and thus a high rate of technological progressiveness.

5. The existence of unavoidably homogeneous products may lead to severe price competition and low levels of profitability.

However, what such an analysis omits is any form of feedback or reaction on the part of firms – particularly a reaction to unsatisfactory levels of profitability from the point of view of individual firms in a market. Low levels of profitability may induce certain changes in conduct – for example, a change in pricing tactics, in product policy or promotional expenditures – which may change structure through decreasing product substitutability, making competitive entry more difficult, or increasing the ratio of fixed (selling) costs to total. Falling profitability may also stimulate merger activity. This problem of a multi-directional chain of events within the basic model also produces difficulties of distinguishing between cause and effect. Does seller concentration encourage technological innovation; or does such innovation normally bring about changes in cost structures which dictate a larger optimum size of firm in the market and therefore, *ceteris paribus*, a higher degree of concentration? Thus,

> 'The emphasis on structure–performance links has failed to recognise that the contrary relationship may hold. For example, there have been many studies of the concentration–profits relation with apparently no concern for possible causality. Might not poor profits performance affect structure by leading to the exit of some firms from an industry and, conversely, might not high profits alter structure by attracting the entry of new firms into an industry? Similarly, even a perfect statistical correlation between concentration and technical progress would not prove that the concentration had induced the technical change. Again the contrary relationship might hold. Moreover, although participants in the market may be constrained by the existing structure of the market, the conduct of at least some of the participants may be directed towards altering that structure.'[7]

Some of the statistical relationships which have been established between dimensions of structure, conduct and performance are examined below. A knowledge of these is vital to an understanding of how markets work, and may be the basis for public policy in this area.

(*a*) *Firm size, market concentration, and profitability*

Data under this heading are vital to arguments about the efficiency of large firms, and must condition Government policy on monopoly and merger. The survey by Samuels and Smyth, covering 186 U.K. companies for the period 1954–63, came to three interesting conclusions: (1) There was overall a negative relationship between profit rates and firm size, i.e. larger firms were found to be less profitable than smaller ones. (2) The time variability of profit rates (as measured by the residual variance around the trend) was negatively related to firm size; and variability of profit rates in any one year was greater within small-firm groups than among large firms. This indicates that large firms have a less erratic profit performance over time than small firms, and that as a group they are more homogeneous with regard to profitability than small firms. (3) Using 1951 concentration ratio data, firms in high concentration ratio industries (especially where $CR_3 > 30\%$ – rather low by modern standards) had a lower time variability of profits.[8] Support for the first of the above conclusions (on the negative relationship between firm size and profitability) is given by Barron, although he found that this relationship did not apply in all cases when data were examined at the industry level.[9] Hart, using somewhat imperfect data from the early 1950s to the early 1960s, supported point (3) above in finding no relationship between the degree of concentration in a market and the *level* of profitability, but confirming a slight negative relationship between market concentration and profit variability.[10] The most recent study, covering the period 1970–3 and using the 500 largest U.K. industrial companies, confirmed the existence of a negative relationship between profitability and size – using net assets as a denominator in the profit ratio and as a measure of size – and again found no relationship between the profit ratio and market concentration.[11] However, so far as profit variability is concerned, these more recent results conflict with the earlier findings of Samuels and Smyth. No significant difference was found between different size classes of firms either in respect of profit variability at any one time or with regard to the time variability of profit rates.[12]

The findings of these and other U.K. studies[13] appear to cast doubt on the 'efficiency' of large firms. A similar lack of clear conviction on the part of U.S. studies, however, suggests either that the underlying data are unreliable and the statistical problems not completely resolved (and the findings of Smyth *et al.* clearly suggest this as a possibility), or that unresolved conflicting tendencies are being measured which sometimes throw up one set of results and sometimes another.[14] For example, large firms in concentrated markets may dissipate potential monopoly gains by purely prestigeous investment, lack of general cost control and other forms of X-inefficiency or managerial slack.

(*b*) *Size, growth and profitability*

Having already examined the issue of size and company profits, this subsection looks at the issues of growth and profitability, and growth and size.

So far as growth and profitability are concerned, financial considerations would emphasise the latter as a constraint upon the former. In respect of internally-financed growth, according to this view, a limit is set to the growth rate by the rate of return upon capital employed multiplied by the rate of corporate earnings retention.[15] Profitability also influences growth to the extent that high profits and dividends increase the firm's share price and so make external finance cheaper and more easily available. The relationship between growth as an independent variable, and profits is recognised as being more complex. Basically in graphical form, and measuring growth on the horizontal axis, the relationship is an inverted U. Initially, as the rate of company growth rises the effect is to increase profitability. Beyond a certain point, however, faster rates of growth tend to involve excessive managerial, etc., costs which reduce profitability. Given the fact that growth is likely to be a planned process, and therefore likely to proceed in a regular manner, while profits, as a residual, would tend to fluctuate from year to year, one might expect the statistical results in this area to be inconclusive. However, Marris's survey of U.K. studies in this area revealed, in the author's words, 'a degree of regularity which is quite surprising'.[16] The same was found to be the case with Eatwell's survey of empirical studies.[17] It is interesting, however, to note the conflicting results of Meeks and Whittington. These authors contrast the different performance of large firms so far as internally *vis à vis* externally financed growth is concerned. This recent study has pointed out that larger firms can grow more rapidly than smaller ones despite the greater profitability of the latter. This is because of the greater opportunities for raising external finance open to larger companies, particularly when this takes the form of share-exchange acquisitions of other companies.[18]

So far as size and growth is concerned the usual starting point is Gibrat's Law of Proportionate Effect. This law is based upon the assumption that the forces which generate business growth act in a random manner, such that over any period the rate of growth is independent of the initial size of the firm. Gibrat's Law, therefore, implies that different size groups of firms have the same mean proportionate growth rate and the same dispersion of rates around this mean.[19] This, it should be noted, would certainly imply a tendency to increased market concentration in the economy. The evidence here, however, is contradictory. Some studies have found Gibrat's Law a reasonable approximation to events in the U.K. economy;[20] some have found that large firms grow proportionately faster than smaller ones;[21] while others have discovered that smaller firms have achieved faster growth rates than larger companies.[22]

(*c*) *Market structure and research and development*

To the extent that much of the increase in welfare in an economy comes from the reduction in real prices which should follow from successful innovation in products or production methods, research and development performance by firms is of considerable significance.[23] In terms of the basic model the primary concern here is with the relationship between market structure and technological progress.

J. K. Galbraith has no illusions on the topic.

> 'A benign providence . . . has made the modern industry of a few large firms an excellent instrument for inducing technical change. It is admirably equipped for financing technical development. Its organization provides strong incentives for undertaking development and for putting it into use. The competition of the competitive model, by contrast, almost completely precludes technical development.'[24]

Galbraith's argument is essentially this: oligopolists have an incentive to compete on the technological front (rather than engage in price competition) and also the financial resources to do so (a product of their size, and possibly also of their 'monopoly' profits). He also argues that the nature of oligopolistic competition ensures that the benefits of technological change will accrue largely to the innovative firm rather than be forcibly shared with its competitors as in the case of structurally more competitive markets. Galbraith evidently has little faith in the operation of an effective patent system.[25]

The alternative *a priori* view is supported by Jewkes, Sawers and Stillerman. Regarding the relationship between market structure and research and development performance, these authors identify three forces: (1) the fear of being supplanted – the fear that if one does not take part in research activity one's products, etc., will become out of date; (2) the fear of being dispossessed – the fear that others may reap the fruits of one's research labours; (3) the hope of expansion – the hope of expanding one's share of the market on the basis of successful research.[26] This approach would suggest that the greatest force for technical advance would lie in unconcentrated markets: where the fear of being supplanted and the hope of expansion are greatest – the fear of being dispossessed hopefully being mitigated by an effective patent system. Monopolists would tend to react sluggishly on research within this framework, as their fear of being supplanted and hope of expansion, one would expect, would both be limited.

It is this type of *a priori* analysis which has influenced empirical studies in this area. Thus, although there are felt by some authors to be more complex issues involved (including the relationship between R. and D. behaviour and output, firm and industry price elasticities of demand, and anticipated reactions of market rivals – along a number of dimensions) most of the empirical work has involved correlation of market concentration or firm size and technological progress.[27] The basic test, then, is: are measures of market concentration and/or firm size correlated with increases in technological progress?[28]

As an example of earlier work in this area Phillips – using a small sample of U.S. data relating to the period prior to 1939 – correlated market concentration and firm size with technological change. The last was measured as decreases in the ratio of employment per unit of output, and increases in the ratio of horsepower per employee. Phillips certainly found significant correlation between increased technological change and concentration, between increased technological change and scale of plant, and between increased technological change and concentration combined with large scale. Moreover, these relationships continued to apply among the very largest firms and most concentrated industries. However, as the author himself stressed, the results should be treated with 'extreme caution'. Not only were the major parameters far from ideally specified; but the statistical tests used did not enable any *causal* relationships to be identified. The author himself left open the possibility that certain technical changes induce changes in scale and concentration.[29]

The general conclusion of review studies, however, is that large firms and concentrated markets have by no means demonstrated a unique record on invention or innovation.[30] Despite the fact that data show that the vast bulk of research in industrial economies is accounted for by the largest firms in the market,[31] studies relating firm size and market concentration to R. and D. inputs (e.g. employment) or output ('technical progress' or patents registered) cast severe doubt on the Galbraithian or Schumpeterian thesis. The Kennedy and Thirlwall survey of U.K. and U.S. studies, for example, concluded:

> 'As it stands, the evidence appears to be heavily weighted against the hypothesis that a necessary condition for technological change and progressiveness is that firms should be large scale and dominate the market in which they operate. From the very origins of technical change, in the work that is put into research, to the commercial application of new knowledge, it does not appear that large firms or monopolistic industries are necessarily more dynamic or progressive, or produce more fundamental technical change. After a certain threshold size there is even evidence that R. and D. activity and the number of patents issued appear to increase less than proportionately with size. Moreover, there is some evidence that it is not always the largest firms that innovate the quickest despite their presumably more favourable access to resources. Large firms by no means have a monopoly of fundamental changes either. Major technological breakthroughs come from a variety of sources.'[32]

The only caveat to be added to these conclusions relates to the concept of a minimum scale of research activity which appears to be necessary. Most surveys point out that below a certain minimum firm size, or in totally unconcentrated markets, almost no research is carried out; and Johnson quotes certain figures relating to minimum levels of expenditure on research deemed to be necessary before such efforts are likely to bear fruit: £8m in the case of communications satellites.[33] This concept of a threshold is held to apply particularly to innovation as opposed to invention.

Kamein and Schwartz went somewhat further in their analysis of U.S. evidence in this area. Not only did they cast doubt upon the existence of economies of scale in research (in the sense of the effectiveness of total research programmes of different sizes), but they also doubted the efficiency of large firms in terms of the research output from a given volume of research input. From this, and again in respect only of those firms which carried out an appreciable amount of research, these authors concluded:

> 'Roughly speaking, combination of research efficiency that decreases with firm size beyond a quite moderate size, and research input intensity that increases and then decreases beyond some point leads to anticipation that research output, relative to firm size, should increase with size but then decline with further increases in firm size. Within most industries, we would expect that the peak research output intensity would occur at a smaller firm size than the peak research input intensity, due to decreasing efficiency. In fact the evidence indicates that research output intensity does tend to increase and then decrease with increasing firm size.'[34]

A particular example of this relationship has been established by Reekie in respect of firms operating in the U.K. pharmaceutical market over the period 1959–66. Reekie found that beyond a certain firm size R. and D. intensity (R. and D. Expenditure/Sales) increased at a diminishing rate, and that in respect of very large firms the intensity ratio fell. Furthermore, with respect to the 'productivity' of such expenditures (measured as Patents/R. and D. Expenditure), Reekie concluded, 'the relationship . . . is not perfectly linear. Increasing returns are apparent initially up to the group including . . . (the company ranked 12th out of 20 by sales). Very intense diminishing returns then set in at R. and D. levels, in 1966 values, of somewhere under £2 million per annum'.[35]

The conclusion which our present state of knowledge allows us to derive from this survey is that although small firms find considerable difficulty in making a contribution to the total of research and development in the economy (particularly as regards innovation), beyond a certain threshold size of firm or degree of market concentration, market imperfections and their attendant static allocative inefficiency are unlikely to be significantly offset by superior performance in the dimension of technical progress.[36]

(*d*) *Advertising, concentration and profitability*

This relationship has attracted attention because of the fear that advertising may create or consolidate oligopoly situations, and, by reinforcing barriers to entry, may allow persistent monopoly profits to be earned. It has not always been clear, however, which of the above variables should be treated as dependent and which independent. There are, in fact, three relationships worth examining: (1) that between advertising as an independent variable and market structure; (2) structure as an explanatory variable in respect of advertising levels; and (3) advertising as a causal factor in respect of high rates of return.

As was noted from the very much earlier work, high ratios of advertising to sales were associated with oligopoly markets. More recent empirical studies based upon U.S. data have found significant correlation between concentration and advertising,[37] and also between advertising intensity and profitability.[38] The assumption in these studies was that advertising expenditure (as a ratio of sales) was the (an) independent variable.

Advertising may be held to affect market concentration if the economies of scale in this function dictate a larger optimum firm size than is necessary on the basis of economies of scale in, say, production or distribution. Such advertising economies of scale may arise for either or both of the following reasons: there may be economies in purchasing advertising, i.e. the more advertising a firm buys the lower is the unit cost; or there may be economies in advertising effectiveness beyond a certain level, when, for example, a firm with a number of brands in the market creates a sufficient 'presence' that advertising for each individual brand has beneficial 'spillover' effects in creating goodwill for other brands. Although there is some controversy over the existence and significance of scale economies in this function, one recent study of U.K. data has interestingly concluded:

> 'our general results point to the conclusion that advertising expenditures are subject to economies of scale up to some point greater than that to which multiplant economies of scale are in evidence, so that the influence of heavy advertising expenditures would be to increase the minimum efficient size of the firm.'[39]

So far as U.K. studies of the impact of market structure upon advertising levels are concerned, a more complex relationship appears to emerge between size and advertising intensity. Taking advertising expenditure as dependent upon market structure, and assuming that firms seek to maximise the expected return from such expenditure, Sutton hypothesises that such returns will be greatest for firms in oligopoly markets. Sutton argues that the individual firm in unconcentrated markets is unlikely to achieve significant benefits from advertising expenditure, given the smallness of existing market share, the difficulty of achieving a sustained market share increase *vis à vis* rivals in the market, and the disproportionate cost of effective advertising for small firms. Small firms in unconcentrated markets would also find it difficult to erect entry barriers to their markets. Monopolists, Sutton argues, have little to gain from advertising in terms of taking sales from smaller rivals.

Oligopolists, by contrast, stand to gain from advertising through increased sales taken from the fringe of smaller firms in the market, and can afford the expense of advertising. They may also have an incentive to use advertising to promote the smaller number of brands in the market; and may regard advertising as a less 'dangerous' competitive weapon among themselves than price reductions. Sutton substantiates this general hypothesis by data showing an 'inverted U' shape relationship between market concentration (measured on the horizontal axis) and advertising/sales ratios.[40] Further statistical support for this view, given the use of certain concentration measures, is provided from U.K. data by Cowling *et al.*[41]

So far as the impact of advertising intensity upon profitability is concerned, advertising here is assumed to be acting as a barrier to entry. This barrier will allow firms to earn supernormal profits without the fear that these may be eroded by competitive entry. Recent U.K. studies have lent some support to this view. Cowling *et al.* found that in the U.K. food industry differences in advertising expenditures at the firm level had an impact upon price-cost margins;[42] and other U.K. studies have tended to support this finding.[43]

(*e*) *Conclusions*

The purpose of this section has been to review some of the major findings of empirical studies on structure, conduct and performance relationships. A full appreciation of the value of these cannot be gained without an intermediate understanding of statistical methods and a working knowledge of the sources of the underlying data. Without such empirical studies, however, there would be a real gap in our understanding of the workings of industrial markets; and it has been suggested that the relative lack of such knowledge in this country *vis à vis* the United States has been responsible for the rather different approach to the issues of monopoly and merger in these two economies.[44]

D. Workable Competition

A further advantage of the structure, conduct and performance model stressed previously was that it permitted us to accept certain structures, imperfect though they might be in terms of more conventional microeconomic market analysis, if they led to, or were at least associated with, 'workable' performance. The concept of workable competition, stemming from the work of J. M. Clark,[45] is an essentially pragmatic one. It is concerned, in the words of one writer responsible for a considerable development of the ideas, with indicating 'what practically attainable states of affairs are socially desirable in the condition of individual capitalistic markets'.[46] Bain puts the task in context by assuming certain macroeconomic goals (for example, full employment, maximum volume and reasonable stability of output, a desired rate of growth of output, a satisfactory composition of output, and an acceptable distribution of incomes in the community), and then considering what sort of individual-industry structure, conduct and performance is most conducive to these macro goals. This crucial relationship between individual-industry performance and the attainment of established macroeconomic welfare goals is based upon a belief that, although other factors such as the attitudes of Government and organised labour enter into the analysis, it is the operation of business firms in the economy which is a central force; and upon the economic theory of general equilibrium analysis.[47] Having given itself a macroeconomic setting, workable competition then seeks to establish performance norms at the level of individual markets. These often become hideously complex, and certainly in some cases non-operational. But among the conceptually fairly (!) simple of Sosnick's performance norms are the following:

Performance dimension	Norm
Profitability	Should not vary from the normal level except to compensate for risk or innovation, or to bring about reallocation of resources
Output	No excess demand or stockbuilding should occur; and should generate normal profits
Promotional activity	Should be no more than necessary to inform consumers

Others of Sosnick's performance norms are less helpful: as when he suggests that 'the quality, variety, standardization, and location of sale of products should be curtailed only to effect the compromise between economy and individuality which informed customers would choose by an appropriate direct ballot'.[48]

Despite problems of establishing norms and specifying operational criteria, workable competition and the existence of the basic structure, conduct and performance model, have enabled policy makers to escape from an obligation to demand perfectly competitive markets in seeking to achieve the macro goals discussed above. Thus, instancing (*inter alia*) the absence of optimum conditions in all markets, the existence of external economies and diseconomies, the problem of incorrect and inconsistent expectations, and imperfect mobility of factors, Sosnick concludes that 'what they amount to is recognition that the perfectly competitive structure and conduct are unattainable in any real market, that closer approximations to them may entail worse performance than more distant, and that the closest possible approximation would entail actual and even equilibrium performance of dubious desirability'.[49]

At a practical level, and taking agriculture as a classic example, Maunder points out that 'industries which approach the conditions required for perfect competition characteristically do not give good market performance. By contrast, although industries characterised by a high degree of concentration of production may in theory lead to restricted output, excess monopoly profits, tardy innovation and exploited returns to factors of production, in practice they may be noted for low profits and prices and a high degree of technological progressiveness'.[50] Particularly pertinent in the light of the concern of most countries to increase the rate of technical progress is Galbraith's observation that 'industries which are distinguished by a close approach to the competitive model are also distinguished, one can say almost without exception, by a near absence of research and technical development'.[51]

The value of the concept of workable competition lies, first, in recognising the impossibility *and* the undesirability of achieving perfectly competitive market structures. Second, through the establishment of performance norms it lays down certain pragmatic criteria by which individual markets may be judged satisfactory or not. Third, it uses the relationships of the structure, conduct and performance approach to establish norms of structure and conduct. This last condition may give authorities guidelines for interfering in the structure and behaviour of firms in private-enterprise economies: a remedy for unsatisfactory performance which is likely to be more acceptable to both parties than direct long-term intervention or control over prices or profits.

There are those, however, who are critical of the use of the workable competition 'shopping list' of norms on anything but the most general basis. One reference to the criteria of workable competition speaks of 'a series of unrelated measuring rods of indeterminate length and with no units marked on them'.[52] The real criticism of the approach is directed at the lack of a coherent theoretical base – although it is considered that in this area no one coherent theory could be developed; and Bain himself speaks of the element of 'horseback judgement' involved in the approach. But this lack of theory does pose real problems. For example, what relative weights are we to give to performance in various dimensions; what are the policy implications for an industry characterised by monopoly profits *and* a fine record of technological progressiveness; in this case how much lower profits and how much less technical progress would be acceptable?[53] However, if workable competition and its associated norms are used as a means of highlighting 'areas for inspection', and if the norms themselves are accepted in a relative rather than absolute form and are not used for any exact evaluation, then the process does at least have the not inconsiderable virtue of drawing attention to gross divergencies on the part of some firms or markets from the market or sector norm. It is in this sense that although the identification and measurement of a single ideal is difficult it should be possible to distinguish a band or range of performance which is acceptable – performance outside this being regarded by implication as unacceptable, and, *prima facie*, open to inspection and judgement.

References

1. For example in linoleum Nairn Williamson is a Unilever subsidiary, and Barry & Staines is owned by British Steel Constructions.
2. O. Morganstern, *On the Accuracy of Economic Observations*, Princeton U. P., Princeton, 2nd ed. (1963), p. 81

3. See J. L. Eatwell, Growth, Profitability and Size: The Empirical Evidence in R. Marris and A. Wood (eds.), *The Corporate Economy*, Macmillan, London (1971), p. 391
4. See J. Bates, Some Problems in the Interpretation of the Accounts of Unquoted Companies, *Business Ratios* (Spring 1969), 30–1
5. G. Polanyi, *Detergents: A Question of Monopoly?* I.E.A., London (1970), p. 18
6. C. K. Rowley, *Antitrust and Economic Efficiency*, Macmillan, London (1973), pp. 10–11. In addition to the problems posed by Rowley, there are others raised by those who question whether the traditional measure of rate of return is sufficiently dynamic (and who would rather think in discounted cash flow terms), and also the issue of whether rate of return on capital alone (as opposed to measures of technical efficiency) is an accurate means of appraising business efficiency. See G. C. Harcourt, Investment-Decision Criteria, Investment Incentives and the Choice of Technique, *Economic Journal*, Vol. LXXVIII (1968), 77–95; and R. C. Skinner, Return on Capital Employed as a Measure of Efficiency, *Accountancy* (June 1965), 530–33
7. R. T. Nelson, An Outline of Industrial Economics, *Economics*, Vol. X (1974), 212
8. See J. M. Samuels & D. J. Smyth, Profits, Variability of Profits and Firm Size, *Economica*, Vol. XXXV (1968), 127–39. Readers interested in detailed specification of the variables and tests used and the significance levels of individual tests should consult the original studies.
9. See M. J. Barron, The Effect of the Size of the Firm on Profitability, *Business Ratios*, (Spring 1967), 13–15. Barron's data covered a similar period to that of Samuels and Smyth.
10. See P. E. Hart, Competition and Rate of Return on Capital in U.K. Industry, *Business Ratios*, (Spring 1968), 3–11
11. See D. J. Smyth *et al., Size, Growth, Profits and Executive Compensation in the Large Corporation*, Macmillan, London (1975), Ch. 6.
12. *Ibid.*, Ch. 7. This apparent conflict may be attributable to the inclusion in the earlier study of a number of smaller firms.
13. See, for example, the findings across only four industries of A. Singh and G. Whittington, *Growth, Profitability and Valuation*, C.U.P., Cambridge (1968), Ch. 6; and H. K. Radice, Control Type, Profitability, and Growth in Large Firms, *Economic Journal*, Vol. LXXXI (1971), 547–62
14. For a wider review of the literature see J. L. Eatwell, Ref. 3, pp. 389–421; and for some conceptual and statistical issues see A.

Phillips, A Critique of Empirical Studies of Relations between Market Structure and Profitability, *Journal of Industrial Economics*, Vol. XXIV (1976), 241–9

15. If E = total earnings, C = capital employed, and R = retentions, the maximum rate of internal growth, R/C, is $E/C \times R/E$.
16. See R. L. Marris, Profitability and Growth in the Industrial Firm, *Business Ratios* (Autumn 1967), 11–12
17. J. L. Eatwell, Ref. 3, pp. 409–17
18. See G. Meeks and G. Whittington, Giant Companies in the United Kingdom, *Economic Journal*, Vol. LXXXV (1975), 824–43
19. J. L. Eatwell, Ref. 3, pp. 402
20. *Ibid*., pp. 405–6; and J. Bates, in P. E. Hart, *Studies in Profit, Business Saving and Investment in the United Kingdom, 1960–62*, Allen and Unwin, London (1965), p. 180
21. G. Meeks and G. Whittington, Ref. 18. Furthermore, in an extension of their original study (Ref. 13 above) Singh and Whittington, using data on 2,000 quoted companies across 21 industries 1948–60, found evidence of a small positive relationship between firm size and growth rates, and also greater uniformity of growth rates among large firms, i.e. a lower standard deviation of growth rates around a higher mean. See A. Singh and G. Whittington, The Size and Growth of Firms, *Review of Economic Studies*, Vol. XLII (1975), 15–26
22. D. J. Smyth *et al.*, Ref. 11, 37
23. For example Johnson quotes Denison's study *Why Growth Rates Differ* which indicates that over the period 1950–62, 12–34% of the annual growth rate of Western economies resulted from a 'residual factor' related to extensions or increased application of technological knowledge. See P. S. Johnson, Firm Size and Technological Change, *Moorgate and Wall Street* (Spring 1970), 5. One would also, of course, need to know the composition of such expenditures on research and development. Britain, for example, is held to devote the highest proportion of resources in the world to R. and D., and yet has one of the lowest growth rates. See R. Winsbury, Science and Government in E. Moonman (ed.), *Science and Technology in Europe*, Penguin, Harmondsworth (1968), p. 91
24. J. K. Galbraith, *American Capitalism*, Hamish Hamilton, London (1957) p. 100
25. See generally *ibid.*, Ch. 7. This thesis also has an earlier ancestry: see J. A. Schumpeter, *Capitalism, Socialism and Democracy*, Allen and Unwin, London, 2nd ed. (1943), Ch. 7
26. See J. Jewkes, D. Sawers and R. Stillerman, *The Sources of Invention*, Macmillan, London, 2nd. ed. (1969), p. 135

27. For issues in the more complex analysis see D. Needham, Market Structure and Firms' R. and D. Behavior, *Journal of Industrial Economics*, Vol. XXIII (1975), 241–55
28. Jewkes, *et al.* would propose stronger tests than this. They want to know whether, within concentrated markets, new ideas come from the largest firms; whether each of the large firms makes an equal contribution to invention; whether long-standing concentration in a market breeds a particularly good record of technical progress; whether a change from a competitive structure to concentration rapidly generates increased research; and whether, in industries comprising concentrated and unconcentrated sectors, appropriate differences can be observed in the record of research and development. See J. Jewkes *et al.*, *ibid.*, 130–1
29. See A. Phillips, Concentration, Scale and Technological Change in Selected Manufacturing Industries 1899–1939, *Journal of Industrial Economics*, Vol. IV (1956), 179–93
30. Invention is regarded as being the creation of an idea and its expression in practical terms. Innovation is the conversion of an invention into a potential commercial proposition. For a further review of findings in this area see B. Lloyd, Invention Innovation and Size, *Moorgate and Wall Street* (Autumn 1970), 35–62
31. See P. S. Johnson, *ibid.*, 9
32. C. Kennedy and A. P. Thirlwall, Technical Progress, *Economic Journal*, Vol. LXXXII (1972), 61
33. P. S. Johnson, Ref. 23, 10
34. M. I. Kamein and N. L. Schwartz, Market Structure and Innovation: A Survey, *Journal of Economic Literature*, Vol. XIII (1975), 3
35. W. D. Reekie, Location and Relative Efficiency of Research and Development in the Pharmaceutical Industry, *Business Ratios* (Spring 1969), 6–9
36. One rather interesting additional comment on the research and development effort by large firms relates to the short-lived, low risk nature of much innovatory activity. U.K. data relating to R. and D. expenditures by large firms in 1971–2 show that 60% of such projects are completed in two years or less, and that 80% of projects are expected to be brought into use within a period of two years. See K. Schott, Investment in Private Industrial Research and Development in Britain, *Journal of Industrial Economics*, Vol. XXV (1976), at 83–87
37. See H. M. Mann, J. A. Henning and J. W. Meehan Jr., Advertising and Concentration: An Empirical Investigation, *Journal of Industrial Economics*, Vol. XVI (1967) 34–45; W. S. Comanor and

T. A. Wilson, Advertising, Market Structure and Performance, *Review of Economics and Statistics*, Vol. XLIX (1967), 423–40; and L. A. Guth, Advertising and Market Structure Revisited, *Journal of Industrial Economics*, Vol. XIX (1971), 179–98

38. See R. A. Miller, Market Structure and Industrial Performance: Relation of Profit Ratio to Concentration, Advertising Intensity, and Diversity, *Journal of Industrial Economics*, Vol. XVII (1969), 104–18; and W. S. Comanor and T. A. Wilson, On Advertising and Profitability, *Review of Economics and Statistics*, Vol. LIII (1971), 408–10
39. K. Cowling, J. Cable, M. Kelly and T. McGuinness, *Advertising and Economic Behaviour*, Macmillan, London (1975), p. 110
40. See C. J. Sutton, Advertising, Concentration and Competition, *Economic Journal*, Vol. LXXXIV (1974), 56–69
41. K. Cowling *et al.*, Ref. 39, pp. 89 and 93
42. *Ibid.*, pp. 125–6
43. J. Khalilzadeh-Shirazi, Market Structure and Price-Cost Margins in U.K. Manufacturing Industries, *Review of Economics and Statistics*, Vol. LVI (1974), 67–76.
44. S. E. Holtermann, Market Structure and Economic Performance in U.K. Manufacturing Industry, *Journal of Industrial Economics*, Vol. XXII (1973), 119–20
45. See J. M. Clark, Toward a Concept of Workable Competition, *American Economic Review*, Vol. XXX (1940) 241–56
46. S. H. Sosnick, A Critique of Concepts of Workable Competition, *Quarterly Journal of Economics*, Vol. LXXII (1958), 383
47. See J. S. Bain, *Industrial Organization*, Wiley, New York, 2nd ed. (1968), pp. 13–14 and 22–25
48. For Sosnick's performance norms see S. H. Sosnick, Ref. 46, pp. 416–18
49. *Ibid.*, p. 384
50. W. P. J. Maunder, Workable Competition and the Assessment of Market Performance, *Loughborough Journal of Social Studies*, Vol. II (1969), 22
51. J. K. Galbraith, Ref. 24, 105
52. D. Swann, D. P. O'Brien, W. P. J. Maunder and W. S. Howe, *Competition in British Industry*, Allen and Unwin, London (1974), p. 109
53. See *ibid.*, pp. 103–109 for amplification of these criticisms.

Chapter V

The Economics of Vertical Integration

Overview

This chapter deals with the phenomenon of combining a number of successive stages of production or distribution under the common control of one business organisation. The principal discussion centres around the advantages or otherwise of such a means of co-ordination, as opposed to a market or 'arms length' relationship, and how business men attempt to achieve the benefits of this strategy without the disadvantages.

A. Vertical Integration and its Extent

Integration of economic activities can be said to occur when a single business undertakes more than one successive stage in the total process of moving from a set of raw materials to the placing of the finished product in the hands of the final consumer. To this extent most businesses are 'integrated' in some way. However, the real interest centres around the decision on the part of any business to undertake functions preceding or succeeding its main activity which could have been performed by a separate company whose services the former could have bought. It is this conscious policy of integration which is of concern to economists. Furthermore, because technical considerations often more or less dictate the need to carry out several successive stages of production at one location (for example, in order to conserve heat in the case of steel rolling mills, or to avoid excessive transport costs in a weight-losing production process such as timber pulp and paper making) these are only to a lesser degree situations in which a business has exercised a conscious decision to become an integrated organisation. Of much more concern is why multiple retailers do or do not manufacture their own food, dresses or shoes; and why beer and petroleum manufacturers wish to control their distribution points. Vertical integration is normally broken down into two types: backward, when a producer integrates into a previous stage of manufacture; and forward, when the firm moves into a succeeding area of activity.

The extent of integration in the economy is not susceptible to precise measurement, although it has been suggested that the ratio of value added to turnover would in principle give a reasonable indication.[1] Unfortunately no empirical studies have been carried out at the aggregated level in this area, with the result that we have little idea of the current extent of the practice, nor of the direction or speed of any trends.

B. Reasons for Integration

A large number of reasons has been put forward to explain the attractiveness of vertical integration for individual firms, and these can be classified under a variety of headings. There are also varying degrees of abstractness in terms of which the advantages and disadvantages may be discussed. It is proposed to discuss the question under three main headings in this section.

(*a*) *Conceptual advantages of vertical integration*

One of the reasons most commonly put forward in this context to support a policy of vertical integration is that the strategy eliminates 'unnecessary' market or transaction costs. In the first place the whole activity of haggling and bargaining may be eliminated if two formerly independent companies become successive divisions under common corporate ownership.[2] In particular advertising and promotional expenses formerly incurred by the preceding stage of operations are no longer necessary. This last point may be generalised by saying that there is a saving in the whole cost of gathering, processing and using information. Neither should there be such a large purchasing function within the latter group. Other costs that may be avoided, or at least substantially reduced, are those physical and financial expenses associated with stockholding. None of this is, however, to deny that vertical integration itself also has its associated administrative costs; and it will be found, for example, in Chapter VIII that the technique of transfer pricing for costing services moving from one division to another within a firm has difficulties of its own. One of the costs which business men apparently consider it most worthwhile to try to eliminate is the 'unnecessary' profit margin on goods bought in.[3] These people presumably recognise that all business functions, including capital and entrepreneurship, must be adequately rewarded. However, if a manufacturer at one stage of production considers that his suppliers are making 'supernormal' profits (because, for example, they constitute a monopoly or oligopoly group), or if the manufacturer considers that he is more efficient in general terms than his suppliers, or if under particular circumstances the manufacturer has some spare capacity (either physical or managerial) which he considers is costless in terms of opportunity earnings, then the manufacturer may be tempted to integrate backwards in the market. This, of course, is often the ultimate threat which manufacturers can use to induce their suppliers to lower their prices.

Vertical integration may also be a means of reducing certain business risks and the costs associated with these. Stockholding, mentioned above, is one of these. Stocks of raw materials and of finished goods are held basically because the incidence of their requirement is unknown, or may only be predicted within wide limits. Following vertical integration, holding of finished goods by the preceding division, and of those same material inputs by the succeeding division can be amalgamated and reduced. An example of a further risk which may be absorbed, if not eliminated, as a result of vertical integration is that of price changes. In the case of two distinct businesses the seller may accept a fixed-price contract, in which case he bears the brunt of unforeseen cost increases, or 'escalation clauses' may be built into a contract which allow the seller to pass on cost increases via a rise in price on the basis of prearranged formulae. Either of these arrangements may reduce the element of risk for one party. Vertical integration internalises and so further reduces the risk of a combined concern. However, there is also inflexibility in this. A business which integrates backwards to acquire a source of inputs may lose the opportunity to buy those same inputs at a lower price in the market. The familiar example of this is Unilever's purchase of sources of several of its primary commodity inputs in Africa. Unfamiliarity with the management of these, and a fall in the world market price of the commodities meant that backward vertical integration 'instead of bringing independence, security and profit, . . . could bring bondage, insecurity and loss'.[4]

Finally, and more tentatively, it may be suggested that some categories of integration, in the form of undertaking services that precede or succeed others, may capture some externalities which would otherwise be missed. Where one service is consumed with another each is creating an external benefit for the other. If the two services are run by separate corporate entities this interdependence, while it may be casually recognised, may not be rigorously analysed or quantified. Only the threat of one business going out of existence because of continuous operating deficits will bring the value of the externality to light. Nove gives a characteristically homely example of a shipping service and a hotel on an island.[5] As separate entities neither is concerned about its effect on the other or *vice versa.* Ultimately if *either* was running at a loss *both* might be forced out of business. This would not, however, have to occur if the concerns were integrated under one management. This would be an excellent example of the efficiency of internalising externalities. The same policy consideration would apply to all cases of integrated transport and accommodation operations, etc., and the argument could equally apply to the strategy of diversification.

(*b*) *Examples of increased communications and control*

When a business requires component parts which have to be made to a very high standard of accuracy, or where the standard required cannot be the subject of exact specification, then the operation of two successive stages of production may be better carried on under a single management. This will encourage a closer relationship between those at the operational level, and this may be reinforced by a common superior management. Edwards and Townsend stress this encouragement to integration, and give examples from the steel industry where cutlers or nut and bolt manufacturers may wish to operate their own forges or have their own steel-making capacity in order to ensure the necessary quality of inputs and co-operation between successive stages of production.[6] It should be noted that this is the result of a conscious management decision which is quite divorced from the purely technical considerations such as heat conservation in continuous steel making.

This question of control over component production has been extended in the case of the motor car assembly firms to embrace security of supplies. Thus there has been a history since 1945 of assembly firms acquiring body building capacity, culminating in 1966 in the disappearance of the last independent supplier of mass-produced car bodies in Britain with B.M.C.'s acquisition of Pressed Steel. The principal arguments put forward by B.M.C. in favour of the merger were that it would lead to increased coordination and certainty of component supplies, and to greater stability of operations.[7]

Two well-known cases of forward vertical integration for increased control are those of brewing and petroleum distribution. Two factors are common to these markets: first, there are restrictions on the number of outlets, which increases the difficulty of internal expansion in the market; second, the manufacturers feel that control over distribution helps to ensure increased turnover of their particular brand of the product. In the case of brewing this has led to a situation where in 1967 the brewing firms owned 48% of licensed outlets, including some 78% of on-licensed premises (basically public houses).[8] In the case of petroleum distribution the refiners' arrangement with the distributors (garages) was not based entirely upon corporate ownership (although an estimated 28% of U.K. sites are actually 'company' owned)[9] but upon a 'solus site' arrangement under which, in return for certain financial advantages such as low-interest loans, the individual garages agreed to sell only one brand of petrol and other petroleum products. Again the emphasis here must be on the contribution which this makes to certainty of turnover in an industry characterised by large expenditures on exploration, drilling and production undertaken considerably in advance of retail sales. It is also claimed by the petroleum companies that garage ownership and solus site arrangements help to reduce the cost of physical distribution, and improve administrative efficiency.[10] There may be a further incentive to forward vertical integration of this type where manufacturers are faced with a relatively static or declining market. This is clearly the case with the U.K. bread market where the major milling groups have integrated forward to ensure a market for their bread flour;[11] and the same process of ensuring outlets for production can be seen in the extent of vertical integration in the textile industry from spinning thread to retailing the final product.[12] A similar trend may also be found in the footwear market. In aggregate this industry appears to be faced with a low income elasticity of demand; and at the same time competition from imports is severe. In this market increased mechanisation of production together with the use of synthetic materials and the potential for production economies of scale have been accompanied by vertical integration, though some of this has resulted from the large multiple retailing groups (e.g. British Shoe Corporation, a Sears Holdings subsidiary) establishing manufacturing capacity.[13]

(*c*) *Vertical integration and development of the market*

Some of the examples above have particularly emphasised the desire to control subsequent stages of a market as a motivation for vertical integration, with an emphasis on forward movement in the market. There are cases, however, of a market remaining integrated from an early stage in its development because of the slowness with which separate functions (which could be made available through market transactions between companies) developed, or because developments at one stage of the total market process could not otherwise easily be kept in step with others. This appears to have occurred in a number of industries having otherwise little in common. Thus, commenting on the extent of vertical integration in the chemical industry two authors pointed out,

> 'Companies making chemicals have been anxious to ensure their supplies of petrochemicals by merging with oil companies; oil companies have tried to ensure outlets for their petrochemicals by taking over chemical companies. Further down the chain of processes, firms making plastics have tried to ensure their markets by going in for plastics fabrication and firms making paint raw materials have decided to enter the paint market itself.'[14]

With particular reference to the oil industry Adelman stressed:

> 'The structure derives from a history starting before World War I. Low-cost sources and profitable markets beckoned in distant places. Companies knew how to make money in finding, processing, and selling oil. Their skills could not be sold or leased, they could only be used. Those who found crude oil did not care to sell to a few buyers; they built their own refineries. Those who had built sales outlets for refined products did not care to buy crude from a few sellers; they looked for crude oil. A concentrated integrated market structure thereby perpetuated itself.'[15]

A similar structure in manufacture and retailing of men's clothing is explained in terms of the history of the industry.

> 'The reason for the industry's vertical integration from retailing to manufacturing dates back to earlier in the century, when the suit market was clearly divided into a limited range of ready-to-wear suits for the working-class, and made-to-measure suits for the better off. However, Montague Burton – a general outfitter – decided to expand by offering bespoke tailoring at the cheaper end of the scale. Burton had all the ingredients for success, and by

> 1929 when the group went public there were 300 retail shops in operation and many other retailers followed his example.
>
> Most of the groups had to expand into manufacturing because their retailing operations were running ahead of their suppliers' ability to manufacture suits. Once involved in manufacturing, the retailers found themselves more or less forced into opening more and more new shops in order to satisfy the output that their factories were capable of.'[16]

Some of these examples would seem to confirm Stigler's view that while vertical integration may be necessary in the early stages of the development of a market, subsequent expansion of the market would facilitate greater specialisation of functions and the replacement of integration by a market relationship. Thus,

> 'If one considers the full life of industries, the dominance of vertical disintegration is surely to be expected. Young industries are often strangers to the established economic system. They require new kinds or qualities of materials and hence make their own; they must overcome technical problems in the use of their products and cannot wait for potential users to overcome them; they must persuade customers to abandon other commodities and find no specialized merchants to undertake this task. These young industries must design their specialized equipment and often manufacture it, and they must undertake to recruit (historically, often to import) skilled labor. When the industry has attained a certain size and prospects, many of these tasks are sufficiently important to be turned over to specialists. It becomes profitable for other firms to supply equipment and raw materials, to undertake the marketing of the product and the utilization of by-products, and even to train skilled labor.'[17]

It would seem, however, that this tendency could not be expected to operate in all cases, and that some circumstances would tend to encourage more mature industries to increase integration. This could be expected to be the case where maturity and increased technological complexity work together. In this case research and development spillover effects, the internal marketing of by-products or reusing of waste or scrap materials may lead to increased vertical integration as the industry matures.

C. Disadvantages

There may, however, be potential disadvantages associated with vertical integration so far as individual firms are concerned. Among the more specific of these are the disparities which can arise between the productive capacity of successive stages of operation, the loss of the advantages of specialisation, inability to adjust output levels rapidly in response to changes in the economic environment, problems of loss of management control, and failure to subject intermediate operations to the test of market efficiency. This last problem may be attacked through the use of a transfer pricing system. One of the most formidable problems is that of matching the output of intermediate product groups to the requirements of succeeding stages of manufacture. A shortfall or excess of these inputs as a regular occurrence could lead to serious inefficiency. The result, as one financial journalist put it, is that a firm ends up competing with its suppliers or supplying its competitors.[18] By this was meant that production by one unit surplus to the requirements of a succeeding unit might have to be sold at marginal cost to competitors, while any shortfall has to be bought in from firms who normally regard one as competing with them and where goodwill will therefore be limited.

It is this type of situation which may have tended to bring about a relationship between some firms which Blois has termed vertical quasi integration. The goal of the purchasing firm in these cases is to achieve the advantages of vertical integration without assuming the risks, rigidity or responsibility of corporate ownership.[19] This position is achieved by the purchasing firm becoming a 'large customer' of the supplier in terms of taking a significant proportion of the output of the latter, and of being in a position to withdraw this custom in favour of another supplier or full vertical integration. As a result of this relationship a purchasing firm may receive special treatment in terms of delivery, stockholding, credit, non-standard products, technical services, etc., which the supplier's other customers do not receive, and which the purchasing firm would normally obtain only from a fellow subsidiary. In addition to all this of course the large customer may expect to pay a lower price for the goods than other purchasers.[20] To the extent that these practices exist, then clearly some firms have achieved the advantages of vertical integration without the disadvantages; and furthermore, any formal measure of the degree of vertical integration across the economy may seriously underestimate the extent of the practice through ignoring vertical *market* linkages which operate in the same way as would common corporate ownership of the successive production operations involved.

D. Conclusions

As with many business practices, integration raises a number of questions in the mind of the economist which are centred around efficiency of resource allocation and market performance in general. As will be found again in the following chapter on diversification, it becomes difficult to appraise performance in different economic markets if single corporate units, producing consolidated financial accounts, operate across these market boundaries. This is a problem of sheer lack of information. It may, however, be the case that even when an attempt is made to produce data on, say, profitability in one market an integrated concern may experience difficulties not only in allocating common overhead expenses but also in calculating input and sales data in respect of one market. This is the problem of transfer pricing, detailed in Chapter VIII. As a practical example, the Government has over the past decade conducted a number of investigations into the politically sensitive bread industry, and found that profitability in baking is low. But the major bread makers in the U.K. are in fact large integrated (and diversified) groups with interests in milling and bread retailing as well as baking. It has been suggested that baking profits may have been removed and are to be found among the better returns on milling.[21]

It may also be held that vertical integration has an effect in reducing the degree of competition in a market, especially if this is aggravated by the issue of monopoly on the part of the integrated concern. So far as competitive entry and raw materials are concerned a potential entrant into a market may find that he cannot obtain access to raw materials except via the organisation against whose final product he wishes to compete. Some industries, although characterised by monopoly, remain quite open in this respect. Thus, although Bridon (formerly British Ropes) accounts for around 53% of U.K. wire rope output and does supply some of its competitors with roping wire, the other wire rope manufacturers largely supply their needs from their own drawing mills.[22] A different situation would, however, appear to obtain in respect of some types of electric cables. Here the dominant producer, B.I.C.C., is a significant supplier of copper rod and wire to competitors in the mains cable market. Thus, speaking of B.I.C.C.'s role as price leader in this market, one survey concluded that 'since independent cable firms have relied on it as a source of copper rod they may have felt constrained in their pricing policy in selling cables'.[23] A further documented case is that of Courtaulds which provided cellulosic fibres on more favourable terms (including price) to its own subsidiaries than to their competitors. The Monopolies Commission had particular reservations regarding this practice in the light of Courtaulds' monopoly position in the cellulosic fibres market.[24]

In these respects, therefore, some aspects of vertical integration – especially on the part of companies in a semi-monopoly position – may have harmful effects upon competition in a market. New entrants may be deterred; and existing competitors may be put at a price disadvantage in buying from an integrated concern. All of this is in addition to the detrimental effect of integration in tying up retail outlets, particularly where the availability of these is restricted by legislation as in the case of licensed premises or garages. These problems must be considered when weighing up the advantages of vertical integration to businesses, and arriving at some view as to the net effect upon consumer welfare.

References

1. See J. F. Pickering, *Industrial Structure and Market Conduct*, Martin Robertson, London (1974), pp. 53–4
2. See O. E. Williamson, *Corporate Control and Business Behavior*, Prentice Hall, New Jersey (1970), pp. 15–18
3. See R. S. Edwards and H. Townsend, *Business Enterprise*, Macmillan, London (1958), pp. 204–5
4. C. Wilson, *The History of Unilever*, Cassell, London (1954), Vol. I, p. 265
5. See A. Nove, *Efficiency Criteria for Nationalised Industries*, Allen and Unwin, London (1973), pp. 16–17
6. See R. S. Edwards and H. Townsend, Ref. 3, pp. 205–9. The steel industry in fact provides examples of a variety of forces operating to encourage vertical integration. Dormer, for example, (formerly known as Sheffield Twist Drill & Steel) a major manufacturer of drills, acquired its own steel making, forging and wire mill capacity both in order to have a protected source of supply and to ensure control over quality of materials. The attraction of some of these facilities also lay in the difficulty of securing planning permission to build new forges, etc., in built-up areas. See C. Caulkin, The Drill at Sheffield Twist, *Management Today* (April 1975), 43.
7. See Monopolies Commission, *British Motor Corporation Ltd. and Pressed Steel Company Ltd.*, H.M.S.O. (1966), H.C.P. 46. Prior to the merger B.M C. bought 28% of its total body requirements from Pressed Steel accounting for about 40% by value of the latter's output. A car body represents 35–40% of the unit value of the finished vehicle. See Monopolies Commission, this Ref., paras. 19, 24 and 44
8. Monopolies Commission, *Beer*, H.M.S.O. (1969), Cmnd. 216, paras. 168–70
9. See The Analysis of European Distribution Systems, *International Journal of Physical Distribution*, Vol. III (1972), 35
10. Monopolies Commission, *Petrol*, H.M.S.O. (1965), H.C.P. 241

11. See N.B.P.I., *Bread and Flour*, H.M.S.O. (1965), Cmnd. 2760, para. 12. This integration has in fact been carried through to the retail stage as a feature of the oligopolistic competition in this market where the three largest producers currently account for about 70% of sales. N.B.P.I. (this Ref., paras. 12 and 46) pointed out that 1/6 of bread sales are through producer-owned retail outlets, and R.H.M., A.B.F. and Spillers-French now have over 5,500 outlets either directly owned or 'tied' to them in respect of bread sales. See T.A.C.C., *Bread: An Assessment of the British Bread Industry*, Intermediate Publishing, London (1974), pp. 59–60
12. See T. Lester, Tootal's Vertical Theme, *Management Today* (June 1975), 42
13. See Challenging Times for the Footwear Industry, *Midland Bank Review* (May 1971), 14–19. B.S.C. is estimated to account for just under 10% of U.K. footwear production, and to hold about 35% of the retail market. See E.I.U. *Retail Business* (October 1970), No. 152, 11–33. It is important to be clear that it is not being suggested that vertical integration itself will eliminate the problem of declining markets. What vertical integration may do, however, is to ensure a firm of a reasonable share of an existing market: an important consideration from the point of view of the firm particularly when the total market itself is contracting.
14. B. G. Reuben and M. L. Burstall, *The Chemical Economy*, Longman, London (1973), p. 110
15. M. A. Adelman, The Multinational Corporation in World Petroleum, in C. P. Kindleberger (ed.), *The International Corporation*, M.I.T. Press, Cambridge, Massachusetts (1970), p. 227
16. *Financial Times*, 24 January 1975
17. G. J. Stigler, The Division of Labor is Limited by the Extent of the Market, *Journal of Political Economy*, Vol. LIX (1951), 190. Some support may be given to this view by the findings of a study which suggested that if anything the tendency in U.S. industry was towards a decline in the extent of integration over the period 1929–65. See A. B. Laffer, Vertical Integration by Corporations, 1929–1965, *Review of Economics and Statistics*, Vol. LI (1969), 91–3
18. See R. Heller, Vertical Disintegration, *Times*, 20th June 1971
19. See K. J. Blois, Vertical Quasi-Integration, *Journal of Industrial Economics*, Vol. XX (1972), 253–72
20. The best example of this relationship in practice is that of Marks & Spencer, which has no equity investment in its suppliers but which plays the role of 'large customer' for many of them – a role

described as 'one of benevolent dictatorship rather than ownership'. See *Financial Times*, 31st October 1974

21. T.A.C.C., Ref. 11, p. 63
22. See Monopolies Commission, *Wire and Fibre Ropes*, H.M.S.O. (1973), H.C.P. 2, paras. 28, 76 and 119–20
23. D. Swann, D. P. O'Brien, W. P. J. Maunder and W. S. Howe, *Competition in British Industry: Case Studies*, Loughborough University, Loughborough (1973), p. 347
24. See Monopolies Commission, *Man-made Cellulosic Fibres*, H.M.S.O. (1968), H.C.P. 130, paras. 184–94

Chapter VI

Diversification

Overview

This chapter begins by adopting a working definition of the term diversification. This is followed by an examination of the forces which encourage businesses to diversify from a market in which they are established or to operate from the beginning on a diversified front. It is then asked if there is any particular direction in which firms are likely to diversify from a particular market base. This is followed by a discussion of the ultimate form of diversification – the conglomerate company. The chapter concludes by analysing the wider economic issues for the working of the economy as a whole which are raised by corporate diversification.

A. Definition and Extent

This chapter is concerned with examining why some firms (indeed the great majority of large companies in the U.K.) are not content with producing a single product or narrow range of goods. We want to ask why some of the largest firms have become diversified, in what way they have diversified, and what are the general economic principles surrounding diversification as a corporate strategy. Any distinction between *internal* diversification and *external* diversification, i.e. between purchase of individual assets or acquisition of other firms as a means of diversification, is deferred until Chapter VII.

The term diversification itself can be used in a fairly elastic manner. However, as it is used here the expression refers to any firm which is producing other than a fairly restricted range of goods. The expression, therefore, covers everything from the general electrical engineering groups such as G.E.C., Thorn Electrical Industries and Philips Electronic and Associated Industries to the conglomerate holding companies such as Norcros or Thomas Tilling. Within the general electrical firms, for example, diversification has taken the form of operating in a wide range of product markets – output often being produced or sold on an international basis, with perhaps a common technological core. Sir Joseph Latham, chief executive of A.E.I. immediately prior to its acquisition by G.E.C. in 1968, summed up his company's operations thus:

> 'At the beginning of 1960 A.E.I. was a complex international industrial concern, with annual sales of over £200m. and deliveries to most countries of the world. Its products ranged from the largest turbines to electric kettles; from large radar equipment for tracking and control and early warning to the smallest domestic lamps; from electron microscopes and linear accelerators to washing machines; and from equipment for geothermal power generation in New Zealand to floodlighting for British castles and football grounds.'[1]

Other companies in the electrical field have an even wider range of activities. E.M.I., for example, makes television cameras and X-ray systems, machine tools and gramophone records, runs steak houses and hotels, as well as being a major company in the production, distribution and exhibition of films. But at the farthest end of the spectrum are to be found firms such as Thomas Tilling with the interests as shown in the table opposite.

It is not easy to establish a measure of diversification or therefore to gauge the extent of the practice. This difficulty arises basically because, whereas diversification as a corporate strategy and economic phenomenon is concerned with trading in a number of markets, the Census of Production data upon which we have to rely for empirical studies relate to industries defined in terms of common material inputs or technology. To this extent Census data may imply diversification where none exists (if an enterprise applies more than

Thomas Tilling Ltd. (1976)

Main U.K. Operating Companies*	
Construction:	Palmers Scaffolding William R. Selwood Tilling Construction Services
Engineering:	D.C.E. Vokes Group Gascoigne, Gush & Dent Hobourn Group
Furniture:	Rest Assured
Insurance:	Cornhill Insurance Co.
Medical supplies:	H.V.K. Orthopaedic Services
Publishing:	Cox & Wyman Heinemann Group
Textiles:	Pretty Polly
Pottery:	Pilkington's Tiles Holdings
Distribution:	Stratstone Volkswagen (G.B.) Graham Building Services F. J. Reeves Newey & Eyre

* Each of these companies is 100% owned by Thomas Tilling except William R. Selwood Ltd., where the holding is 90%.

Source: Thomas Tilling Ltd. *1976 Annual Report & Accounts*

one technology in the same economic market), or may fail to identify diversification arising from the application of a common technology in otherwise unrelated markets. There is also the more complex issue of identifying a positive strategy of diversification on the part of a firm as opposed to the application of a given set of material inputs or technology to more than one market. Thus, as was pointed out in the earliest study in this area, 'the point at which an enterprise can be said to have reached a decision to diversity not implicit in the technology of the industry is therefore not evident from the statistics, and must depend on empirical investigation.'[2]

Of the evidence which is available from empirical studies, however, some is very impressionistic; and identification of trends over an extended period is made difficult by a lack of consistency of definitions. Thus, speaking of the behaviour of large firms in the early 1950s, Downie concluded that 'the firm which sprawls over a multiplicity of different industries is quite exceptional, even the largest companies have firm centres of gravity in a very few trades'.[3] On the other hand Amey came to the view, using 1958 data, that 'diversification of the business enterprise is widespread';[4] and a more recently published study found that of enterprises employing 100 or more people, those which could be described as diversified accounted for 55.75% of net output in 1958 and 70.74% in 1963.[5] The result of this trend documented above – and which others have felt more impressionistically may have been going on[6] – has been to make the large diversified company appear to be an increasingly typical form of business enterprise, and therefore the subject of much greater private and Government interest. Once again, however, it would seem necessary to enter a caveat in respect of some of the more impressionistic discussion on the topic. One unpublished paper which analysed data relating to the 200 largest manufacturing firms in 1974 concluded that 'the data for the U.K. on the whole run counter to the popular view of a small number of very large conglomerates with tentacles stretching into every corner of industry'.

Despite the relative lack of a statistical basis for an examination of this characteristic some very useful historical comparative data are available. Studying the top 100 U.K. manufacturing firms of 1970 (size being measured in terms of value of sales) Channon divided these businesses into four categories of diversification: Single Product (95% of sales within a single product area), Dominant Product (firms having secondary products accounting for 30% or less of sales), Related Product (firms having expanded into related markets such that no one product line accounted for 70% of turnover), and Unrelated Product (firms having expanded into new markets or technologies such that no single product line accounted for 70% of turnover).[7] Taking these firms (which Channon estimated accounted in 1970 for around 60% of sales and net assets of U.K. manufacturing industry) and projecting back to 1960 and 1950, the author found the following comparative situation.

U.K. Manufacturing Industry

(100 largest firms (1970) by turnover)

Category	*1950*	*1960*	*1970*
Single Product	34	20	6
Dominant Product	41	35	34
Related Product	23	41	54
Unrelated Product	2	4	6
	100%	100%	100%

Source: D. F. Channon, *op. cit.*, p. 67.

These figures provide an indication of just how diversified the top U.K. businesses are, and of the trend over the past 20 years.

The lesson to be drawn from these paragraphs is that the single-product firm in the U.K. economy is something of a rarity. Economic analysis which proceeds on the assumption that firms in general operate in single markets with single products, and which thus makes highly simplified assumptions about the demand and cost conditions facing such businesses, should, therefore, be treated with caution. It has indeed been admitted that 'the contribution of existing theory (of the firm) nowhere appears more limited than in the explanation of the *modus vivendi* of the ubiquitous multi-product firm, the characteristic, not the atypical, unit of enterprise'.[8] The purpose of this chapter is to add some further realism to our understanding of the theory of the firm.

B. Why Diversification?

The starting point here must be a recognition of the high standing of business growth in terms of corporate objectives. It has been emphasised that significant theories of the firm have centred round the importance of growth to management through its association with higher managerial salaries, reduced risk in business activities and the generally increased status in being associated with high-growth firms. This growth is normally measured in terms of increases in turnover and/or net assets – both of which will obviously be moving up steadily with our current rate of inflation – rather than the ratio of net profit to net assets (which can, however, also be vastly overstated during a period of inflation).[9] But if firms simply wish to grow, why do they not just increase output of existing products? Some firms, of course, do just this. Hoover in domestic appliances, Black & Decker in power tools, Schreiber in furniture (prior to its merger with G.E.C.'s British Domestic Appliances in the latter part of 1974), B.S.R. in gramophone record changers are all examples of firms achieving high growth rates within a particular chosen field. But for reasons discussed in more detail below this path of specialist expansion is not always possible. In this context, however, the following words are a salutary reminder of the dangers to be faced in departing from the straight and narrow path of corporate expansion. The words, incidently, were written by an American international business consultant in 1973.

> ' "Diversification" has long been a magic word among corporate strategists and myriad sins have been committed in its name. *The primary principle that must be grasped is that diversification is fundamentally a negative strategy.* Diversifiers are always running away from something.
> They are escaping something about the present business configuration that is unsatisfactory, threatening, or downright calamitous. If this were not so, any responsible manager would commit all of his accessible resources in the business he knows best and in which his organization has the highest degree of developed competence. In diver-

sifying into new kinds of activities he inherently accepts the risks of undertaking responsiblities for which he is less well qualified than he is for his present ones. He should only accept this risk if he is quite certain that the potential rewards are substantially better than those probably available for continuing to do more of what he knows best.'[10] (Emphasis added.)

From where, then, are the present diversifiers running, and what are they seeking? It is possible to identify a number of conditions under which diversification may be a necessary or attractive corporate policy.

(*a*) Wish to avoid domination of market,
(*b*) Inability to survive in existing market,
(*c*) Slow growth rate in existing market,
(*d*) Risk spreading through diversification.

In fact most of the cases of diversification will feature more than one of the above characteristics; and one may also find cases which fit neatly into none of these categories.[11]

(*a*) *Avoidance of market dominance*

Although there may be attractions to a business in being in a dominant position in any market in which it operates – for example, in being able to play the role of dominant price leader among its competitors, or exercising monopsonistic buying power over input suppliers – there may also be disadvantages. These are more obvious in the U.S. where 'monopolisation' of a market is an offence under the antitrust laws, and where businesses are thus specifically *prohibited* from acquiring a dominant position in any market. Thus one American economist, pointing out that horizontal mergers in the U.S. had fallen from 31.0% of the total in 1948–53 to 9.4% in 1965–8, commented in the early 1970s that 'the Cellar–Kefauver Amendment to the antitrust laws of 1950 is undoubtedly responsible for the changed composition of merger activity in the last two decades'.[12] But even in this country some businesses may wish to avoid the element of potential unwelcome publicity (and expense) which may attach to a Monopolies Commission inquiry into any market which contains a 'statutory monopolist', i.e. a single firm which accounts for 25% or more of that market. The usual reaction of firms in this country which do find themselves about to be subjected to the cost and publicity of the Commission's scrutiny is a mixture of scarcely-veiled annoyance at the inconvenience, and an innocently-protestant 'why us?' Such an unwelcome visitation may be avoided by expansion in other markets.

(*b*) *Failure to survive*

Graham Bannock gives two examples of this form of diversification.[13] In the U.S. Studebaker, originally founded in 1902, was finally forced out of the U.S. motor car market in 1963 despite having merged with Packard in 1954. In 1967 the firm merged with the Worthington Group to form the Studebaker–Worthington Corporation which is now engaged mainly in electrical engineering. Of more immediate interest is Bannock's example of Scribbans–Kemp. This company expanded in the bakery products field up to a peak in the early 1950s when the uncompetitiveness of its position became apparent. By the late 1960s it had sold off its biscuit and cake interests, and also the names Scribbans and Kemp. The firm now survives as S. & K. Holdings and in the food-grocery business: among its better known subsidiaries are Baylis Supermarkets, Budgetts, United Counties Stores, Waller & Hartley, and Barker & Dobson.

A further example of diversification which falls into this category rather than any of the others below is that of the highly localised Dundee jute industry.[14] The market for Dundee jute goods declined both as a result of increased manufacturing capacity in India and Pakistan, and the loss of certain traditional markets such as packaging and sacking in this country. The response of the Dundee firms previously dependent upon this trade was in some cases to move into non-traditional jute markets such as hessian wall coverings. Wider diversification, however, has involved a movement into fairly closely related, though technologically more complex, areas such as spinning rayon staple, weaving carpet backing, and polypropylene. Some firms have, however, moved into paper packaging and the production of other containers, or have utilised their knowledge of jute spinning and weaving machinery to move into other areas of engineering, and also into the provision of oil exploration and drilling equipment.[15]

These are examples of more extreme forms of diversification. It is now proposed to consider businesses which, while continuing to operate in their original markets, have significantly shifted into other fields.

(*c*) *Diversification for growth*

A firm seeking to grow within a single market faces two major constraints: the competition of other firms in the same market, and the aggregate rate of expansion in that market itself. With regard to the former, as a firm expands in any market it is bound to impinge sooner or later upon the ambitions of other firms in the same market – particularly so if the total market is not expanding. This situation may be characterised either by a severe price war among the combatants and/or a takeover of one of the firms by a more aggressive competitor. If for any reason a takeover is not possible or is not desirable, and a mutually destructive price war is to be avoided, then an expansionist firm may seek to fulfil its growth ambition by diversifying into another market.

The aggregate rate of growth of a market may have a more direct impact upon diversification. If a market is growing at a slow rate, then without leaving the field altogether a firm with growth ambitions may also diversify. The U.K. cosmetics and toiletries market, for example, appears to be static. In this context it is not surprising to find Avon, the brand leader in most sectors, diversifying into other fields.[16] It may be suggested that this second type of circumstance may occur more frequently in an economy which is characterised by a rapid rate of technological change – in which individual product markets move with increasing rapidity through the sequence of rapid growth, maturity, stagnation and decline. Thus in the U.S.,

> 'For example, as a result of the impact of the automobile and airplane on the railroads, firms in the railway equipment industry were compelled to enter other industries in

order to maintain growth. A similar set of forces operated on the textile industry with the development of synthetic fibres. The substitution of oil for coal had a similar impact on the coal industry.'[17]

We shall be referring to Guinness in other diversification contexts presently, but it is obvious that some of its diversification strategy has been stimulated by the company's feeling that it may have reached its maximum rate of expansion in the stout field. Thus, commenting on the company's plan to push the share of non-brewing profits beyond 20 per cent of the total, one analyst pointed out:

> 'Like the cigarette manufacturers, Guinness realised a good while ago that it would have to look away from its traditional business for much of its future growth. With its stout brewed in 17 countries and drunk in 120 more it is clearly getting more difficult to find large new markets for expansion.'[18]

It was this latter type of situation which also faced Cadbury in the 1960s. It was reported that by the end of that decade 'not only has Cadbury's run into intense competition, low profitability and slowly growing sales in its traditional lines, but it has chosen to move heavily into even fiercer battles in the grocery trade'.[19] With U.K. confectionery consumption static in *per caput* terms at 7.8 oz. per week (the highest in the world), and Cadbury itself having an estimated 26% of the home market (only marginally ahead of the subsequently-merged Rowntree and Mackintosh), the group diversified into cakes, instant milk, instant potatoes and food drinks to such a degree that even prior to its merger with Schweppes in 1969 chocolate and confectionery accounted for less than half its turnover. This process of diversification was speeded up with the subsequent merger. Indeed prior to the merger Schweppes itself had gone through a process of diversification from its dependence upon sales of carbonated drinks through public houses and supermarkets (suffering from relatively slow growth, and the development of countervailing power respectively) into wines

(Dubonnet), jams (Hartley's, Moorhouse, and Chivers) and tea (Typhoo Tea).[20] The combined group now appears to have moved into faster-growing markets such as convenience goods which it no doubt hopes will permit a greater rate of corporate expansion.

The British Match Corporation can be taken as a further example of a company which carried through a considerable programme of internal diversification away from slow-growing markets before linking up late in 1973 with Wilkinson Sword to form Wilkinson Match and thus secure further diversification. British Match had by 1927 a large share of the U.K. market for matches through Bryant & May and J. John Masters.[21] By the mid-1950s, however, British Match had anticipated a decline in the U.K. match market, although sales overseas were expanding. The result of this forecast was both a rationalisation and re-equipment of its match-making facilities, and a conscious programme of diversification. This resulted in British Match entering the related fields of wood chipboard, printing and packaging, pyrotechnics, steel wool and hardware products, ticket-issuing machines, and industrial fans. The relatively disappointing financial results of this can be seen in the following figures; and it was in the light of these that British Match decided upon the further programme of acquisition or merger which eventually brought about the link with Wilkinson Sword.

British Match Corporation 1972–73

	Turnover (%)	Profits (%)
Matches	53.1	74.3
Wood chipboard	12.2	9.7
Lumber and Plywood	6.0	1.2
Printing and Packaging	11.9	7.6
Miscellaneous	16.8	7.2
	100.0	100.0

Sources: Monopolies Commission, *British Match-Wilkinson Sword* (H.M.S.O., 1973, Cmnd. 6442) para. 13; and British Match, *1973 Annual Report and Accounts*.

(*d*) *Diversification for risk spreading*

Again returning to the earlier analysis of theories of the firm, we find that one of the acknowledged goals of modern management is risk reduction. In the words of the urbanely witty J. K. Galbraith,

> 'The riskiness of modern corporate life is, in fact, the harmless conceit of the modern corporate executive, and that is why it is vigorously proclaimed . . . the development of the modern business enterprise can be understood only as a comprehensive effort to reduce risk. It is not going too far to say that it can be understood in no other terms.'[22]

A firm which is diversifying in order to reduce risk is, albeit implicitly, looking upon its spread of activities as a portfolio which is designed to maximise the return for any given degree of risk, or alternatively to minimise the risk attaching to any target rate of return. Thus it was recognised that with the growth of more diversified companies, and forms of business organisation which replaced the earlier functional administration with greater delegation of decision making, 'the quasi-independent divisions could be likened to a series of portfolio investments which could be bought or sold without serious impact on the overall corporation'.[23] The essence of the combination of activities in such a portfolio is that the correlation between their returns should be perfectly negative. But even if this relationship does not hold in respect of each of the individual market interests in a diversifier's portfolio, as a greater number of activities is added the law of large numbers will at some point have the effect of essentially reducing the element of risk to zero. (We have already seen something of this effect in noticing that the distinguishing characteristic between the earnings of large and small firms is the lower variability, rather than the higher average level, of the former.)

Unfortunately, and insofar as the data used allow any firm conclusion to be drawn, it does not appear on an empirical basis that diversification does reduce profit variability; although in this type of analysis it is not always possible to distinguish between the impact of diversification and internal *vis à vis* external expansion, or the effect of differences in firm size. Utton's findings, using data over the period 1958–67, were that diversified firms appeared to enjoy neither higher nor less variable rates of return on capital employed, although some of the fluctuation in profit performance of the diversified firms may have been brought about by their rapid growth rates.[24] Similarly Hood and Young found that over the period 1964–73 a sample of 400 holding companies performed if anything less well than a control group of industrial and commercial companies in terms of profit growth, and that within their sample increased diversification was not associated with increased profit growth.[25]

There are reasons, additionally, for supposing that this portfolio diversification will not necessarily be taken to its logical extreme outside conglomerate companies. This is because such extreme diversification would, to all intents and purposes, result in a sacrifice of rationalisation, economies of scale or common management techniques. Thus it has been pointed out that most domestic appliance manufacturers make small as well as large appliances, because while the latter suffer in their sales from movements in the trade cycle, the former offer prospects of a more steady turnover. This is diversification for risk reduction; but no one would claim that there is no correlation between sales of large and small appliances. Again, Gillette is one firm which has apparently suffered in the U.K. as a result of being too dependent upon one product – the safety razor. In 1960 Wilkinson Sword brought out its PTFE-coated blade Super Sword-edge (on sales of which it had to pay a royalty of 2½–4% to Gillette as the latter had actually patented the process first), and between 1960 and 1964 profits of Gillette's U.K. subsidiary fell from £6m to £2.3m. Gillette in fact fought back on the technological front with its Silver blade and subsequently with its Super blade to gain an equal share of the stainless steel razor market with Wilkinson: each has about 45% of this market. Gillette's subsequent diversification, however, has been into the closely related field of male toiletries, with such brands as Sure, Right Guard and Old Spice.[26]

Any further diversification, such as the major cigarette and tobacco companies' interests in retailing, food and drink, and cosmetics, or the case of a firm such as Booker McConnell (whose sugar interests have fallen from about half of its profits in the early 1950s to 20% by the early 1970s, and whose income is now derived from supermarkets, North Sea Oil equipment, and royalties from works of Ian Fleming, Agatha Christie and Harold Pinter),[27] tends to be labelled as conglomeration. It is not being suggested that limited diversification does not spread risks. But it should be stressed that, other than those businesses which have converted themselves into conglomerate firms, this strategy has limitations. The case of conglomerates is, however, quite different, and a special section is devoted to them below.

C. The Directions of Diversification

What factors will determine the direction in which a firm diversifies? One of the most obvious is a common technology or a development of existing technology. Dunlop, for example, has moved from rubber tyres through a variety of leisure and sports goods involving polymer technology. Additionally, 'having started with tyres they followed with wheels, later with brakes and hose, and later still with many purely engineering components such as brake controls, compressors, oxygen bottles and so on'.[28] Guinness has largely expanded its original technology into new areas. Edwards and Townsend described it in the late 1950s as 'perhaps the most famous example of a firm which has grown by doing more of what it was doing already'.[29] At that time the firm was characterised, quite uniquely, by its total concentration upon stout or porter, and further by a concentration upon brewing alone. The company owned neither its own maltings nor its retail outlets, i.e. there was neither backward nor forward vertical integration. This situation began to change in the 1960s. First Guinness moved into the lager market in Ireland with Harp in 1960; and with the launching of Harp in England the following year Guinness entered into a partnership with three other brewers to acquire public houses so as to guarantee outlets for sales of Harp lager.[30] Other directions of expansion at this time included a link up with Ind Coope for production and marketing in Ireland of ales; metal cask manufacture; part acquisition of Crookes Laboratories; the construction of Twyford Laboratories for work in the fields of microbiology, biochemistry, virology and organic chemistry; and the acquisition of Callard & Bowser, William Nuttal, Riley's and Lavell's in confectionery manufacture and distribution. Guinness' experience in pharmaceuticals was not an entirely happy one, and some plant was subsequently sold to Boots in 1971. But the company does not appear to regret having taken this growth path.

In other cases firms have been found to follow technological change as market emphasis shifts. For example, selling in a number of fields where its product is an intermediary good, Rockware – which has an almost equal share of two-thirds of the glass container market with D.C.L.'s subsidiary United Glass – planned by the mid-1970s to earn one-third of its profits from plastic containers.[31] Developments in plastics have also taken Bridon (known as British Ropes until mid-1973) from the application of this technology to ropes and twine to vacuum forming of plastic components; and technical developments in the wire field have led the firm into the manufacture of engineering springs, wire filtration screws and electro-mechanical ocean cables.[32]

For other companies the more obvious path of diversification is to make products which can be marketed through channels similar to their existing output. The links between the couturiers and female cosmetics are well known; and the field of male cosmetics and toiletries has been expanded into by safety razor manufacturers. Cadbury Schweppes has moved into convenience foods, cakes and food drinks, utilising the outlets with which they were familiar through producing chocolates, jams and soft drinks.

D. The Conglomerate Company

The ultimate degree of diversification is, of course, the conglomerate holding company. A conglomerate company can be defined in rather negative terms by saying that it is an organisation whose various operations cannot be seen as bearing any market relationship to each other. That is, there is no necessary element of horizontal or vertical integration in the firm's operations; nor may there appear to be any 'rational' or 'logical' element of diversification. This lack of apparent rationality or 'industrial logic' (a phrase coined by the Monopolies Commission) about conglomerate companies has perplexed both the layman and the academic economist. Even business analysts are confused by the 'spectacular financial acrobatics' of these organisations; and writing at the beginning of the 1970s one business correspondent probably summed up the situation fairly accurately in suggesting that 'the conglomerate was and remains one of the most remarkable and ill-understood creations of the past decade'.[33]

But while many economists may have doubts about the logic of some of the conglomerate groupings (Jimmy Ling's Ling–Temco–Vought had its diverse interests in sport goods, pharmaceuticals and food-groceries rationalised on the New York Stock Exchange as golf balls, goof balls and meat balls!), there is in financial terms no reason why these apparently bizarre product combinations should not occur. And this perhaps gives one a clue as to their meaning; for they were in their U.S. origins essentially *financial* organisations; and were justified to shareholders and investment analysts on the basis of their financial performance in the shape of earnings growth and capital appreciation per share. The argument appears to have been that any possible acquisition which could justify itself to a potential acquirer in terms of increasing the earnings per share and the stock-market value of the latter was worth having. In the case of conglomerate firms the situation was aided by the fact that other companies were acquired not for cash but in exchange for the acquiring firm's shares. So long as these had a high value in relation to the firm's profits (i.e. so long as conglomerate firms had high price/earnings ratios) the success of this type of venture seemed assured. Indeed this element of 'dealing' in the businesses in which they are concerned seems to be at the heart of the activities of the most advanced forms of conglomerate corporations. Thus one business journalist summed up the operations of Slater Walker Securities:

'(What it) does is to buy up indifferently run companies, sell off uneconomic bits, reorganize management, install sound business principles, possibly amalgamate similar companies into larger and more viable units – and then sell off part or all of the shares at a greatly enhanced price. Fundamentally, this is a sort of industrial reorganization or rationalization, made possible by the amount (in Slater Walker's view, almost limitless) of underused assets and poor management in the U.K.'[34]

The conglomerate company grew up in the U.S.; and while some of these have been around for a long time – Litton Industries or Textron – and while others such as I.T.T. would not really like to be thought of as conglomerate at all – it has been the newer and more aggressive of the American conglomerates that have hit the headlines on both sides of the Atlantic. Most people have heard of Ling–Temco–Vought, Gulf & Western, Leasco and Studebaker–Worthington. In the light of the financial relapse (or in some cases collapse) of many U.S. conglomerates at the end of the 1960s it is not surprising that economists in this country should be questioning this form of business activity. But in this context it has to be emphasised – and the point has been made by none other than Mr. Jim Slater of Slater Walker Securities[35] – that many of the largest firms in the U.K. are 'conglomerate' in a broad generic sense. Their activities and performance must, therefore, be examined in that context.

In order to understand this, and to appreciate why Mr. Slater suggested that I.C.I., Unilever, G.K.N., Tube Investments and G.E.C. could all well be described as conglomerates, the concept of the conglomerate firm can be broken down into four categories.[36] First, there are companies which may be called *giant conglomerates*. These have diversified so far that it is often difficult to classify them as being in any particular market. Perhaps the most convincing U.K. example is Unilever which since its formation in 1929 through the merger of Lever Bros. and the Margarine Union (itself the result of a merger two years earlier of Jurgens and Van den Berghs) has moved into a wide range of fields. The firm itself breaks down its activities into five main product groups: Food, Detergents, Toilet Preparations, Chemicals, and Paper, Printing, Packaging and Plastics. The general public know the firm as the producer of Sunlight and Lifebuoy soaps, Persil, Domestos, Gibbs S.R., Sunsilk, Astral, Blue Band, Cookeen, Birds Eye, Batchelors, John West, Vesta, Royco, Tree Top, Walls and Mac Fisheries. Into this same category could also be put I.C.I. Second, there are firms which are *large diversifiers* – which have deliberately moved away from an overdependence upon one product or product range. The Rank Organisation, for example, has split its interests between Rank Xerox, which in 1967–8 accounted for 41% of total turnover, and its other leisure-market activities. In the latter group are film production, distribution and exhibition (23% of turnover); hotels (including Butlin's); bowling, dancing and bingo; and television rental.[37] The cigarette and tobacco companies (following the trend in the U.S.)[38] have moved out of their traditional markets in the light of a static tobacco market and adverse publicity on smoking. Imperial Tobacco, which has an estimated two-thirds of the U.K. market, has diversified not only fairly obviously into paper and board but also into food and drink. Golden Wonder Crisps, H.P. Sauce, Norfolk Canneries, Courage breweries and a 27.6% shareholding in Glenlivet Distilleries have together made non-tobacco sales 43% of Imp's. total turnover.[39] The story has been the same at British American Tobacco. In 1962 B.A.T. and Imperial Tobacco jointly established Mardon International in the packaging field, and in 1970 B.A.T. acquired Wiggins Teape in this field. Rather than move into food processing, however, B.A.T. has acquired interests in the cosmetics field (Yardley, Germaine Monteil, Morny, Lentheric and Cyclax) and retailing (International Stores and Pricerite).[40] Companies with a similar spread of interests are Reed International which operates in paper and board, newspapers and periodicals (I.P.C.), wallpaper and paint (W.P.M. and Crown, Sanderson and Polycell), and building products (Twyfords and Key Terrain); as well as the large general electrical companies which, although they could be said to be in the general area of electrical engineering, are in so many different markets that they justify being thought of as large diversifiers. Third, there are the *industrial holding companies*. Tilling and Norcros have been mentioned before; S. Pearson & Son and Carlton Industries are further examples. These are the traditional type of industrial holding company which has a fairly limited portfolio which is reasonably static. Finally come the *classic conglomerates*. In comparison with the industrial holding companies it has been suggested that companies in the last group 'claim to operate on the same financial logic a wide variety of interests. The common factor is strong financial and managerial control, even though profit centres may be far removed from corporate headquarters'.[41] These, then, are the four main classes of conglomerate company. Their similarities and differences can best be seen by examining the economic basis of their operation.

The explanation of how conglomerates work is complex. Without researching into a number of cases in detail one cannot see how much real decentralisation of management power there is, nor easily define the true economic relationship between the headquarters and the subsidiary profit centres. But this relationship is the key one; as, if the individual subsidiaries were left *entirely* alone there would *de facto* be no economic relationship and no conglomerate as an economic phenomenon. The possibilities can be seen from the following schema. If we assume that the function of a conglomerate organisation is to enhance the financial performance of the enterprise as a whole then some of these economic or financial benefits must accrue.

Sources of Economic Advantage in Conglomerate Diversification

A.	*'Operating' Effects*	i. With integration	a. Horizontal integration: economies of scale
			b. Vertical integration: elimination of functions
			c. Advantages of absolute size: purchasing, etc.
		ii. Without integration	a. Provision of technology, marketing knowledge, finance
			b. Provision of managerial ability

continued

Sources of Economic Advantage in Conglomerate Diversification (cont.)

B.	*'Financial' Effects*	a. Higher market value for earnings
		b. Change in capital structure: debt/ equity ratio
		c. Reduction of risk through diversification
		d. As in (c) through size
		e. Accounting treatment: 'creative accounting'
		f. Corporate tax position: 'group relief'

Source: H. H. Lynch, *Financial Performance of Conglomerates* (Boston, 1971) p. 5.

While one would imagine that the 'Operating Effects' are less significant in the context of conglomerate mergers, Lynch points out that these cannot be ignored, and that 'usually economies and efficiencies from assimilation and integration are at least possible'.[42] This would suggest that conglomerates may reap advantages under headings A(i)c. and (ii) above. For many people, however, the rationale of conglomerate companies is financial rather than economic. Thus they achieve their superior performance (in terms of earnings per share growth and capital appreciation) by using their own high-value equity to acquire businesses having low p/e ratios, by raising their ratio of debt to equity capital (i.e. by increased gearing), by reducing the risk element in their earnings, by taking full advantage of all legal accounting procedures (e.g. in valuation of assets and structuring of balance sheets following amalgamation), and gaining from company tax provisions (e.g. in carrying forward losses over time or within a group to offset profits earned elsewhere). Detailed case histories of the operation of conglomerates show some combination of all of these factors above. For example:

> 'The classic example of the Slater Walker technique is Crittall-Hope, created by a merger in 1965 of the two family businesses of Crittall Manufacturing and Henry Hope, to form the biggest metal window business in the world. At that time, it was agreed that facilities (largely

> overlapping) between the two partners should be rationalized. But whose should go? On that they could not agree. So there remained two head offices, two chains of sales offices, two or more factories, working well under capacity – and so on. Just as serious, several subsidiaries were in dire financial trouble.
>
> When Slater Walker took over last year, it found that the German subsidiary was by far the worst of these. It was losing £25,000 a month, and needed £300,000 cash just to keep creditors at bay. It owed £800,000 to the bank. Rather than liquidate, which would have cost £1 million, Horsman agreed to inject £400,000 and then sell it to a buyer for a 'nominal' sum. The cash injection was covered by selling off Hope's London HQ for over £½ million. Three other UK subsidiaries were also liquidated, stopping losses of £150,000 a year, and two subsidiaries were sold off. The assets of the South African subsidiary were sold off, although its quotation on the SA exchange was kept for future use by SW
>
> One and a half factories have been closed: duplicated depots and sales offices have been sorted out: Crittall-Hope's privately owned village in Essex was sold off. These moves altogether 'liberated' (a pet Slater word) about £2 million in cash, and turned £18 million in capital employed, earning £925,000 into £16 million earning more than £2 million, rising in the future to £3 million. Tarling says that in this, as in other cases, the arrival of new, outside owners enabled action to be taken which people previously knew to be desirable, but just could not get through because of opposition or inertia.'[43]

In fact Slater Walker Securities subsequently sold Crittal-Hope to a fellow conglomerate, Norcros, in 1974.

E. Wider Economic Issues of Diversification

In this concluding section consideration is given as to whether corporate diversification poses wider issues for economic analysis or policy.

(*a*) *Information loss from diversification*[44]

One of the most frustrating experiences of a researcher is to find that a constituent company of an industry which one is examining is owned by a diversified group. The 1967 Companies Act provides that if a company's total turnover exceeds £50,000 per annum, and if *in the opinion of the directors* this total falls into two or more classes which are 'substantially' different from one another, then these proportions of aggregate turnover and the respective contributions to overall profits of each class must be given.

The Rank Organisation Ltd.
Analysis of Turnover and Profit

An analysis of the turnover and profits of the various classes of the business carried on by the Company and its subsidiaries for the year ended 31st October, 1973 is as follows:

Class of Business	Turnover/£000's	Profit before Tax (see note below)/£000's	Margin	% of non-Xerox Sales	% of non-Xerox Pre-tax Profits
Leisure					
Film Exhibition					
British Isles	24,482	2,243	9.2	9.4	8.6
Overseas (mainly Canada)	13,581	1,482	10.9	5.2	5.8
Dancing and Bingo	15,503	2,416	15.6	6.0	9.4
Motorports and Restaurants	10,362	277	2.7	4.0	1.1
Film Studios and Laboratories	9,359	1,132	12.1	3.6	4.4
Film Production and Distribution	4,687	(299)	(6.4)	1.8	(1.2)
Hotels	10,622	(744)	(7.0)	4.1	(2.9)
Holiday Centres	24,951	5,024	20.1	9.6	19.6
Audio Visual	26,548	2,167	8.2	10.2	8.5
Radio, Television and Hi-Fi	87,348	8,233	9.4	33.6	32.2
	227,443	21,931		87.5	85.5

continued

Class of Business	Turnover/£000's	Profit before Tax (see note below)/£000's	Margin	% of non-Xerox Sales	% of non-Xerox Pre-tax Profits
Scientific Instruments, Optics and Electronics	20,972	(164)	(0.8)	8.1	(0.6)
Property	5,712	3,363	58.9	2.2	13.1
Other Activities	6,168	477	7.7	2.4	1.8
LESS Unallocated Central Costs		(940)			
	260,293	24,667		100.2*	99.8*
Share of profits before taxation of Associated Companies					
Rank Xerox Group		47,384			
Others		3,963			
Dividends and Interest Receivable		3,619			
		79,633			
LESS Interest Payable		11,223			
	£260,293	£68,410			

NOTE: In the opinion of the Directors it is not practicable to apportion interest payable and certain central costs between the various activities of The Rank Organisation.

* Due to rounding.

Source: The Rank Organisation Ltd. *1973 Annual Report and Accounts*

As these figures stand: (a) we do not know the net profit before tax relating to individual classes of business because of problems of allocating certain central costs and interest; (b) we have no figure for the turnover of Rank Xerox which is attributable to the Rank Organisation, and so cannot calculate the margin of profitability on sales in this area; (c) we have no figures for capital employed in each area, and so cannot calculate the rate of return on capital employed. The best we can do is as follows: calculate the sales margin, and percentage of total turnover and total profit from each activity. This company has at least broken down its activities into fairly small groups. These calculations (to the right of the vertical line in the table above) at least enable one to know the *sales* margin of profitability on each line of business, and allow one to make a crude 'comparative percentages' analysis using the final two columns. Thus it can be seen that although Motorports and Restaurants account for 4.0% of non-Xerox turnover they contribute only 1.1% of comparable profits. Holiday Centres, on the other hand, show the reverse type of situation.

As a further example, pity the researcher inquiring into market performance in the transformer industry: no figures on this are given by G.E.C., Parsons, etc. The loss of detailed figures through corporate diversification is a serious one. Without more detailed published figures (and most companies must surely have the data themselves) accurate outside appraisal of company performance is impossible; misdirection of shareholder investment may occur, i.e. the new issue market will not function efficiently; changes of ownership and management of corporate assets (i.e. takeovers) will not fulfil their function in the 'market for corporate control' if either bidders or biddee shareholders are misinformed or ill-informed; and State policy on monopolies and mergers may be conducted in an informational vacuum. Lack of information on profitability also acts as a passive barrier to the entry of new firms, as potential entrants may be unaware of true profit opportunities in a market.

(*b*) *Diversification and competition*

In most cases corporate diversification is a healthy response to changes in the relative demand for products, and in such markets as confectionery or cigarettes firms which want to grow clearly cannot depend for success upon remaining in those fields. In this context a firm such as B.S.R., which specialises in gramophone record changers and which it is claimed is responsible for half the world output,[45] is an exception, and is only able to remain so because of the growth (which, however, slowed down markedly in 1974) of the market in which it specialises.

However, many economists have also stressed the need to

examine the impact upon competition in the market of certain forms of diversification. As in the case of so many issues in industrial economics, there is no single answer: 'The relationship (between diversification and competition) is a complex one. Competition both encourages diversification and sets limits to it. Diversification in turn may increase the degree of competition or may reduce it.'[46] As far as stimulating competition is concerned, diversification by an established firm may be the only way in which barriers to entry in a protected market may be overcome. This may apply to financial, technological and (if the difference between two markets is not too great) patronage barriers to entry enjoyed by existing firms. The entry by Green Shield Stamps in 1973 into the discount store market with Argos was made easier by the fact that it had experience of similar operations associated with the redemption of its trading stamps, the finance available for such operations (trading stamps are sold for cash to retail outlets long before the customers redeem them) and the name of Mr. Richard Tompkins behind them. The same can be said of I.C.I.'s expansion into paint and pharmaceuticals. The firm which is free (in terms of possessing the necessary finance and technological and managerial ability) to diversify into new markets is thus a potentially pro-competitive force in an economy. However, for further analysis a distinction has to be made between diversification by establishment of new plant, and acquisition of existing producers. So far we have assumed that the diversifying firm was setting up new plant in the market into which it was diversifying. To the extent that new capacity is thereby being established in the market we might assume that the effect of this is pro-competitive. This may not, however, be so in all cases.

A firm which is diversifying is by definition moving away from an established base. If this established base is a highly profitable one then in the shorter term the new entrant may be able to indulge in competitive under-pricing or 'predatory' pricing which, while it would benefit the consumer in the short run, could, if the new entrant thereby eliminated his competitors and established a monopoly position, eventually lead to higher prices for consumers. This potential sequence of events – known in the U.S. as the 'deep pocket' hypothesis – suggests that 'a large conglomerate firm can sell below cost for extended periods of time, driving smaller, single-line rivals out of business. A large, diversified firm can subsidize losses in an individual line of business by drawing upon profits from other activities. The single-line producer has no such recourse and would eventually face bankruptcy'.[47] In this country such fears have been expressed in the context of the domestic electrical appliances sector which is characterised by both specialist producers such as Hoover, Electrolux and Lec, and subsidiaries of the diversified electrical engineers such as G.E.C., Thorn and Philips. It has been pointed out that these latter could squeeze out the former class of competitor by cross-subsidisation from their wide electrical engineering base. A stockbroker's report commented that 'many appliance subsidiaries have been running at a loss, but because of prestige considerations have been financed from profits from other divisions';[48] and a group of economists concluded that 'the moral is that those firms have become brand leaders whose entire venture hinges upon the sales of their line of appliances – *unlike the case of the large integrated firms* – and unless the specialists succeed in selling their wares, they "go to the wall" '.[49] (Emphasis added.) This type of cross-subsidisation potential or predatory pricing – with the outcome being the 'survival of the fattest' – can occur outside the context of diversification. The Monopolies Commission's Report on Industrial and Medical Gases gave a thumbnail sketch of this very form of pricing by B.O.C. in order to eliminate a rival supplier.[50] Conditions for such 'loss leader' selling or predatory pricing are, however, much more favourable in the context of diversification.

A further loss of competition through diversification may arise if reciprocal trading between the constituent members of a diversified concern forecloses such markets to smaller firms or new entrants. Reciprocal trading arises where A and B (both owned by C) agree to buy their respective requirements of a's and b's from each other despite the existence of other suppliers in those markets. The result of such a policy is, of course, to reduce the full potential for price competition in any market so affected.

When one considers diversification by a firm through acquisition of an existing business in the new market then, to the extent that no additional competitive capacity has been added in this field, such a course is not obviously pro-competitive. Indeed if the acquisition is of the largest firm then reciprocal trading or predatory pricing could reduce competition. However, if a small firm in the new field was acquired by a large diversified organisation, this small firm's ability to compete with the leading firms in its own market could be enhanced. Lack of finance, managerial or technical expertise could be overcome by resort to its larger and wealthier parent. This possibility is referred to in the U.S. literature as the 'toehold' hypothesis.

(*c*) *Management efficiency*

On the other hand it may be suggested that conglomerate firms possess certain characteristics which allow them to operate more efficiently than other firms in the economy. This arises because conglomerate businesses in particular lend themselves to a multidivisional organisation structure. Such a business can be broken down into individual operating units – normally based upon distinct product groups – whose economic performance is under the strict surveillance of a central controlling office. To the extent that this top controlling group can be induced to place its principal emphasis upon profit maximisation, and assess each individual divisional manager on a similar basis, the opportunities for the pursuit of goals other than profit maximisation within such businesses are severely limited. From this it may be held that a conglomerate firm will be operated more efficiently than either a non-diversified business of equal total size, or a set of individual businesses of equal aggregate size and degree of diversification. The key to this is the operation of individual divisions as quasi-independent units, and the role of the central controlling group. Each division may be given specific rate-of-return targets to achieve. The salaries of the divisional chief executives (or perhaps in extreme cases their continued employment), and the provision of investment funds are made dependent upon the profit performance of the autonomous divisions. Thus, so far as efficient allocation of investment finance is concerned, 'the conglomerate acts in this respect as a miniature capital market'.[51] It may be assumed that this capital market can operate more effectively than the traditional one insofar as information is available in greater quantity and at less cost, and also that the mechanism for displacing incompetent executives operates with less friction. Normally incompetent top management cannot be replaced except as a result of a board room revolution or in some cases a full-scale takeover. Both of these have high attendant costs and risks.

Is there any evidence that such a quasi capital market system of financial resource allocation operates within conglomerate firms? Certainly it would appear that most of these devolve operating responsibility and authority to autonomous divisions. What may be in question, however, is the ability of the large conglomerate to move rapidly further into or out of any of its existing areas of activity.

> 'If Tilling is effectively prevented from selling off its less attractive investments except at knock-down prices, some of the flexibility of the conglomerates in moving into new growth areas appears to be mythical. A big discount would have to be accepted on the sale of a less-successful venture – not necessarily a loss-maker – and a premium would be needed to buy another company in the chosen growth field. The combination would be sufficient to prevent the parent doing the swap too often without diluting its own equity. Nor, by the time a group reaches Tilling's size, would buying one or two small companies a year allow a very rapid change of direction or improvement in profitability.
>
> The element of chance must also be a serious limiting factor. Tilling cannot decide to go into the hydraulics business, say, if no suitable companies present themselves for purchase.'[52]

It is also necessary to realise that the strategy of multi-divisionalisation is open to large non-diversified businesses. These firms may also gain the efficiency benefits of operating a series of quasi-independent units, with the central organisation carrying out the function of divisional management assessment and capital rationing. This happens most obviously in the case of the more specialist multinational companies where divisionalisation takes place on a geographical basis. To take the motor car market as an example, during the recession of 1974–5 the European vice president of Chrysler, speaking of the U.K. situation, emphasised:

> 'We expect our operations to be self-sufficient, those that generate the capital funds can use them to develop new products . . . a new car for the U.K. will depend on Lander, (Mr. Don Lander, U.K. managing director) generating the funds.'[53]

Businesses which operate on such a multidivisional basis may gain the benefits of this type of organisation structure without diversification.

F. Conclusions

Diversification for businesses is normally a logical reaction to changes in their environment: to falling profitability, a reduced growth rate, or an undesirable degree of perceived risk involved in operating in existing markets. Other organisational factors, however, may also be encouraging a trend to diversification. Studies have indicated that increased diversification is associated with high 'technical personnel ratios',[54] or high levels of spending in the areas of marketing or research and development.[55] George has also called attention to the role of greater professionalisation of management in producing managers (unhampered by active shareholders!) who seek growth and security, and who may use modern management techniques to expand businesses beyond the market horizons of earlier generations of managers. The same author also credits the merger boom of the late 1960s with having influenced the pace of diversifications.[56]

Diversification, like monopoly, may have pro- or anti-competitive effects on the economy. Just as the Government has provided itself with investigative machinery for deciding whether monopolies and mergers do or do not operate in the public interest, a much closer eye might well now be kept upon diversification as such. The first prerequisite for this would be an expansion of our existing knowledge of the extent and impact of the phenomenon at the market level.

References

1. J. Latham, *Takeover: The Facts and the Myths of the GEC-AEI Battle*, Iliffe, London (1969), p. 21
2. L. R. Amey, Diversified Manufacturing Businesses, *Journal of the Royal Statistical Society* Ser. A, Vol. CXXVII (1964), 253
3. J. Downie, *The Competitive Process*, Duckworth, London (1958), p. 146
4. L. R. Amey, Ref. 2, 265
5. P. K. Gorecki, An Inter-Industry Analysis of Diversification in the U.K. Manufacturing Sector, *Journal of Industrial Economics*, Vol. XXIV (1975), 131
6. See G. Whittington, Changes in the Top 100 Quoted Manufacturing Companies in the United Kingdom 1948 to 1968, *Journal of Industrial Economics*, Vol. XXI (1972), 25–27
7. D. F. Channon, *The Strategy and Structure of British Enterprise*, Macmillan, London (1973), pp. 12–13
8. M. R. Fisher, Towards a Theory of Diversification, *Oxford Economic Papers*, Vol. XIII (1961), 293
9. See W. S. Howe, The Inflation Accounting Debate: An Economic Viewpoint, *Moorgate and Wall Street* (Spring 1973), 21–33
10. M. L. Kastens "How much is an Acquisition Worth?, *Long Range Planning*, Vol. VI (1973), 53
11. See H. I. Ansoff, T. A. Anderson, F. Norton and J. F. Weston, Planning for Diversification through Merger in H. I. Ansoff (ed.), *Business Strategy*, Penguin, Harmondsworth (1969), pp. 291–5
12. L. G. Goldberg, The Effect of Conglomerate Mergers on Competition, *Journal of Law and Economics*, Vol. XVI (1973), 138. Sec. 18 of the Celler-Kefauver Amendment (1950) prohibits the acquisition of 'the whole or any part of the assets of another corporation engaged also in commerce where in any line of commerce in any section of the country, the effect of such acquisition may be substantially to lessen competition, or to tend to create a monopoly.'
13. G. Bannock, *The Juggernauts*, Weidenfeld and Nicolson, London (1971), p. 989

14. In the early 1960s, for example, Dundee and district accounted for 89.2% of U.K. jute spinning and 94.2% of the industry's weaving capacity. At this time 20% of the insured population of Dundee was employed directly in jute manufacture. See A. M. Carstairs and A. V. Cole, Recent Developments in the Jute Industry, *Scottish Journal of Political Economy*, Vol. VII (1960), 117
15. See J. H. Leveson, *Industrial Organisation of the Jute Manufacturing Industry: Decline and Diversification*, Dundee College of Technology, Dundee (1973)
16. See Cosmetics, *Financial Times* (24 August 1974)
17. J. F. Weston, The Nature and Significance of Conglomerate Firms, *St. John's Law Review*, Vol. XLIV (1970), 71
18. R. Dafter, Why plastics is good for Guinness, *Financial Times* (20th September, 1974)
19. D. Thomas, Why Cadbury's had to change, *Management Today*, (July 1968), 52
20. See A Vice, Blending Cadbury Schweppes in *The Strategy of Takeovers*, McGraw Hill, Maidenhead (1971), pp. 63–81
21. These details are taken from Monopolies Commission, *British Match Corporation Ltd. and Wilkinson Sword Ltd.*, H.M.S.O. (1973), Cmnd 5442
22. J. K. Galbraith, *The Affluent Society*, Hamish Hamilton, London, 2nd ed. (1969), pp. 98 and 100
23. D. F. Channon, Ref. 7, pp. 3–4
24. See M. A. Utton, Diversification, Mergers and Profit Stability, *Business Ratios* (Spring 1969), pp. 24–27. As further examples of research in this area see: Econtel Research Ltd., *Conglomerates*, London (1969); and A-M. Kumps, Conglomerate Mergers: The Case of Great Britain, *Document de Travail C.R.I.D.E.*, No. 751 (1975)
25. See N. Hood and S. Young, Growth, Performance and Strategy in 400 U.K. Holding Companies, unpublished paper, Paisley College of Technology (1975)
26. G. Foster, Blunt Truth at Wilkinson Sword, *Management Today* (June 1965), 46. See also J. Thackray, Close Shave at Gillette, (May 1968), 102–5
27. A. Moreton, Bookers: the great unknown, *The Director* (July 1972), 56–9
28. R. S. Edwards and H. Townsend, *Business Enterprise*, Macmillan, London (1958), p. 55
29. *Ibid.*, p. 45. See also the same authors' *Business Growth*, Macmillan, London (1966), pp. 193–201; and A. Moreton, The surprising saga of Guinness, *The Director* (October 1971), 80–85
30. Harp Lager is now owned 50% by Guinness, 25% by Courage (Imperial Tobacco) and 25% by Scottish and Newcastle Breweries.
31. S. Caulkin, Rockware's Remoulding, *Management Today* (April 1974), 77

32. *Bridon: The Significance of 50 years*, Doncaster (1974)
33. J. Thackray, The Conglomerate Catastrophes, *Management Today* (June 1971), 75
34. R. Winsbury, Slater Walker's Non Conglomerate, *Management Today* (August 1969), 82. For examples of the success which has attended this policy in the past see: A. Vice, *op. cit.* 1–11, How Jim Slater Bought Forestal; and also an account of how S.W.S. acquired Greengate and Irwell Rubber Co. in C. F. Pratten, A Case Study of a Conglomerate Merger, *Moorgate and Wall Street* (Spring 1970), 27–54
35. See his article, Conglomerates: case for more mergers, *Financial Times* (15 February 1969) and also his letter in *The Times* (9 April 1969)
36. This categorisation was suggested in R. V. Buxton, Conglomerates in the Cold, *Management Today* (November 1969), 93
37. See Monopolies Commission, *The Rank Organisation Ltd. and The De La Rue Co. Ltd.*, H.M.S.O. (1969), Cmnd 298, para. 12
38. See G. Bannock, Ref. 13, p. 97
39. See D. Thomas, What Marketing Means for Imps, *Management Today* (April 1968), 78–83
40. See S. McLachlan, The Strategic Spread of B.A.T., *Financial Times* (15 May 1973); and E. Foster and G. Bull, The new man astride the B.A.T. colossus, *The Director* (September 1971), 334–8
41. R. V. Buxton, Ref. 36, 93
42. H. H. Lynch, *Financial Performance of Conglomerates*, Harvard University Press, Boston (1971), p. 9
43. R. Winsbury, Ref. 34, 87. For the other side of the story on this particular acquisition see M. Hope, On Being Taken Over by Slater Walker, *Journal of Industrial Economics*, Vol. XXIV (1976), 161–79
44. For a more detailed treatment of this, see S. E. Boyle and P. W. Jaynes, *Conglomerate Merger Performance*, United States Federal Trade Commission, Washington (1972), Ch. V, Information Loss from Conglomerate Expansion.
45. See T. Lester, B.S.R.'s Record Round-Up, *Management Today* (June 1971), 96
46. K. D. George, *Industrial Organization*, Allen and Unwin, London (1971), p. 46
47. S. E. Boyle and P. W. Jaynes, Ref. 44, p. 5.
48. Hoare and Co. Investment Research, *Domestic Electrical Appliances*, London (1969), p. 35
49. N. A. H. Stacey *et al.*, Domestic Electrical Appliances – A Look into the Future, *15th British Electrical Power Convention Proceedings*, London (1963), p. 221
50. Monopolies and Restrictive Practices Commission, *Report on the Supply of Certain Industrial and Medical Gases*, H.M.S.O. (1959), HCP 13, paras. 52–3

51. O. E. Williamson, *Corporate Control and Business Behaviour*, Prentice Hall, New Jersey (1970), p. 143
52. T. Lester, Tilling's Three-Way Testing, *Management Today* (August 1971), 43
53. *Financial Times* (14th June, 1975)
54. J. Hassid, Recent Evidence on Conglomerate Diversification in U.K. Manufacturing Industry, *Manchester School*, Vol. XLIII, (1975), 388–9
55. C. J. Sutton, Management Behaviour and a Theory of Diversification, *Scottish Journal of Political Economy*, Vol. XX (1973), 29–30 and 34–36
56. K. D. George, The Changing Structure of Competitive Industry, *Economic Journal*, Vol. LXXXII (1972), 355–7

Chapter VII

Mergers

Overview

After an introduction in which merger is defined and an indication is given of the significance of mergers in the U.K. economy, we consider why the topic currently deserves such close attention. This is followed by a discussion, with examples, of the reasons for mergers; after which we look in more detail at the financial nature of the corporate merger decision and the economic implications of this. Consideration of the phenomenon of merger cycles and of business survival is followed by a concluding section on the wider economic implications of mergers. Discussion of Government policy on mergers is delayed until Chapter IX.

A. Introduction

One of the most significant characteristics of the contemporary industrial scene is the expansion of some firms by the taking over of others, or the coming together of two or more firms on a voluntary basis. The former of these two processes is normally referred to as takeover, while the latter is usually called merger. Apart from the diversity of methods of distinguishing between these two processes, and the difficulty of applying the criteria in any one case, there seems to be little point in labouring the dichotomy; and since they both embrace the characteristic of *external* corporate expansion we shall refer to them by the generic title of industrial merger. Some idea of the magnitude of the sums involved in mergers and of the types of firms concerned can be gained from the data, in table III.

Mergers may be classified according to whether they are

horizontal, vertical or diversified; and the following data relates to those mergers which fell within the scope of the 1965 Monopolies and Mergers Act: basically those where market dominance was involved, or where assets of more than £5m were being acquired (table IV).

TABLE III

Acquisitions by Quoted Companies in Manufacturing, Distribution and Services

	No.	Value (£m)	Proportion of applications (%)**
1954	275	114	9.2
1955	294	97	6.5
1956	246	119	8.1
1957	301	128	8.2
1958	341	121	9.5
1959	559	277	14.7
1960	736	328	14.1
1961	632	374	17.5
1962	636	306	16.1
1963	885	307	13.3
1964	939	445	16.7
1965	995	472	15.9
1966	805	357	13.3
1967	763	709	22.2
1968	942	1,251	32.6
1969*	846	1,069	12.8
1970	793	1,123	10.9
1971	884	911	12.6
1972	1,210	2,532	7.6
1973	1,205	1,304	7.5
1974	504	508	4.3
1975	315	291	3.4
1976	353	426	2.5

* Figures since 1968 are not strictly comparable with those of 1954–68.

** I.E. proportion of total uses or applications of company funds involved in acquiring subsidiaries.

Sources: *Economic Trends*, April 1963 No. 114 *Ibid.*, November 1965 No. 145 *Trade and Industry*, 2 December 1970 *Acquisitions and Mergers of Companies*, Business Monitor (M7) H.M.S.O., *Financial Statistics*, H.M.S.O.

What is shown most clearly in table IV is the vast increase in the significance of conglomerate mergers: from 5% (by value) in 1967 to 51% in 1972. This has been accompanied by a fall in the corresponding figures for horizontal mergers from 91% to 40%. While it may be thought that one result of this trend is that mergers which lead to consolidation and increased market concentration (horizontal) have given way

TABLE IV
Industrial, Commercial and Financial Mergers Classified by Type of Integration (%)

	1965		1966		1967		1968		1969	
Type	No.	Value	No.	Value	No.	Value	No.	Value	No.	Value
Horizontal	78	75	76	84	86	91	81	79	80	83
Vertical	12	13	12	9	5	4	4	4	2	1
Diversified	10	12	12	7	9	5	15	17	18	16
	100	100	100	100	100	100	100	100	100	100

	1970		1971		1972		1973		1974	
	No.	Value	No.	Value	No.	Value	No.	Value	No.	Value
Horizontal	84	70	75	62	65	40	70	76	68	65
Vertical	1	–	6	4	7	9	4	2	5	2
Diversified	15	30	19	34	28	51	26	22	27	33
	100	100	100	100	100	100	100	100	100	100

Source: J. D. Gribbin, 'The Operation of the Mergers Panel since 1965', *Trade and Industry*, 17 January 1974, p. 71. The author is grateful to the Office of Fair Trading for subsequently updating the data.

to (conglomerate) mergers which may have pro-competitive effects, it must be remembered that the efficiency of diversified companies is not beyond question (see previous chapter). Conglomerate mergers are not to this extent any more or less desirable than horizontal mergers.

B. The Importance of Mergers

Increased merger activity would appear to have accompanied industrial development on both sides of the Atlantic. One observer has commented that 'it is generally recognised that in both countries (U.S. and U.K.) since the middle 1950s the level and significance of merger activity has been one of the major factors reshaping industrial structure'.[1] Certainly in this country the incidence of merger activity has increased greatly over the past decade. We have seen the data relating to the increased level of merger activity in Tables III and IV above. Three other factors encourage us to look further into mergers. These are the contribution of the 'merger boom' to increased concentration and the development of oligopoly in a number of markets; the growing criticism of U.K. Government merger policy on the part of academic economists and business writers, combined with suggestions on the part of the Government of further action in this particular field; and finally the disenchantment of many business people and academic economists with the subsequent economic performance of many merged businesses.

The merger movement in an economy acquires its real significance from the changes which it brings about in the structure and competitiveness of markets. Surveys of U.K. manufacturing business over the past decades concur in finding increased concentration at all levels of aggregation and with the use of varying measures of the phenomenon. Some of the work in this field has comprised analysis of Census of Production figures and similar work at an aggregated level, while more detailed evidence at the level of individual markets is available from the increasing volume of case-study material.[2] Some indication of the aggregate position may be gathered from data given by Dr. S. J. Prais of the National Institute of Economic and Social Research showing the rise in the share of total net output of the 100 largest companies in the U.K. from 20% in 1950 to almost 50% in 1970.[3] In respect of individual product markets, it was claimed early in 1970 that there were 156 companies holding half or more of the British market for their product;[4] while the D.T.I. reported three years later that it had identified at least 115 product sectors where a single company was considered to be responsible for between a quarter and a third of production.[5]

In addition to this, the much more complex question of the role of mergers in increased concentration has been examined by Dr. Michael Utton of Reading University. The existence of increased merger activity and concurrent increased market concentration does not establish a causal relationship. But by using sophisticated statistical methods Utton has shown that *over the period 1954–65 up to 49% of the concentration change in manufacturing industry was due to merger activity*, and that in Food, Drink, and Metal Manufacture the proportion was about two-thirds.[6] Elsewhere the same author and colleagues have concluded that 'with the intensification of merger activity after 1965 one inference is that the rate of increase in business concentration has increased as a consequence'.[7] What we emphasise here is, firstly, (as documented very briefly above), that mergers lead to, or are a significant causal factor in, increased market concentration; and secondly (as recognised in economic textbooks and borne out in empirical studies), that market concentration may lead to a loss of consumer economic welfare under the headings of higher prices and reduced output, the possibility that the best production methods *available* will not be used (X-inefficiency) nor maximum *existing* market opportunities exploited, or that innovation in production and products will be reduced.[8] Evidence on some of these matters is scanty, and methodological difficulties in empirical research abound. But on the question of the influence of market concentration upon prices, profits, resource allocation and innovatory activity a recent survey of empirical studies concluded that while

> 'It is . . . difficult to say whether the vindication of the traditional approach (i.e. that embodied in economic theory) means that monopoly and high levels of concentration are so serious a matter that public policy intervention is imperative. . . . Nevertheless, . . . (the survey) shows at least that a general attitude of vigilance towards monopoly and high levels of concentration can be founded on something more substantial than economic dogma or a mistaken appreciation of the realities of contemporary industrial and commercial markets.'[9]

U.K. Government policy on mergers, as in the case of monopoly in general, is based upon pragmatism and flexibility – or the absence of a coherent policy and total lack of guidance for industry and the Monopolies and Mergers Commission alike, if one disagrees with present policy! The Conservative Government in 1964, while recognising the contribution of mergers in the economy, admitted that 'there is, however, a small minority of mergers which may have harmful results';[10] and proposed that the Monopolies Commission should have power, at the direction of the then Board of Trade, to investigate monopoly mergers. These intentions were translated into somewhat more severe legislation by the succeeding Labour Government in the 1965 Monopolies and Mergers Act. Power was given to the Board of Trade to authorise investigation of monopoly mergers or those cases where assets exceeding £5m were acquired; such mergers could be held up pending inquiry by the Commission, and such proposed or completed mergers could be prohibited or unscrambled upon the direction of the Board of Trade. These provisions have been restated within the 1973 Fair Trading Act.

Academic criticism of Government merger policy in this country has been based upon the Government's failure to use existing legislation thoroughly enough as much as upon the need for tougher legislation itself; although there is also criticism of a lack of consistency or a real sense of direction in merger policy. For example, on the basis of Board of Trade data over the period 1965–73 there were 833 'qualifying' mergers (plus a further 47 newspaper, banking and building society mergers, which should either be considered as exceptional or for which there are special procedures), from which only *20* references (2.4%) were made to the Commission.[11] Other writers have gone much further in suggesting a radical tightening up of merger policy;[12] in one case claiming that for all qualifying mergers the Commission should want to inquire whether a merger is specifically in the public interest, and that merger activity by the top 25 companies should be virtually prohibited.[13]

The final point to be made in this section relates to the economic performance of merged companies. The statistical problems in such analysis are not inconsiderable, the greatest difficulty being to avoid attributing to a corporate merger benefits or detriments which are in fact the result of other changes in the business environment. A large number of such studies has been carried out with a fairly uniform finding that merging companies perform badly when compared with either average industry performance or the previous performance of the unmerged constituents of a subsequent merger. Among the more recent studies, Farrant took per-annum growth in earnings per share among the 85 largest (by sales) British companies; and over the period 1959–68 of the 30 major 'acquirers' only one in five achieved above-median profitability.[14] A more rigorous examination of U.K. data over the period 1955–60 was carried out by Singh. His approach was to compare the weighted average profitability (as measured by pre-tax profits on net assets relative to the industry-year average) of the acquiring and acquired firms with the subsequent profitability of the combined acquiring firm one and two years later. The general finding was a decline in profitability subsequent to merger, and his conclusion from his data was that:

> 'This strongly suggests, although it by no means proves, that it is on balance very unlikely that the reshuffling of economic resources which takes place as a result of the take-over process leads to any more profitable utilisation of these resources.'[15]

A survey of such studies – 13 in all – was carried out by Utton. His finding was that 'the commonest results are either that merging firms' profit performance was no better than non-merging firms or that it was significantly worse'. Utton's own study led him to conclude that 'the performance of the merger intensive sample of U.K. manufacturing firms for the period 1961–70 suggests that . . . mergers led to a worsened performance'.[16]

C. The Reasons for Mergers

So many opinions are expressed in this area that it is almost impossible to offer firm suggestions (on economic bases) as to the true reasons for mergers. This has led one author despairingly to conclude that 'there is at present no general economic theory of mergers comparable to the theories that have been developed in other branches of the science'.[17]

The American economist S. R. Reid concluded from his studies that 'a merger is an investment decision that will generally be rationalised on economic grounds, promoted to serve narrow self interests, and consummated for a variety of noneconomic factors in addition to the usual economic ones',[18] and this general view has been repeated in respect of the U.K. by Newbould.[19] At the individual level one of the lessons which Graham Turner derived from his account of the whole series of mergers and takeovers in the British motor industry – culminating in the takeover of British Motor Holdings by Leyland Motors in 1968 – was that

> 'It provides . . . a number of graphic illustrations of the truth that, in business in general and mergers in particular, it is the self-interest of the key personalities involved – not the interests of the shareholders or the country or even of the company itself – which often dictates events.'[20]

From the mouth of a business man himself has come the comment that 'many of the benefits of amalgamation are more imagined than real and the real motive for many take-overs is megalomania rather than industrial efficiency'.[21]

Criticism of the approach of business managers to merger strategy and acquisition pricing is in fact widespread. The American business economist John Kitching found that even *if* mergers were treated as an aspect of planned strategic growth (and this was not necessarily the case), 'the business thinking that lay behind the acquisition is often dangerously shallow';[22] while one firm of merger brokers is characterised as feeling that 'if there is community of interest, the price is almost a formality'.[23]

But to concentrate upon the more obvious tactical reasons for carrying out mergers, we can suggest that in merging with another firm a business is attempting to achieve one or more of the following objectives:

(i) Growth.
(ii) Market dominance.

(iii) Integration.
(iv) Diversification.

We have already commented upon managerial attitudes to corporate growth in the context of the theory of the firm. In an economic environment characterised by growth on the part of some sectors or firms others may have a particular incentive to follow. This applies especially to external expansion. Thus Lord Nelson of Stafford, chairman of the newly-created G.E.C.-English Electric, declared in 1969 that 'we now have the base on which to build a business comparable (in size) with those Continental competitors who have been steadily increasing their market penetration'.[24] In the case of insurance there has been a less direct chain of events. Speaking of the 1968 amalgamation of the Guardian and Royal Exchange assurance companies the point has been made that 'Mergers in other industries, and the creation of ever bigger risks as factories, fleets, etc., were built up after the war, virtually guaranteed a parallel concentration in insurance. It was clearly a case of swallow or be swallowed, and the Guardian board elected to take the active role'.[25] This is the type of situation encountered in a large number of markets. Concentration breeds further concentration as merger is matched by merger. Thus in the late 1960s the remaining British U.K. car manufacturers found themselves in an international market dominated by U.S. and other large European firms. The situation which precipitated the 1968 merger of Leyland and British Motor Holdings was, therefore, that 'in the long run, Leyland was certainly going to have to link with someone, to become part of one of the 10 or so motor companies that will sooner or later straddle and monopolize world markets'.[26] Although, as we shall see shortly, management may regard merger as being subject to greater managerial risks and complications than internal growth, from an economic point of view external expansion may appear to offer a faster and less competitive means of achieving growth or market dominance. Thus 'growth by acquisition is superior to organic (i.e. internal) growth since the latter, based on price competition, is uncertain in effect, slower in achieving the same result and always subject to retaliation from other would-be aspirants to a claim on a market's growth'.[27]

Since merger involves absorption of one firm by another, then if the firms are in the same market and if one of the firms is already relatively large, market dominance is likely to emerge. A further question is whether management specifically seeks to achieve this market dominance. Certainly Newbould found that in his large sample of mergers in 1967 and 1968 27% of the aggregate responses relating to the reasons for mergers involved market dominance.[28] Obviously, other than in answer to anonymous questionnaires, managers are normally unlikely to admit that market dominance is a specific aim of their merger policy. However, the large proportion of mergers which involves increased market concentration suggests that there is scope for this motive. It should also be noted that market dominance also confers benefits on firms in dealing with suppliers and customers. These are the benefits of monopoly and monopsony. It may be going too far to suggest that mergers at one stage in a productive process always generate mergers at previous or subsequent stages; but a more detailed consideration of the facts suggests that this may have been the case in the U.K. food industries over the last two decades.[29] Certainly Mr. Adrian Cadbury (Managing Director of Cadbury Schweppes) pointed out subsequently to the 1969 Cadbury Schweppes merger that one of the advantages of size following a merger is 'the ability to obtain better terms from suppliers and to resist similar demands from customers. Some (trade) discounts . . . can be improved by making use of the leverage that comes with size'.[30]

Diversification through merger may be considered the most appropriate method of spreading risks, etc. The business which is considering diversification may be particularly drawn to *external* expansion in the light of its existing management's relative unfamiliarity with the new field. Through diversifying by merger a business is buying the managerial expertise as well as the physical and other human assets required. Although it was suggested in the previous chapter that Dunlop had diversified some distance away from its basic product, the pneumatic tyre, in fact at the beginning of the 1970s tyres still accounted for 62% of turnover. The merger in 1971 with Pirelli (with only 40% or less of turnover accounted for by tyres, and a sound foothold in the cable field) thus offered a solid basis for diversified expansion.[31] Diversification, particularly to escape from relatively stagnant markets, is also to be found in some of the food/grocery mergers of the late 1960s. In these cases – for example the merger of Brooke-Bond and Leibig in 1968, or Cadbury and Schweppes in the following year[32] – the firms were hoping to find together what they could not gain as individual businesses: size and a broader market base.

Having devoted an earlier chapter to integration we simply need to comment here upon the particular issue of backward or forward integration by merger. The most important issue here relates to capacity. Integration by merger will occur where either the manufacturer has no wish to increase retail capacity as a result of his forward integration, or where the retail capacity is already limited by regulation – as for example in petrol retailing or licensed premises. Where a manufacturer feels that he can expand the number of retail outlets through internal integration without upsetting the total pattern of trading in the market he may well adopt this policy. However, the integrated men's tailoring concerns such as Montague Burton or United Drapery Stores (through John Collier, Alexandre etc.) have tended to acquire retail outlets through takeover. The same has been true of Sears Holdings in footwear. Backward integration is normally associated with difficulty in obtaining input supplies.

In cases where the number of retail outlets for a good is subject to legal control, then not only is a manufacturer who wishes to expand into retailing obliged to accomplish this by external means, but the producer may feel especially obliged to expand forward in these circumstances to ensure a favourable distribution of his products *vis à vis* those of his competitors. In petrol retailing, for example, the strictness of town and country planning regulations results in 90% of applications for erection of new petrol stations being refused.[33] The result of this situation, combined with an oligopoly among petroleum refiners, has in the past been a scramble on the part of these large firms either to acquire garages outright or to enter into long-term agreements with proprietors. The Monopolies Commission criticised this system in its report in 1965;[34] but an estimated 28% of sites in the U.K. are company owned.[35] A similar situation in brewing results in each member of the brewing oligopoly placing a high premium upon public house ownership. The situation here for aggressive, expansionist brewers is that 'with demand stagnant, or at best slowly rising, markets were primarily extended by the purchase of firms, not so much for their breweries but for their tied outlets and distribution areas'.[36]

D. The Corporate Acquisition Decision

The purpose of this section is to examine briefly the nature of the corporate acquisition decision. In detail this topic forms part of the subject area of financial economics. However, it is felt that some appreciation of the concepts involved is desirable for those wishing to understand the subject of mergers in the context of industrial economics.

A merger at the individual-firm level is essentially a capital investment appraisal situation for the acquiring firm. This firm is making an initial investment (the purchase consideration of the acquired firm) in respect of an anticipated future stream of earnings (the incremental cash flow arising from the merger). The practical difficulties involved in such a computation are considerable, and many interesting issues such as changed company tax position will be involved. We would suggest, however, that such a computation, however tentative, should be undertaken by all acquiring firms in respect of each acquisition. Indeed, to base the purchase price of an acquisition on any other data is incorrect and could lead to significant losses in equity shareholder welfare.

What should be emphasised is that all of the relevant factors can, and indeed must, be built into this assessment of the maximum price to be paid for an acquisition. These factors may include gains (in the form of increased selling prices or reduced input costs) through market dominance, or a reduced uncertainty of earnings from the same source. A further interesting phenomenon should also be accommodated. Professor Rose, in speaking of what are acknowledged to have been premium prices paid for acquisitions in the past, has pointed out that

> 'the evidence suggests that the price eventually paid has reflected, not only the increase in profits expected over time, but also the *loss* of profits feared in the event of the bid being lost to a rival.'[37]

The application of these principles will determine the maximum price which should be paid for an acquisition as a going concern. This does not mean to say that this price will be paid, but certainly no more should be offered. Despite the inevitable involvement of qualitative or non-quantifiable factors in a takeover situation we consider that the major factors can be subsumed within the above approach.

How 'rationally' business people approach a merger decision is impossible to say. The views quoted at the beginning of this chapter might appear to suggest that a great many personal factors are involved along with financial calculations. Certainly a reading of some of the Monopolies Commission's merger reports leaves one with the impression that little quantitative work is done in forecasting the potential gains to be had from proposed mergers. On the one hand few people can have been impressed by learning in November 1968 that 'Lord Cole and Sir Derek Pritchard began talking about a link between their two companies – Unilever and Allied Breweries (combined capital employed at the time £1,354m.) – last Monday night. They were in Pritchard's flat, not really for that purpose, but simply meeting as old friends with some common business problems'.[38] On the other hand from other sources it would seem that management do not enter lightly into merger discussions. Nor does it appear that business people overestimate their own ability unduly. A publication issued by some of the leading U.K. business people stressed that 'perhaps the generalisation that can be made with most confidence is that a merger is normally one of the most intricate operations that a company is ever called upon to perform';[39] while the U.S. executives whom Kitching interviewed in his study in fact appeared to attach a higher degree of risk to external than to internal expansion. One manager was 'quite sceptical about the existence of synergy'; and, speaking of managerial talent, another manager commented:

'Don't think it's hard to release synergy; it's not. It's damn near impossible'.[40] In the light of this, it may be that if management can be seen to be attempting acquisition goals which are clearly in economic terms quite unrealistic, this would be *prima facie* evidence of non-economic motivations. Newbould's approach to this is most enlightening. Considering U.K. mergers in 1967 and 1968 where the price paid for the 'victim' firm was £1m+, Newbould solved the accepted D.C.F. formula to determine the required post-merger earnings growth rate implied by the purchase price of the acquired firm (table V).

TABLE V
Required Compound Rates of Growth to achieve 10% Return

Rate (%)	No. of firms	%
Less than 3½	53	21.9
3½ –	23	9.5
7 –	17	7.0
10 –	30	12.4
15 –	34	14.1
20 –	63	26.0
50 –	22	9.1
	242	100.0

Source: G. D. Newbould, 'Implications of Financial Analysis of Takeovers' in J. M. Samuels (ed.), *Readings on Mergers and Takeovers* (London, 1972) p. 22.

Bearing in mind that these are *annual compound* required rates of growth over the specified period, it must be conceded that the unreality of the purchase price can hardly be explained by acquiring-firm managerial optimism alone. Non-economic factors must be involved.

Do these arise because the techniques of financial analysis are inapplicable in merger situations, or is there a willing disregard of the discipline? Elsewhere, Newbould and another colleague have come to the conclusion that 'to examine the prescribed role of merger finance in the typical large company is not to review the extent of that role, but to question whether it exists at all in the prescribed form'.[41] Newbould and Jackson specifically claim that external investment potentials are looked at by expanding firms in a radically different manner from internal investments of funds. They claim that the *opportunity* to make the former occurs fortuitously as a result of the personal factors involved, that finance for these projects cannot, therefore, be budgeted for in the normal way, that the purchase price paid where the purpose of the acquisition is clearly market dominance or the avoidance of being dominated cannot be finely calculated, and that 'management is emerging as the force behind merger activity, a force acting in its own right, in its own interest, and replacing the impersonal dicta of finance and economics'.[42]

E. Merger Cycles

It is common experience on both sides of the Atlantic that mergers occur in waves – that there is a cyclical incidence of mergers over time. Can we account for this in terms of traditional economic reasoning? Two sets of economic conditions appear to be necessary to sustain a merger wave: the continued *incentive* to amalgamation as a form of expansion, and the *feasibility* of this. In respect of the first set of conditions Cook and Cohen give particular emphasis to intense and persistent short-term competition, and to economies of scale.[43] The first of these circumstances, they suggest, will obtain under conditions of non-differentiated products, high overhead costs, raw material price fluctuations, excess capacity, inability to agree upon common prices among producers, and/or opportunities for price discrimination by producers. The existence of potential economies of scale in any area of business is of course an incentive to expansion, *ceteris paribus*. Having established *incentives* to external expansion (and we should not exclude the drive for market dominance), we can go on to suggest that whether expansion occurs internally or externally will in many cases, r, depend upon the relative *feasibility* of these two of expansion – the second of the two economic ns outlined at the beginning of this section. Econ- lysis would lead us to suppose that internal expan- ost difficult in imperfect markets characterised by ifferentiation and thus patronage barriers to in- -expansion which could only be overcome by innovatory activity – Schumpeterian competition – on the part of expansionist firms. Outside financial constraints such as the difficulty of obtaining new finance would also apply here. Furthermore, expansion on the part of one firm in any market will be more difficult when the total market is in decline, or when the aggregate market rate of expansion is lower that that desired by an individual firm. We would, therefore, expect mergers to be a particular characteristic of declining industries and of expansionist activity in imperfect markets. Not all of this, however, would appear to be wholly satisfactory. Some of the above variables – such as the extent of product differentiation – cannot be measured accurately; while product homogeneity on the one hand appears to encourage amalgamation through intensifying direct price competition, while on the other allows for internal expansion rather than external growth characteristic of imperfect markets. The technical advances introducing the potential for economies of scale are likely to come about at a different pace and at different times over a number of industries. These changed technical conditions as such, therefore, cannot of themselves account for merger waves. Likewise, the effect of industrial concentration upon individual-firm profit performance (involving basically a decline in the degree of variability of profits rather than a statistically significant rise in the level of earnings) is something which is always available as a merger incentive, and cannot therefore account for the *cyclical* pattern of merger activity.

Again, as in the case of examination of merger activity at the individual-firm level, we must be aware of a complex of non-quantifiable factors involved in analysis of merger cycles. Hunter examined the causes of mergers under the headings of Long-term Objectives, Immediate Motivations, and External Conditions. His conclusion on merger cycle analysis was:

> 'It is possible, on examining the structure of a particular industry and its surrounding circumstances, to predict with some assurance that mergers will take place in some forthcoming period. But it is very much less feasible to isolate the main factor at work which creates, at one period rather than another, waves of mergers. And certainly it is not possible to point to a predominant principle of explanation for the occurrence of mergers which will solve, for all purposes, the problems of the policy-maker.'[44]

This would seem to substantiate the conclusion of more recent researchers that 'there are so many different reasons for mergers that it is not possible to subsume them into one, or into a few, financial ratios. There seems to be no short-cut statistical method of assessing the causes and effects of recent merger activity'.[45]

As an alternative approach, and one which may be more attractive to some insofar as a certain amount of statistical analysis may be applied to the data, some authors have forsaken the search for *a fortiori causes* of mergers in favour of analysis of *correlation* of merger cycles with various indices of economic and other activity. This could, of course, be the first step in establishing *a priori* causal relationships between merger activity and such other economic variables. Thus, the U.S. literature in this field is characterised by attempts to trace the causes of merger cycles through correlation of certain economic and financial variables with recognised merger waves. S. R. Reid covers this area of research; and while he found a number of characteristics individual to each of the U.S. merger waves (1898–1902, 1925–9, and 1955–), there were found to be a number of macroeconomic variables which coincided with each merger wave.[46] The most significant factors from our point of view can be summed up in Reid's own words:

> 'A period of relative prosperity accompanied by a buoyant stock market has been in evidence during each merger wave. Similarly, periods of declining economic conditions have witnessed a decline in merger activity. The economic

> environment of realised or anticipated prosperity as evidenced by security prices has been a contributing factor to increased merger activity. . . . Depressed economic conditions in the form of a recession and/or depression followed the peaks of merger activity in both the turn-of-the-century merger wave and the later 1920s merger wave.'[47]

This would appear to be a promising area in which to find some explanation of merger cycle patterns. The only caveat is that, as Reid himself points out (and a phenomenon which is not satisfactorily explained in economic theory), merger cycles may *create* stock-market cycles. This would appear to be a real possibility in respect of the ending of stock-market and merger cycles. In this case the poor subsequent performance of merged companies which were brought together at the beginning of the merger boom may bring about a bear market. There may be a number of pitfalls involved in this approach; but since we shall subsequently place some emphasis at the individual-firm level on stock-market valuations of firms *vis-à-vis* valuation by other persons, then if we can show that there are periods in economic history when such gaps between valuations given to a firm by its existing shareholders and potential purchasers have been great, and if there is a common economic environment of these occasions, then we may have a more reliable guide to the incidence of merger cycles.[48]

Little work of this kind has been carried out in respect of the earliest merger waves in the U.K. The period 1888–1912 (or in particular the years 1895–1902) witnessed a considerable merger boom in this country. What one commentator stresses, however, as the dominant force behind these turn-of-the-century mergers is the depressed market conditions of the time. Thus:

> 'The argument which recurs again and again in the prospectuses and reports of preliminary meetings between interested firms is of the need to eliminate severe short term price competition which reduced profits and accentuated the burden of excess capacity.'[49]

On the other hand mergers over the period 1886–1914 in the U.K. have been shown to be positively correlated with movements in national income. This has been explained in terms of *financial* factors, and in particular the fact that high share prices produced in times of economic boom provided an additional incentive both for the existing owner-managers to sell their shares to those wishing to establish large horizontal consolidations, and to company promoters who would in times of prosperity maximise the forecast advantages of mergers to potential new shareholders and also reap large promotional fees for themselves.[50]

It would seem to be impossible to find a direct causal relationship between mergers and aggregated economic data,[51] although the comments on the U.K. situation immediately above seem to be in line with the generally buoyant economic conditions which characterised the 'gay-nineties' merger wave in America.[52] Although the U.K. merger wave of 1882–1912 represented significant market concentration in many fields – in excess of 66% of the market in 10 out of 16 cases presented by Utton – the resulting consolidations experienced considerable financial and administrative difficulties. The interwar merger wave in this country was horizontal in type and further contributed to market concentration.

It is not, however, until we examine the post-World War II merger wave in this country that we find financial factors of considerable importance. It was in fact in the opinion of many people the gap between the potential earnings or asset value of companies and their current stock-market value which was largely responsible for the spate of mergers of the 1950s. During this period stock-market prices were depressed relative to potential earnings for a number of reasons. Stock-market prices, most people would agree, are heavily influenced by the current level of dividends.[53] These latter were discouraged in the period after 1945 by differential corporate taxation in favour of retentions, political pressure on dividend limitation, and the need which many companies felt for a high level of retentions with which to replace war-damaged plant and catch up with the post-1945 increase in demand at a time when the Capital Issues Committee limited new issues of shares. On the other hand some firms had accumulated large cash balances which were clearly not being used, and which were in part declining in real value as inflation occurred particularly up to 1952. This was, therefore, a period during which takeovers based upon 'financial disparities' were common.[54] The early 1950s was the era of Wolfson, Clore and Fraser – individuals who took full advantage of the undervaluation of corporate assets and earning power.

The personalised glamour of their era has been preserved by some financial journalists;[55] but it would seem that the mergers of the 1960s have been characterised by the quest for industrial rationalisation – the effects of which may not be *immediately* realisable in financial terms – rather than immediate financial gain. Thus, although it is possible to read a comparatively recent example of how within one year Slater Walker Securities bought a firm for £10.5m. and sold off its assets individually for a total of £18.1m.,[56] and although 'asset stripping' is still written of with opprobrium in the financial press, it would seem that the concensus of informed opinion is that 'the typical take-over bids of the 1950s which thrived on the undervaluation of fixed assets, particularly freehold land and buildings, have slowly given way to the 1960-style mergers and take-overs when the accent is on rationalization'.[57] Thus, more recent financial analysis of mergers has concluded that by the 1960s

> 'equity prices had reached levels which could no longer be recognised as being 'obviously' low in relation to asset values or earning capacity, and company liquidity had fallen. Purely 'financial' considerations therefore played a smaller part after 1959 in promoting acquisitions, in which commercial factors must have become more important.'[58]

We contend, however, that these broader 'commercial' factors can, and indeed must, be subject to financial analysis at the individual-firm level of acquisition decisions. An explanation of merger cycles couched in 'purely financial' terms may therefore be valid. An example is Gort's 'economic disturbance' theory of mergers. While not denying the incentive which potential or anticipated synergy offers to merger movements, Gort suggests that 'forces which generate discrepancies in valuation are decisive in determining variations in merger rates both among industries and over time'.[59] In essence this theory is simple: firm A places a greater value upon firm B than do B's present owners. This takeover potential situation can arise either because the potential net cash flows from B are greater in the mind of A than for B's owners, or because the discount rate which A is applying to B's net cash flows is different from (i.e. *lower* than) that applied by B's existing owners. This discount rate would reflect both the respective (opportunity) costs of capital facing A and B, and also the risk factor which each is building into the discount rate to be applied to B's net cash flows. In order to explain merger cycles one must envisage conditions existing at one time and across industries under which a sufficient number of non-owners of firms put a higher valuation upon the firms than existing owners. Gort claims that changes in technology and stock-price movements are of importance here. The former condition will make future net cash flow prediction difficult; while stock-price fluctuation – particularly above the long-run mean – will facilitate acquisition as 'growth' company shares tend to rise faster and further than average shares. Gort also suggests that entry barriers and demand growth in the industry will stimulate mergers. The usefulness of Gort's article is partly in his ability to discount (on substantial grounds insofar as this is possible) any of the other reasons advanced to account for mergers and merger cycles. These other reasons including the desire to achieve economies of scale, to eliminate competition, or the acquisition of 'bargain' companies.

Some economists have appeared to be lukewarm in accepting this approach to takeover analysis; and yet we may find it the only viable approach to merger cycle analysis. Thus Penrose has admitted that firms, faced with the choice between direct asset purchase and acquisition of corporate possessors of such assets, will choose the more profitable course of action. But such authors yet appear to be reluctant to pursue further analysis of such 'valuation discrepancies'. The implication is that existing owners are 'unwisely' undervaluing their company's shares. This can, however, only occur where someone else is relatively 'unwisely' (?) overvaluing the same shares. Thus, speaking of 'special situations' in regard to merger finance, Penrose says:

> 'An undervaluation by the market of the shares of a firm may be another reason why a particular firm may be acquired relatively cheaply. There may be a variety of special conditions at any given time which lead to undervaluation of the publicly traded stock of a firm, but probably the most important general conditions are a lack of knowledge on the part of the investing public of the value of the firm, a lack of confidence in its management, or a discounting of the less marketable stocks for lack of liquidity.'[60]

Our conclusion on merger cycles is that these must be explained in terms which apply across a large part of industry at one time. Conditions of relative expansion or economic depression would seem to be a common background; and in either case some firms must see the elimination of their rivals as a prerequisite to their increased economic wellbeing. High levels or considerable durability of fixed investment may be significant factors in depressed markets; while patronage barriers to rapid expansion or shortage of necessary inputs may quicken the pace of mergers during economic expansion. In either case we can expect valuation discrepancies to arise, making formerly independent businesses seem 'good-buys' in the minds of competing, or perhaps economically unrelated, firms. These are the conditions obtaining under the personalised glamour of the G.E.C.–A.E.I.–English Electric, Imperial Tobacco–Ross Group, Sears Holdings–British Shoe Corporation, Consolidated Gold Fields–Amey Group, Cavenham Foods–Allied Suppliers, Glynwed–Allied Ironfounders takeovers and mergers. In some cases rationalisation was found to be necessary in contracting markets, in others (Cadbury–Schweppes, Rowntree–Mackintosh) a realignment of forces was taking place in a relatively static market; and one clearly cannot rule out the repercussive effects across a whole industry of one principal merger.

F. Business Survival

The approach adopted here is parallel to that used in Section D above. That is, we shall consider business survival in the context of the financial approach to the corporate acquisition decision. The question we pose is, can we explain in terms of the economic theory of mergers the survival or demise of businesses according to their economic or financial performance? It might also be thought that one should examine the contribution of this branch of economic theory to the prediction of which firms will *initiate* successful takeovers. This is a significant matter as, if 'poor' firms (in terms of past profitability) are successful acquirers (in terms of accomplished acquisitions), then it could be that the economic performance of the economy as a whole will suffer. Work has been carried out in this field, but we shall restrict ourselves to examination of the takeover mechanism as it affects 'victim' companies.

The starting point here must be the relative valuations of a business by its existing shareholders and potential bidders, *and* the relative attractiveness (taking into consideration all economic factors) of external *vis-à-vis* internal expansion by the potential acquirer. Thus, for a firm Alpha to be acquired by Beta it would have to be the case that the price at which 51% of Alpha shareholders will dispose of their holdings is lower than the cost to Beta of otherwise buying the appropriate assets, welding them together to earn a profit, and penetrating Alpha's markets. So long as Alpha's shares are more expensive than this to purchase then Alpha should be immune from takeover. To quote a U.S. source on this:

> 'if they (expanding firms) are profit-oriented, they will *always* compare the desirability of entry by internal means and entry by acquisition and then choose the means most consistent with their objective of increasing profitability.'[61]

Fundamental to this decision is for the acquiring management to believe that they could utilise the assets of a potential acquisition more effectively than its existing management. An American consultant recently summed it up by emphasising that 'the most business-like (technique for evaluating acquisitions) is to look at the transaction as the purchase of a money machine. You are buying an instrument to generate earnings, or even more accurately, to generate cash flow'.[62] To this extent our theory of merger activity is essentially based upon treating a takeover situation in the eyes of the acquiring firm as being a complex fixed-asset-acquisition and therefore investment-appraisal situation. This is the approach adopted by Manne in setting out his concept of the market for corporate control.[63] Giving a smaller role than many to the realisation of economies of scale or monopoly profits as incentives to takeover, Manne – taking the present share price of a company as an indication of existing managerial efficiency, and the relative (to similar companies or to the market as a whole) share price as a measure of possible capital gain to acquiring management – sees takeover as occurring when a firm's share value is below that which it would be under improved management. Thus,

> 'The lower the stock price, relative to what it could be with more efficient management, the more attractive the take-over becomes to those who believe that they can manage the company more efficiently.'[64]

Despite their apparent reservations about rate of return on capital employed and/or share prices as an indicator of managerial or economic efficiency, and some doubts about the efficacy of the market in corporate control, this view of takeover is supported by Samuels and Wilkes.[65] Apart from the above-mentioned reservation these two authors explicitly take a financial-asset-acquisition view of corporate takeover. To quote again from an American source:

> 'For the acquisition route to be competitive with, or superior to, the internal route, a firm contemplating entry into a profitable industry (or market) has to be convinced that a particular candidate for acquisition is selling at a price which is significantly *less* than what the (acquiring) firm thinks the intrinsic value of the candidate is.'[66]

Having established that an acquiring firm will take over another if it considers that it can manage the acquired resources more efficiently than existing management, is there an index by which we can measure the relative cost of internal (i.e. purchase of assets) and external (i.e. acquisition of existing corporate possessors of such assets) expansion? Whittaker has taken as a point of departure the acquisition of a firm (as a going concern) as an alternative to the purchase of an identical set of assets in the normal factor input markets. It is this latter cost which Whittaker has referred to as the takeover support level: the point at which it becomes cheaper for an expanding firm to acquire the corporate possessor of the desired assets for expansion rather than to buy these as separate inputs in the market.[67] Thus, where $M > B$ (if M is the stock-market value of a firm with desirable assets, and B is some approximation to the cost of acquiring these in the factor market) the firm owning the assets should be immune from takeover to the extent that expansion in the market is cheaper via direct asset acquisition. M must be arrived at by inflating the existing market value of the desirable acquisition by the market premium which inevitably arises during a public takeover – about one-thrid according to Rose and Newbould.[68] B, to be a realistic alternative, must represent the replacement cost of all assets, adjusted for any Government grants, allowances, etc., in respect of fixed-asset investment. This would appear to be a more realistic form of valuation-ratio analysis than that traditionally used – which so far has yielded poor predictive results for survival of firms.[69] The point is that the traditional valuation ratio (V), on a per-share basis, merely expresses the stock-market's appraisal of the worth of a company (based upon past dividends and future earnings and distributions) as a numerator upon the net equity book value of the assets. The point is not that the computational problems of the valuation ratio render it a difficult tool to use, but that the denominator must only in a very minimum of cases be of any interest to a potential acquiring company. Rubner has wittily blown a hole in the idea of underlying corporate assets being any indication as to the 'value' of the firm – pointing out in the process that whereas in 1964 the market valuation of Marks & Spencer was four times that of the net equity assets, for Cunard the stock market was valuing each £1 of underlying assets at 25p.[70]

Again on an empirical basis we can ask, are businesses with high valuation ratios protected from takeover? Can businesses with low valuation ratios survive? A summary article led two notable authors in the field to conclude that 'low stock-exchange valuation has a substantial and significant effect on the chance of being taken over, *provided the hypothesis is framed in such a way as to allow for the likelihood that there will be considerable differences between firms as regards how low their quotations may fall before the take-over danger becomes critical*'.[71] (Emphasis added.) On a wider basis Singh selected variables to describe the economic and financial characteristics of firms in an attempt to distinguish between taken-over and non-taken-over firms. These ratios included measures of profitability, growth, size, retentions, distributions, liquidity, gearing, and the valuation ratio. Singh's conclusions on the basis of univariate analysis (i.e. comparing only *one* characteristic at a time between the two groups of firms) were that while there were no significant differences in profitability between the two groups at the individual-industry level, taken-over firms were smaller and retained a greater proportion of profits than non-taken-over firms. Individually, however, none of the variables considered was a good discriminator between the two groups. On the basis of multivariate analysis (i.e. comparing a number of characteristics simultaneously) Singh found the same difficulty of distinguishing between the two groups. Singh further analysed firms by 'matching' taken-over with non-taken-over firms of the same size and industry, and compared other ratios including *V*. Again, poor discrimination was achieved. But Singh's most significant finding was that the relationship between profitability and likelihood of takeover is not linear; that once a 'threshold' level of profitability has been achieved, profit improvement beyond this level does not markedly decrease the risk of being taken over. Furthermore, it would appear that for a medium or large firm the best way to reduce the risk of takeover is to increase size rather than profitability as, at certain existing levels of size and profitability, this would seem to be the more certain way of reducing the statistical likelihood of being acquired.[72]

The general conclusion of this sub-section would appear to be that the takeover mechanism does not necessarily discriminate 'efficiently' between those firms which are or are not taken over. Particularly disturbing is Singh's conclusion as to the 'survival of the fattest'. If this were to be a permanent feature of the market in corporate control, then it might be that such a mechanism should not be allowed to operate without additional correction/impetus from the Government.

G. Wider Economic Implicatons

As was stressed at the beginning of this chapter, mergers and takeovers have significant implications for the working of the economy. There are also obvious political and social implications arising from the high levels of *aggregate* concentration in the economy indicated by Prais's data quoted above. It may, for example, be felt to be wrong for a society to allow vast concentration of economic power to lie in the hands of a fairly small group of private individuals or corporations. Such concentration of economic power could imply, or result in, the wielding of political influence, or the creation of a social divide between those possessing such power and those subject to it. These may appear to be much wider considerations relating to mergers which are outside the province of economics. But it was in just this context that the Conservative minister formerly concerned with Government policy on mergers stated quite openly that 'the decisions and behaviour of large firms are matters of legitimate public interest'.[73] Certainly the interests of current shareholders, suppliers, employees, customers, and even citizens of present and future generations are involved in merger decisions. For example, a merger may have significant implications for income distribution, regional policy, balance of payments, or rate of consumption of finite natural resources.

So far as detailed consideration of the effects of mergers is concerned, however, economics is usually involved in an assessment of the efficiency aspects of the problem. Do mergers create a more economically efficient environment? This question itself is more complex than may appear at first glance. It can be suggested that our basic question above really poses three issues. What implications arise from mergers for economic allocative efficiency, for technical progressiveness and X-efficiency, and for the pattern of national income distribution?[74] Thus we are asking, do mergers lead to more competitive product markets, to improved technological performance or elimination of managerial slack, or to a more optimal distribution of national income. Much optimism is often expressed in this area. Thus Dr. Brian Hindley has suggested that 'there is only one constraint which can, in principle, compel managers to attempt to maximise returns to the owners. It is the take-over bid'.[75] And even in the context of a discussion of asset stripping one company director commented:

> 'There are many managements in existence which are not as good as they could or should be. There is equally little doubt that shareholders in general, and institutions in particular, are not effective enough in gingering up or removing such managements. The threat of bankruptcy or a take-over bid is an extremely powerful social tool to remedy this deficiency'.[76]

However, not only has doubt been cast on this optimism on the methodological ground that there is no possibility of comparing the merger situation with the non-merger situation, but the operation of the market for corporate control – competition in the capital market as opposed to the traditional economic natural selection via competition in the product market – has also been questioned.[77]

Mergers do not necessarily, as a matter of arithmetic, raise the degree of concentration in a market. There may be no change in concentration in a single market following a conglomerate merger. Furthermore, mergers by specialist firms within a single market *may reduce* the degree of concentration as measured by the dispersion of firm size if mergers take place among the small or medium-sized firms. This process may also have the effect of setting up more viable competitors to the largest firms in the market. Mergers do, however, by definition, create larger firms, and we have already noted the role which mergers have been found to play in increasing concentration.

Certainly such evidence as exists does not suggest that large firms perform better than smaller firms. A summary of one recent study would seem to be that although 'giant' firms grew faster than other quoted firms over the period 1948–69, the greater part of this growth was the result of acquiring other quoted companies, and that the rate of growth of new fixed capital formation was lower among giant companies. Furthermore, despite the higher levels of capital gearing enjoyed by the giants (perhaps as a result of their more stable pattern of earnings), their rate of return on equity capital was lower than that for other quoted companies.[78]

So far as mergers are concerned we have already seen that the economic performance of merger-intensive companies, or of merged companies relative to the pre-merger performance of constituents, does not suggest that mergers automatically lead to increased efficiency. Many economists too are sceptical regarding the motivation of business men in merger situations, or the *wider* economic, as opposed to firm-centred, benefits to be gained from mergers. For example, it has been pointed out that so far as economies of scale are concerned the real benefits to industrial structure and efficiency are likely to come from mergers among smaller firms, not acquisitions by already large businesses.[79]

Finally it bears repetition that the takeover process as some form of 'market for corporate control' appears to act in a rather crude manner so far as distinguishing between good and bad corporate performance is concerned. In updating his research to cover the period 1967–70 Singh (whose earlier results have already been examined) concluded that 'during the later 1960s, it is clear that although (in most respects) taken-over companies have on average worse records than surviving ones (and are smaller in size), there is an *extremely* large degree of overlap between the characteristics of the two groups of firms'.[81] (original emphasis) Two further writers in this field were forced to conclude, somewhat whimsically,

> 'The acquiring firms themselves however seem to be in a variety of conditions. One way of summarising the results might be that a firm which has a dip in its fortune, reduces its rate of dividend increase, performs poorly on the share market and hence also in VR and p/e ratios, becomes a target for acquisition. If such a firm were big enough, it could become an acquiring firm!'[81]

The place of mergers in the economy, and therefore surely in texts on industrial economics, is significant. It is also, however, in both locations, uncertain. Merged businesses, and for that matter large firms as a whole, do not appear to be efficient by conventional measurement. Their role in the theory of the firm is also thereby confused. At best inefficient or weak firms are allowed to survive; and their chances of so doing are materially increased if they are large. At worst somewhat more profitable firms become less profitable as a result of merger activity. It is in the light of these features that Government intervention in industrial structure is examined in the final chapter.

References

1. M. A. Utton, The Effect of Mergers on Concentration: U.K. Manufacturing Industry, 1954–1965, *Journal of Industrial Economics*, Vol. XX (1971), 43
2. See for example W. G. Shepherd, Changes in British Industrial Concentration, 1951–58, *Oxford Economic Papers*, Vol. XXIII (1966), 126–32; and M. C. Sawyer, Concentration in British Manufacturing Industry, *Oxford Economic Papers*, Vol. XXVIII (1971), 352–83. See also S. Aaronovitch and M. C. Sawyer, The Concentration of British Manufacturing, *Lloyds Bank Review* (October 1974), 14–23. Up-to-date figures at the individual-industry level are to be found in trade journals, the E.I.U. *Retail Business*, and in stockbroker circulars.

3. See report on the research of Professor S. J. Prais in National Institute of Economic and Social Research *30th Annual Report*, 1972, (1973), p. 10; see also the same author's A New Look at the Growth of Industrial Concentration, *Oxford Economic Papers*, Vol. XXVI (1974), 273–288
4. Hansard 799 H. C. Deb. (5th Ser.) pp. *24–27* (6th April 1970)
5. See *The Times* (19th March 1973)
6. See M. A. Utton, Ref. 1
7. P. E. Hart, M. A. Utton and G. Walshe, *Mergers and Concentration in British Industry*, C.U.P., Cambridge (1973), p. 4
8. See M. Beesley, Mergers and Economic Welfare, in I.E.A., *Mergers, Take-overs and the Structure of Industry*, I.E.A., London (1973), p. 73
9. B. S. Yamey, Do Monopoly and Near-Monopoly Matter?, in M. Peston and B. Corry (eds.), *Essays in Honour of Lord Robbins*, Weidenfeld and Nicholson, London (1972), pp. 322–23
10. *Monopolies, Mergers and Restrictive Practices*, H.M.S.O., (1964), Cmnd. 2299, para. 22
11. See J. D. Gribbin, The Operation of the Mergers Panel Since 1965, *Trade and Industry* (17 January 1974), 72
12. See M. Howe, British Merger Policy Proposals and American Experience, *Scottish Journal of Political Economy*, Vol. XIX (1972), 37–61
13. A. Sutherland, The Management of Mergers Policy, in A. Cairncross, (ed.) *The Managed Economy*, Blackwell, Oxford (1970), pp. 106–34
14. P. Farrant, The Truth about Mergers, *Management Today* (May 1970), 120
15. A. Singh, *Take-Overs: Their Relevance to the Stock Market and the Theory of the Firm*, C.U.P., Cambridge (1971), p. 165
16. See M. A. Utton, On Measuring the Effects of Industrial Mergers, *Scottish Journal of Political Economy*, Vol. XXI (1974), 13–28
17. F. R. Jervis, *The Economics of Mergers*, Routledge and Paul, London (1971), p. 133
18. S. R. Reid, *Mergers, Managers and the Economy*, McGraw Hill, London (1968), p. 128
19. G. D. Newbould, *Management and Merger Activity*, Guthstead, Liverpool (1970)
20. G. Turner, *The Leyland Papers*, Eyre and Spottiswoode, London (1971), p. 208
21. Quoted in, Mergers, Amalgamations and Company Size, *The Director* (August 1972), 184
22. J. Kitching, The Strategy of Merging, *Management Today* (October 1969), 75

23. T. Lester, The Business Marriage Brokers, *Management Today* (October 1969), 58
24. G.E.C.-English Electric, *1969 Annual Report*, p. 4
25. G. Foster, How the GRE Grew, *Management Today* (August 1974), 53
26. R. Winsbury, The Labours of British Leyland, *Management Today* (October 1969), 67
27. W. P. J. Maunder, Technical Progress, Competition and Mergers: Some Empirical Evidence for British Competition Policy, *Economics*, Vol. X (1974), 236
28. G. D. Newbould, Ref. 19, p. 139
29. See W. S. Howe, Bilateral Oligopoly and Competition in the U.K. Food Trades, *The Business Economist*, Vol. V (1973), 77–78, and references therein
30. G. A. H. Cadbury, Mergers, *The Business Economist*, Vol. V (1973), 160
31. D. Thomas, Dunlop-Pirelli's Squeezed Start, *Management Today* (November 1971), 64 and 71
32. See G. Foster, Blending Brooke Bond Liebig, *Management Today* (October 1969), 82; and the same author's, The Cadbury Schweppes Mix, *Management Today* (April 1970), 64–73
33. H. Townsend, Competition in Petrol Retailing, *Three Banks Review* (March 1966), 21
34. Monopolies Commission, *Report on Petrol Supply to Retailers*, H.M.S.O., (1965), H.C.P. 241
35. The Analysis of European Distribution Systems, *International Journal of Physical Distribution*, Vol. III (1972), 35
36. J. Mark, The British Brewing Industry, *Lloyds Bank Review* (April 1974), 33
37. H. B. Rose, in foreword to A. Vice, *The Strategy of Takeovers*, McGraw Hill, Maidenhead (1971), p. xvi
38. *Financial Times* (30 November 1968)
39. Industrial Policy Group, *Merger Policy*, London (1971), para. 5
40. J. Kitching, Why do Mergers Miscarry?, *Harvard Business Review*, Vol. XLV (1967), 88 and 90
41. G. D. Newbould and A. S. Jackson, *The Receding Ideal*, Guthstead, Liverpool (1972), p. 109
42. *Ibid.*, p. 114
43. P. L. Cook and R. L. Cohen, *Effects of Mergers*, Allen and Unwin, Cambridge (1958), pp. 433–43
44. A. Hunter, Mergers and Industry Concentration in Britain, *Banca Nazionale del Lavoro Quarterly Review*, Vol. XXII (1969), 382
45. P. E. Hart, M. A. Utton and G. Walshe, Ref. 7, p. 6
46. S. R. Reid, Ref. 18, Part I

47. *Ibid.*, p. 124
48. Unfortunately analysis correlating the business cycle and merger activity has been carried out largely in the U.S. and the existence of any correlation, let alone the interpretation of such findings, has been questioned. See C. Maule, A Note on Mergers and the Business Cycle, *Journal of Industrial Economics*, Vol. XVI (1968), 99–105. Typical of the uncertain state of knowledge here is the comment: 'Consistently, the most positive correlation (against merger activity) has been found with measures of the general level of stock market prices. At the same time, the explanations which have been offered for this are less than convincing'.
49. M. A. Utton, Some Features of the Early Merger Movements in British Manufacturing Industry, *University of Reading Discussion Papers in Economics*, No. 27 (1970), p. 4
50. See L. Hannah, Mergers in British Manufacturing Industry, 1880–1918, *Oxford Economic Papers*, Vol. XXVI (1974), 1–20
51. A detailed paper covering this aspect of mergers and using U.S. data 1919–61 is R. L. Nelson's Business Cycle Factors in the choice between Internal and External Growth in W. W. Alberts and J. E. Segall (eds.) *The Corporate Merger*, University of Chicago, Chicago, 2nd ed. (1974), pp. 52–70
52. See S. R. Reid, Ref. 18, pp. 47–9
53. There is a considerable body of academic literature on this, and in purely rational terms shareholders ought to be indifferent between retentions and distributions. In fact many shareholders have a significant preference for regular dividend distributions. See R. J. Briston and C. R. Tomkins, Dividend Policy, Shareholder Satisfaction, and the Valuation of Shares, *Journal of Business Finance*, Vol. II (1970), 17–24
54. See A. Vice, Balance Sheet for Takeovers, in *Radical Reaction*, I.E.A., London (1961), pp. 168–70
55. See W. Davis, *Merger Mania*, Constable, London (1970)
56. See, How Jim Slater Bought Forestal, in A. Vice, Ref. 37 (1971), pp. 1–11. Vice also gives a similar example (p. 46) in relation to I.P.C.'s takeover of Amalgamated Press in 1959
57. R. W. Moon, *Business Mergers and Take-Over Bids*, Gee, London, 3rd ed. (1968), p. 119
58. H. B. Rose and G. D. Newbould, The 1967 Take-Over Boom, *Moorgate and Wall Street* (Summer 1967), 7–8
59. M. Gort, An Economic Disturbance Theory of Mergers, *Quarterly Journal of Economics*, Vol. LXXXIII (1969), 624
60. See E. T. Penrose, *The Theory of the Growth of the Firm*, Blackwell, Oxford (1959), pp. 155 and 160

61. W. W. Alberts, Conglomerate Growth by Acquisition Revisited, in W. W. Alberts and J. E. Segall (eds.), Ref. 51, pp. 52–70
62. M. L. Kastens, How Much is an Acquisition Worth?, *Long Range Planning* (1973), 54
63. See H. G. Manne, Mergers and the Market for Corporate Control, *Journal of Political Economy*, Vol. LXXIII (1965), 110–20
64. *Ibid.*, 113
65. See J. M. Samuels and F. M. Wilkes, *Management of Company Finance*, Nelson, London (1971), pp. 362–4. Evidence supporting the view that those companies which are currently 'undervalued' tend to be subject to takeover is given in J. M. Samuels and J. Tzoannos, Takeovers and Share Price Evaluation, *Business Ratios*, No. 2 (1969), 12–16
66. W. W. Alberts and J. E. Segall (eds.), Ref. 51, xvi
67. See J. Whittaker, What Level for Share Prices?, *Lloyds Bank Review* (1968), pp. 1–14
68. See H. B. Rose and G. D. Newbould, Ref. 58, 23
69. See, for example, D. A. Kuehn, Stock Market Valuation and Acquisitions: An Empirical Test of one Component of Managerial Utility, *Journal of Industrial Economics*, Vol. XVII (1969), 132–44. For more recent analysis see D. Kuehn, *Takeovers and the Theory of the Firm*, Macmillan, London (1975). Newbould, on the basis of statistical analysis covering U.K. mergers in the years 1967 and 1968, found V (in absolute or relative terms) 'irrelevant to the incidence of mergers'. See G. D. Newbould, Ref. 19, pp. 95–107. On the other hand Hindley, using U.S. data, found that firms which were most frequently raided had lower values for V than unraided firms. See B. Hindley, Separation of Ownership and Control in the Modern Corporation, *Journal of Law and Economics*, Vol. XIII (1970), 185–221
70. See A. Rubner, *The Ensnared Shareholder*, Penguin, London (1965), pp. 123–6
71. D. A. Kuehn and R. L. Marris, New Light on Take-Overs, *The Banker* (1973), 758
72. These sentences have offered a very brief synopsis of Dr. Singh's results. It is hoped that they do some justice to Dr. Singh's full account of his findings. See A. Singh, *ibid.*, Ref. 15, chs. III–VI
73. Sir Geoffrey Howe, Government Policy on Mergers, *Trade and Industry* (1st November 1973), 232
74. See a discussion of this in J. F. Pickering, *Industrial Structure and Market Conduct*, Martin Robertson, London (1974) pp. 137–44
75. B. Hindley, *Industrial Merger and Public Policy*, I.E.A., London (1970), p. 18

76. Quoted in, Mergers, Amalgamations and Company Size, *The Director* (August 1972), 179
77. See O. E. Williamson, *The Economics of Discretionary Behaviour: Managerial Objectives in a Theory of the Firm*, Kershaw, London (1974), pp. 21–25
78. See G. Meeks and G. Whittington, Giant Companies in the United Kingdom 1948–69, *Economic Journal*, Vol. LXXXV (1975), 824–43. Some further support for the relationship between company size and acquisition intensity is given in S. Aaronovitch and M. C. Sawyer, Mergers, Growth, and Concentration, *Oxford Economic Papers*, Vol. XXVII (1975), 139–41
79. See K. D. George and A. Silberston, The Causes and Effects of Mergers, *Scottish Journal of Political Economy*, Vol. XXII (1975), 183
80. A. Singh, Take-overs, Economic Natural Selection, and the Theory of the Firm, *Economic Journal*, Vol. LXXXV (1975), 503
81. S. Aaronovitch and M. C. Sawyer, *Big Business*, Macmillan, London (1975), p. 190

Chapter VIII

Business Pricing

Overview

This chapter opens with a discussion of the contrast between the assumptions made in basic economic analysis regarding pricing decisions and those business decisions in practice. The subject is then looked at under the headings of pricing objectives, policies and procedures; and in a subsequent section particular attention is paid to empirical findings on business pricing.

A. Pricing and Economic Analysis

The pricing decision is surely one of the most important which a business has to make at fairly frequent intervals. Yet, as a practising manager has noted, 'company pricing policy is an area where the academic world has long since retreated in despair of ascribing consistency of principles or rationality of practice'.[1] Basically this situation has arisen because in much of traditional economic analysis firms do not have to engage in positive pricing decisions at all. The business firm in a perfectly competitive market environment is given the market price. This price is, indeed must be, accepted by the firm, which is thus designated a price taker. Even businesses in somewhat less perfectly competitive markets can be said to accept their demand curve as largely given to them and move towards the profit-maximising equilibrium – where, as one economist put it cryptically, 'marginal everything is equal to marginal everything else'[2] – by adjusting levels of output. This is part of the understanding of market pricing which is the core of microeconomics. The analysis of pricing behaviour in this context is concerned with the role of pricing and the market mechanism in ensuring the 'optimal' allocation of scarce resources in the economy. A different approach must be adopted in looking at the actual behaviour of individual businesses in setting prices. As an American economist has pointed out, 'price theory has been developed primarily for use in the analysis of the effects of broad economic changes and the evaluation of social controls. It is too much to expect that the tools that are useful for social economics would also be useful in the same degree for the price maker'.[3]

Before proceeding, however, a further caveat should be entered on the treatment of pricing in this context. Even a fairly extended treatment of pricing may, to those with some experience of industry, appear superficial. Not all of the complexities of the actual operation of pricing policies in the business world are reflected in many economics texts on pricing. In the first instance 'price' itself is often a meaningless concept unless we distinguish clearly between manufacturer, wholesale or retail prices, and in particular between quoted prices or those used as a basis for Government price indices, and prices actually tendered or charged to buyers. This is an important point insofar as most business pricing decisions are made in the context of selling to other businesses (i.e. in industrial as opposed to consumer goods markets), one implication being that demand in these circumstances is likely to be fairly inelastic. Furthermore, the complexity of the pricing decision is added to for many firms by the fact that they are selling, and pricing, a large number of products. Not only does this produce 'accounting' problems of the allocation of joint overhead expenses among a number of product lines, but customers may buy more than one product from a firm and thus be interested in the price of a 'package' of goods rather than individual products. Finally, no detailed analysis of customers' perception of price and the relationship between price and perception of utility is undertaken in this text.

The more practical treatment of business pricing in this text arises from the increased discretion which firms now have in setting prices, and from the practical and almost intuitive nature of the pricing decision itself. It is often suggested that few business prices can now be described as market prices insofar as these are established by impersonal market forces. Rather we now by and large have a system of *administered* pricing, with prices being established as a result of conscious, positive decision making within firms. These businesses are price makers, not price takers. This initiative or flexibility in pricing has come about partly as the price of a product has become less important than is assumed in traditional analysis. In the language of marketing, price is only one of several factors in the 'marketing mix'. Branding, packaging and other forms of product promotion may be considered to be of equal of significance in wooing consumers. Furthermore,

> 'Price policy and administered pricing mean that there is some discretionary latitude in pricing, within which meaningful decisions are made by the enterprise individually or by groups of enterprises. In almost all business pricing, except for some segments of the primary industries, there is at least a narrow zone of choice among alternatives. Even when sellers are numerous, product differentiation and heterogeneity and the chain linking of products and of types of enterprises may create conditions favourable to and opportunities for the exercise of discretion in pricing by individual firms.'[4]

In other words it is also the structural imperfections of markets which allow modern businesses to break away from the passive role of price taking and to adopt active pricing policies. But is it only structural imperfections in product markets which make the neo-classical theory of price less relevant to our purpose?

> 'The circumstances in which many of these price and investment decisions are reached have altered radically over recent decades. With greater industrial concentration, an extension of the area of public ownership, a strengthening of collective power in labour bargaining and technological developments that on balance favour size, the

> determination of prices has increasingly become a matter of conscious calculation – and of a calculation that involves taking account of long-term factors, including a cost appraisal that must look at likely technical developments over a period of years ahead.'[5]

Thus in addition to making the heroic assumption of profit maximisation as the sole corporate goal, and conducting the analysis in terms of single-product firms, such an approach neglects the question of time. It is insufficiently dynamic. This leads it to neglect the phenomena of the product life cycle, of cross-subsidisation of one product by another, of loss-leader selling, fighting companies and the effect of price upon competitive entry. The business man asking questions such as these may receive little help from traditional economic analysis.

> 'What are the dynamic implications of my pricing decision? What effect will today's prices have on tomorrow's sales and therefore on costs and prices? What effect will today's prices have on the likelihood of new entry and therefore on my long-term share of the market? What effect will today's prices have on the growth of the market? If allowed to do so by law, should we build-in future anticipated cost changes in our current pricing decision?'[6]

Additionally, economic phenomena such as the multi-product firm and vertical integration have introduced into this area accounting problems of the allocation of joint overhead expenses and transfer pricing to which there are seldom clear-cut solutions.

A further reason for a practical approach to the pricing decision lies in the large number of unknowns in this area. We must drop the assumption of costless omniscience on the part of business decision takers which is so often part of basic economic analysis. One author has suggested three points to bear in mind: (a) the immense variety of conditions under which pricing decisions have to be made; (b) the lack of information upon which either to make pricing decisions or to analyse subsequently the correctness or otherwise of previous policies; and hence (c) 'the intuitive judgment which dominates most decisions'.[7] The purpose of the next short section is to break down the elements of pricing decisions into meaningful categories so that a logical step-by-step approach can be adopted.

B. Pricing Goals, Policies and Procedures

At the broadest level we must assume that a firm, or a division within a firm, has some overall goal in setting prices. The complexity of the pricing decision may be gathered from the following list.[8]

Possible Pricing Goals

Profit maximisation – long- or short-run
Maximisation of rate of return on capital employed
D.C.F. rate of return
Sales revenue maximisation
Market share maximisation
Price stability
'Satisficing' goals
Ethical pricing goals

These goals provide only a very general guide to management. They will, however, probably indicate the use of some rather than other of the pricing policies and procedures discussed below. It should be noted that if such factors as long-run performance, product market cycle, and reactions of competitors are taken into account the simplicity and the 'non-operational' characteristic of profit maximisation as a pricing goal become apparent. The aim of a maximum or target rate of return on capital employed is included because at the practical level this is how financial analysts most frequently measure average company performance, and because of the use of such a ratio as a management performance target found in the U.S. literature.[9] The use of discounted cash flow (D.C.F.) procedures is recommended for major projects in U.K. nationalised industries, and the discount rate may be used as a financial target.[10] Sales revenue maximisation and market share maximisation as corporate goals have been previously discussed in considering the theory of the firm. The adoption of either of these goals has implications for pricing policies and procedures. Price stability may often assume the role of a pricing goal – or at least a sub-goal. The normal objections to frequent changes of price on the part of a business are that they impose large administrative costs (especially where there are numerous product lines), that it may not be possible, or easy, to return to the original price should business conditions change again, or that customers dislike price changes (even downward ones?) as this will in time complicate their own price setting. Thus many firms may not follow the traditional rational entrepreneur in adjusting price and output levels following changes in cost or demand conditions. Finally, it may be suggested, particularly in the light of the poor information available to businesses in this area, that firms follow satisficing behaviour, and that wider, non-business aims may be taken into account in setting prices. One interesting finding from a more recent field study was that eight out of the thirteen firms covered were considered to be satisficers rather than maximisers in pricing objectives, and that some of the maximisers 'appeared a little half-hearted'. The author makes the point that 'even our whole-hearted maximisers could only *attempt* to maximise: none had enough information to be certain they *were* maximising, given changing external conditions'; and concluded that 'there is no doubt that there is a great deal of satisficing in making pricing decisions'.[11] Particularly in a satisficing context it is difficult to identify positively ethical goals. It is, nevertheless, important to recognise that such wider views of the firm's responsibilities are held within businesses. Thus it has been argued by one eminent business man that 'it is not the business of the professional manager to look after the owners to the exclusion of customers, creditors, workers and the public, but to reconcile these interests'.[12]

We shall now deal with the broad pricing policies and the somewhat more specific procedures or tactics, giving a separate section to each of the broad groups. Under the heading of pricing policies we shall confine ourselves to a discussion of marginal cost pricing and full cost pricing, while under the heading of procedures we shall deal with a variety of approaches used in pricing individual products or groups of products.

C. Pricing Policies: Marginal Cost and Full Cost Pricing

One of the major areas of discussion in business pricing is whether businesses should or in fact do follow either of these two broad approaches. Here we shall examine the general case, and defer to a subsequent section a discussion of the empirical findings.

Marginal cost pricing refers to the application of two basic rules. (a) The level of output at which a business should aim is that at which marginal cost (MC) is equal to marginal revenue (MR).[13] (b) In the short run any price which covers MC should be accepted. This is, of course, the standard economic tool for pricing, and in a perfect world price should be set equal to MC (suitably adjusted so as to arrive at the marginal social cost). There are, however, at least five reasons for which this policy may not be applied in business.

- (a) Business men do not understand the approach;
- (b) the necessary data to implement the policy are not available;
- (c) the approach is not applicable where there is a high level of fixed overhead costs;
- (d) there may be a dislike of the frequent price changes which the adoption of this approach implies;
- (e) there is no guarantee that the fixed costs will be covered.

Of the points above (a) would probably not be as acceptable now as when the original studies of business pricing behaviour by economists were carried out in the late 1930s. Point (c) is based upon a misunderstanding of the approach in that it appears to concentrate exclusively upon incremental or marginal costs and ignores the heavy cost of fixed plant, etc., to the firm. One can nonetheless sympathise with business men on this point. As one economist put it in the context of a survey of pricing behaviour, 'The accountant's traditional allocation of fixed costs has an undoubted 'systematic' appeal whereas marginal costing has no equally obvious plan for the recovery of fixed costs'.[14] Point (d) we have already discussed above. This leaves points (b) and (e) which represent the real reasons for businesses not adopting a marginal cost approach to pricing. Few firms can know the values of MC, or particularly MR, as the latter depends upon an awareness of the slope of the demand curve, i.e. of the price elasticity of demand. The business man is also correct in having reservations under point (e). What he is concerned with is the balance of total cost and revenue – or average cost and revenue as seen by the economist. It is, of course, feasible to have $MC = MR$ and $AC > AR$; and to reply to the business man that he is at the loss minimising point may be of little comfort.

It is in fact the strong desire to ensure that overhead costs are covered which encourages business men to adopt a full-cost approach to pricing. Direct costs and overhead costs are each explicitly accounted for by this approach. The direct costs (e.g. materials bought in, wages for operatives, etc.) for each unit of output are usually known from basic cost accounting data. The unit overhead cost is obtained by dividing the total of overhead expenses (rates, heat and light, management salaries, the apportionment of the cost of fixed assets such as plant and machinery) by the expected level of output. To this is sometimes added a customary percentage margin to allow for inaccurate data or the need to provide for new funds for capital spending out of profits. As an example, assume the following data apply:

Cost of a Pair of Men's Shoes

(a) Direct cost per pair:		(b) Annual overhead costs:	
leather	£1	light and power	£15 000
wages	£2	rates	5 000
		salaries	30 000
		depreciation	50 000
total direct	£3		£100 000

Estimated annual output 10 000 pairs
∴ total full cost per pair £3 + (£100 000/10 000) = £13.

Two points can be made about this approach. Firstly, the output or demand data is being used as a major determinant of price, whereas in economics we regard demand as being a function of, *inter alia*, price. Secondly, if overhead costs are high in relation to direct costs then a slight change in estimated output could have a large impact upon the full-cost price. Also consider the following:

$$P_{FC} = d + \frac{OH}{Q} \qquad \text{where } P_{FC} = \text{full cost price}$$

d = direct costs per unit

OH = total overhead costs

Q = unit sales (demand)

If d and OH are taken as given, then the equality above will hold for a range of combinations of P_{FC} and Q. We saw that P_{FC} = £13 and Q = 10 000 applied; so do P_{FC} = £10, Q = 14 286, and P_{FC} = £15, Q = 8 333. We do not know how to set P so as to maximise total profit unless we know the demand function. We know what the unit cost of 14 286 or 10 000 or 8 333 pairs of shoes is; but we do not know how many pairs of shoes we could sell at £10, £13 or £15. Only a demand curve could tell us. The problem, then, is that full cost pricing looks only at costs. Thus,

> 'The main line of criticism against full-cost pricing is that it disregards demand. It is a mechanical pricing method and, in terms of profitability, the price arrived at is not necessarily the best. Employed dogmatically, the firm can make maximum profit only by chance. Buyers are sometimes prepared to pay a higher price for the product than the one fixed on a full-cost basis. A firm may produce some more attractive product at a lower cost than its rivals because of its better management and more efficient production. Such a firm could earn a higher profit if it departed from full-cost pricing and this would be a reward for its superior efficiency. It is also sometimes a wise policy to adjust prices of various products in the light of market requirements and thus earn different rates of profit from them. By this method a higher total profit may be achieved.'[15]

Considerable discussion has inevitably taken place both at a general *a priori* and also empirical level as to the relative merits of marginal cost and full cost pricing. The space constraint prevents a full development of this theme here, although a few points may be made. On the side of full cost pricing we may say that the data are largely available, and that business men will be reassured to find that overhead costs and the effect of capacity variations on total unit cost have been fully taken into account. Indeed the need to have a realistic view as to the level of output is one of the main forecasting problems involved in full cost pricing. On the other hand some writers appear to suggest that there is almost something too reassuring about the accounting data used in the full-cost approach, and that firms ought to adopt a more dynamic approach to product pricing – taking into account competitive reactions and the product life cycle as well as the effects of learning on costs.[16] Additionally, considerable discussion has centred around whether the admitted flexibility and departures from the pure principles of full-cost pricing do not constitute a crude form of marginalism. For example the late Professor P. W. S. Andrews – normally assumed to be a leader among the full-cost school of thought – summarised as follows:

> 'The application of his costing rules and the resulting costing-margin will yield the business man what we shall call his costing price, and he will quote that price as a rule, never quoting above it in normal circumstances, and going below it only when the competition of others convinces him that he has made a mistake in the rightness of his costing rules. The costing-margin, and with it the business man's price, will thus be arrived at by competition or, in the case of a business man producing what he believes to be a unique product, by his idea of the margin at which he would, in the long run, have to face competition.'[17]

As one later writer commented, envisaging the reaction of such a procedure to an exogenous cost increase,

> 'We may suspect that in such circumstances a business man will sometimes be led to revise his costing margin; whether

he does so or whether he continues to add the old margin will depend on his close knowledge of the market – which may be translated into the elasticity of demand for his product, and the whole marginal apparatus may apply.'[18]

We shall see in examining the empirical pricing studies that although very few businesses claim to be marginal cost pricers, most firms which adopt a full-cost approach frequently modify the price arrived at by the formula to reflect demand conditions.

D. Pricing Procedures

We have now come to the stage where we can discuss some of the range of pricing tactics relating to individual products or particular conditions of demand.

Pricing Procedures

Penetration pricing – market skimming
Price discrimination
Transfer pricing

(*a*) *Penetration pricing and market skimming*[19]

These are two contrasting techniques adopted in the pricing of new products. In particular they give attention to the life cycle of the products concerned. Penetration pricing involves the setting of a price as low as long-term cost conditions will allow. This is an appropriate tactic: (i) where the price elasticity of demand for the product against existing competitors is high, such that setting a comparatively low price will have a significant effect in increasing demand; (ii) closely tied up with (i) is the question of production economies of scale: if these are potentially great then penetration pricing will 'pay for itself' – high demand and economies of scale justifying a low product price; (iii) the low price associated with penetration pricing may be designed to prevent or discourage further competitive entry into the field if this is felt to be a threat; (iv) to some extent penetration pricing may be unavoidable if there is no possibility of creating a distinct niche for a product at the premium end of the market. The pricing behaviour of the Japanese in motor cycle export markets provides a good example of this technique in practice. In the U.S. in the 1960s the Japanese firms of Honda, Yamaha and Suzuki were well prepared to sell at losses to build up their market penetration. The productivity gains from economies of scale are large in this field, and the Japanese largely avoided the expensive 'superbike' market catered for by Triumph in the U.K. and B.M.W. in Germany.[20] The technique of market skimming is used in the opposite conditions: where consumers are relatively insensitive to price, where potential economies of scale are limited, where there is little fear of competitive entry, or where a unique product situation has been created.

(*b*) *Price discrimination*

We can describe this phenomena generally by saying that it occurs whenever a different price is paid by different consumers for what is essentially an identical product. More formally, 'the essence of (price) discrimination is that prices charged for different units of a firm's output are not in proportion to the costs attributable to the production and supply of these units'.[21] Why should this occur, and under what conditions is a producer able to practise price discrimination? Consider the following simple demand schedule:

Price	Quantity
10p	200
9	220
8	250
7	270
6	300

If the producer wishes to set his output at 300 (because, for example, at this level of output MC = MR) then his total revenue will be £18, providing the same price (6p) is charged for each unit. We know, however, that 200 of the 300 units could have been sold at 10p each, a further 20 at 9p and so on. Had this ideal form of price discrimination been in operation the total revenue from 300 units could have been £37.40 rather than £18. In terms of microeconomic theory this situation arises because the producer may be able to eliminate some of the element of consumer surplus, which is the value above the price charged which some consumers would be willing to pay.

Under what conditions may this practice occur? Normally three conditions are necessary: it must be possible to identify clearly and distinguish different classes of consumer; these different classes should each have a different scale of preference for the product; there must be no opportunity for consumers to 'trade' between the two markets, i.e. to buy in the cheaper and resell in the more expensive. The practice of publishers of academic journals and periodicals of setting different subscription rates for institutions and for private individuals is a good example. A library will often have to pay a subscription rate two or three times that of a personal subscriber to a periodical. The basis of this is a clear separation of two markets with different willingness or ability to pay. It is also not normally possible to buy at the personal subscription rate and resell to an institution at the higher rate. There are many examples in other fields, frequently reinforced by the practice of market segmentation or the creation of distinct markets where the differences in the goods being sold are more apparent than real. This could be said to apply to different prices for different seats in the cinema or theatre, or to first and second class rail travel.

Sometimes price discrimination may be part of a long-term marketing policy, as when students obtain free banking facilities in order to encourage them to become life-time customers. A further documented instance of this same general policy lies in the different prices at which motor component suppliers sell to the large car assembly firms (initial equipment) and to garages for sale to the public (replacement sales). So far as electrical components are concerned (e.g. batteries, ignition coils, plugs, lamps and dynamos, etc.) the situation was such at the time of the

Monopolies Commission's Report (1963) that some component suppliers were making considerable losses on initial equipment sales which were only compensated for by large profits in the replacement sales market. This situation appears to have been accepted by the suppliers because of the replacement-market sales which were created by the initial-equipment use of a particular brand of electrical component, by the regularity of orders from the large motor car assemblers, and also because of the bargaining power of initial equipment buyers brought about by the size of their orders and, of course, the power to withdraw these.[22] A more recent example in the same field was that of the manufacturers of clutch mechanisms who were making very much larger profit margins in the replacement sales market than on initial equipment.[23]

Price discrimination raises a number of issues for economists. On the one hand it could be argued that 'discrimination' which reflects a genuine cost difference in dealing with different customers leads to greater allocative efficiency. This would apply to delivered (as opposed to ex-works) prices to consumers in different parts of the country, and to some quantity discount schemes. [24] The lower charges made by banks to students in the expectation of future custom could also be defended as long-run profit maximisation. Those practices which do raise policy questions are massive quantity discounts which have the effect of tying customers to an existing supplier (or, in the case of aggregated rebates, to an existing group of suppliers); discounts which discriminate between different categories of customers (e.g. wholesaler and retailer) and which may have only a tenuous relationship with the performance of different functions;[25] the taking of much larger profit margins on some products than on others by multi-product firms; and the use of 'fighting companies'. This last practice involves a firm in deliberately underpricing a rival business for a short period in order to eliminate this (usually smaller) rival. The Monopolies Commission criticised the use by B.O.C. of undisclosed subsidiaries as fighting companies. These subsidiaries were established to sell in some parts of the country, where competition was more fierce, at less than B.O.C.'s national prices, and this was in fact a contributing factor to the demise of one of B.O.C.'s competitors.[26]

(*c*) *Transfer pricing*

This is a technique by which products which are being passed from one division to another within the same firm can be priced. This must obviously occur when the two, or more, divisions concerned are successive stages in a vertically integrated business. In this case the output of one division (semi-finished goods) becomes the material input for a successive division (final product). A system of transfer pricing enables the financial performance of each of the divisions to be judged on a profit-and-loss basis, as the transfer price between the two divisions fulfils the function of a selling price for the former and a material input price for the latter. Each division may, therefore, compile a separate Profit and Loss Account. The technique is held to be of advantage in ensuring adequate control over vertically-integrated sections of a business, or indeed as a substitute for a market-determined price in any situation in which one division of a business is providing goods or services for another.

Transfer pricing in this context is essentially a tool of managerial economics. Its twin function is to contribute to the assessment of managers of autonomous divisions within a larger business unit, and also to contribute to the maximisation of profits of the total business.[27] How are such prices determined? So far as economic theory is concerned (and where a competitive market exists for the transferred product) the solution is that each of the two divisions concerned would consume that output where marginal cost = marginal revenue. This approach would result in the maximisation of total group profits.[28]

Thus figure 7 gives MC_T and D_T as the relevant cost and revenue conditions facing the transferring division, with an optimal output of the semi-finished product from T to F of Q_T ($MC_T = MR_T$). So far as optimal consumption and output

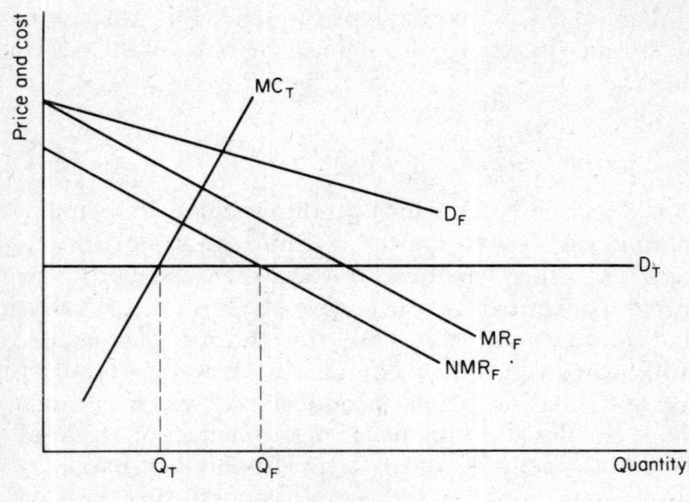

FIGURE 7

for division F is concerned, this is also obtained by comparing the relevant marginal values. MC_F and MR_F are compared indirectly by measuring D_T and MR_F *minus* all other marginal costs for F except those bought from T.[29] Thus F's consumption of Q_F is given by $D_T = NMR_F$. Any difference between the output of the former unit, Q_T, and consumption of the latter, Q_F, would be made up for either by F buying in some of its requirements from outside suppliers at the market price, or conversely, T selling its 'surplus' output in that market (i.e. any Q_T surplus to F's requirements). In those cases where there is either no external market for the semi-finished good, or where the market for that product is imperfect, then the *group* profit-maximising price for T's output is the marginal cost. It is this implication of the theoretical model which has undoubtedly led to its neglect in practice; for as has been pointed out in the context of a practical application of the techniques, 'the manufacturing division will operate at a lower profit level (perhaps even a loss) than it would if dealing with an independent customer and the distribution division will operate at a higher profit level than if it was buying from an independent supplier."[30]

The issue of transfer pricing normally arises in the context of the assessment of managerial efficiency within a large firm. However, the matter is of some concern in the analysis of the activities of multinational companies. In this context the transfer pricing technique raises questions of the measurement of the efficiency of national subsidiaries of multinational companies, the possible disguising of excess profits by these companies, and the level of tax revenue of the Governments of the different countries concerned. One of the most significant industries in which this situation arises is petroleum production and refining. Thus,

> 'The companies' published estimates of earnings from operations abroad are not reproducible and not explained. We have no indication of where, e.g., a tanker company is incorporated and its profit or losses credited. More important, within the integrated company there is no market checkpoint or interface to set the value of transfers. Because we do not know the foreign profits of the multinational oil companies, we do not know their contribution to the balance of payments or the national product, even though we cannot doubt it is large.'[31]

Other industries, however, have not been exempted from suspicion. In addition to more recent criticism of the level of their reported profits, an earlier report expressed some dissatisfaction at the transfer pricing policies of the multinational pharmaceutical companies and the possible revenue loss to U.K. tax authorities arising from these.

> 'Foreign firms reported a much higher cost of materials as a percentage of the total cost of manufacture than did British firms and we believe that the propriety of such costs should be investigated. We are aware that the United Kingdom tax authorities have a right to investigate these transfer prices in order to ensure that foreign-owned manufacturing or distributing companies in this country (no matter in what industry) are not reducing the apparent amount of their profits in the United Kingdom by inflating the transfer prices that they pay to their foreign parents.

The tax authorities of other countries have and operate similar powers. We recommend that the attention of the British tax authorities should be drawn to the transfer prices of pharmaceutical raw materials or intermediates, and that the Ministry, in assessing the Standard Cost Returns of foreign-owned manufacturing companies, should make use of the ability of chemical engineers to form reasonable assessments of the production costs of chemical materials.'[32]

It is in just this context of minimising the multinational corporation total tax burden that transfer pricing of resources between subsidiaries, or between parent and subsidiary, has been most discussed. Consider the following simple arithmetic example:

Subsidiary

	Case (1)	Case (2)
Domestic inputs	£100	£100
Sales (to parent)	120	200
Pre-tax profit	20	100
Corporate tax (50%)	10	50
Post-tax profit	10	50

Parent

	Case (1)	Case (2)
Purchases from subsid.	£120	£200
Domestic inputs	50	50
Sales	300	300
Pre-tax profit	130	50
Corporate tax (20%)	26	10
Post-tax profit	104	40
Total net profits	114	90
Total tax	36	60
Total tax rate	24%	40%

In this case since the parent is located in a lower corporate tax area than the subsidiary there is an incentive for the subsidiary to *underprice* its sales, and so understate its profits to minimise its corporate tax burden. Transfer pricing may also be used as a means of circumventing restrictions on the transfer of capital or earnings between countries – as when a parent company charges a subsidiary more than a fair price for resources provided as an alternative to the formal repatriation of dividends.[33] If it is borne in mind that a significant part of international trade is accounted for by product transfers between constituent parts of multinational companies then the issue of transfer pricing is one which is of vital consideration in determining international trade and money flows.[34]

So far as empirical studies of the practice of transfer pricing in the U.K. are concerned there has until quite recently been little evidence. Dependence has had to be placed upon reference to service divisions in large companies 'selling' their services to product divisions in competition with outside competitors.[35] Two published empirical studies have, however, been carried out. These indicate that for individual companies transfer pricing is not a major issue: in the earlier (1967) study 232 firms out of 400 responded, and only 100 of these used a transfer pricing system; in the 1971 B.I.M. survey 193 out of 293 respondents used a system of transfer pricing, but for the largest part of these the system applied to less than 10% of total sales.[36] A diversity of practices is thrown up by these studies. They indicate a significant departure from the rules established via the formal economic models; and some of the guidelines laid down by companies themselves appear to be mutually inconsistent. For example, 61% of the respondents to the 1967 survey used some form of 'full cost' as a basis for arriving at the transfer price in spite of the emphasis on variable or marginal costs in the economic literature. Furthermore, some senior managements expect divisional managers to behave in a 'commercial' manner, while transfer prices are determined by headquarters staff.[37] The real problem seems to be one of deciding why transfer pricing is being used, and of choosing a system conducive to the achievement of the objectives. The purpose of the Hirshleifer model is to maximise total *group* profits. But this can only be achieved by motivating the transferring division management appropriately. The latter may not appreciate the virtues of a system which involves them in selling at marginal cost if fixed costs are a high proportion of total. Profit and cost accountability in the transferring division are, therefore, essential.

E. Empirical Pricing Studies

The purpose of this section is to examine the findings of empirical research into business pricing decisions, although no attempt has been made to offer a comprehensive review of the literature in this area. The intention is to highlight the principal findings – emphasising the motivation of business people in making pricing decisions, and the pricing techniques adopted.

Although the question of company objectives has been quite fully discussed in the context of the theory of the firm, it is worthwhile reminding ourselves of the variety of those which have been encountered specifically in pricing studies. This will tell us what it is that business men are attempting to achieve in making pricing decisions, and this may influence their approach. It may be, for example, that it is the failure of many business managers to follow a strict path of profit maximisation that accounts for their equal failure to appreciate the value of the economist's technique of marginal cost pricing. On the question of business aims Shackle's study of a small number of Merseyside business men revealed the following attitudes. Shackle gave his respondents a series of possible targets which business men might be 'chiefly anxious to increase', and asked them to award marks on a scale 1–10 for the accuracy of the statements.

Possible Business Objectives

	Marks		
	Possible	Actual	%
Net profit before tax	130	30	23
Net profit after tax	130	68	52
Net profit up to one year	130	73	56
Net profit over the next five years	130	76	58
Net profit over the next ten years	130	41	32
Net profit over the next thirty years	130	21	16
Net profit over a period, with greater weight placed on the immediate future	130	117	90
General prosperity of the business	130	50	38
Firm's estimate of its own net worth	130	50	38
Firm's balance-sheet strength	130	74	57
Firm's general prestige	130	117	90
Business man's reputation and prestige	130	58	45

Source: G. L. S. Shackle, Business Men on Business Decisions, *Scottish Journal of Political Economy*, 1955, Vol. II, 45.

These answers, and the very similar data given by Barback as a result of using an adapted version of Shackle's questionnaire,[38] imply, in Shackle's own words, 'that firms are more far-sighted and prudent, and also less materially minded, than the economist's ordinary assumptions suggest'.[39] It is perhaps worth pointing out also that in the case of Barback's research all of the firms covered were 'entrepreneurial' in terms of size and owner-management patterns: they were by and large small family businesses. In Shackle's sample too small firms were predominant. Even if due allowance is made for the fact that, as Hague emphasises in his more recent study, profit maximisation is made very difficult, if not impossible, by the firm's lack of knowledge of its own cost/output relationships or of competitor's reactions,[40] it is difficult not to conclude from a detailed reading of, say, Barback's study that the matter goes further than this. Business people seem, in the words of one of Barback's respondents, to be 'happy, if, at the end of the year, profits were "reasonable" '.[41] Clearly there is room for considerable research into the pricing policies of firms; and in particular into the relationship between pricing behaviour and firm size, ownership pattern, organisation structure, and the degree of competition in the product market.[42]

The failure of profit maximisation adequately to cover business pricing objectives probably accounts for a further feature of business pricing behaviour which economists find difficult fully to accept: the apparent disregard by many business men of concepts such as price elasticity of demand, or of marginal analysis in general.[43] For example, Hague in his study found that 'within unstated, but fairly broad limits, firms felt that total demand was unresponsive to changes in price';[44] and there seemed to be little belief on the part of some of Barback's respondents that a price reduction on the part of one supplier would increase his sales.[45] This latter view appears to have been based not so much upon any fear as to the consequence of reducing price on the lower (inelastic) section of an oligopolistic kinked demand curve so much as upon the feeling that the existence of goodwill, habit or inertia might significantly mute the reaction of buyers to price reductions. As a further specific example, a book publisher has suggested that 'the market (for books) does not in fact have the (price) elasticity which most authors and economists assume. . . . What can be said with certainty is that if the public want a book they will buy it at a price that seems to them fair, but if they do not, they will not be tempted by comparative cheapness'.[46]

From this disbelief or uncertainty surrounding the concept of price elasticity of demand probably stems a similar lack of faith in formal marginal analysis on the part of business men. This in turn is almost certainly the reason for the popularity of full-cost or cost-plus pricing.[47] Barback, for example, found that having suggested to one business man that output might be set at the level where marginal cost was equal to marginal revenue, 'his reaction to the statement was one of outspoken rejection of it as a description of what he did, mingled with a kind of amused disbelief that anyone would wish to think in this way'.[48] Shackle's data on this, derived from the inquiry on which we have already drawn, are interesting.

Pricing Decisions

	Marks		
	Possible	Actual	%
'Marginal pricing'	130	51	39
Business man ignores competitors	130	23	18
Acknowledged existence of kinked demand curve	130	53	23
'Full-cost pricing'	130	75	58
'Modified full cost'	130	66	51

Source: G. L. S. Shackle, *op. cit.*, p. 45.

In fact the results here give no strong support to any of the suggested approaches to pricing. Neither marginal pricing nor full-cost pricing (even in a modified form, which involves taking account of the reaction of competitors) received overwhelming support; and this impression is reinforced by Barback's findings based upon a similar series of questions.[49]

In fact it is fairly clear from more detailed case studies that although a large proportion of firms *start* their price calculations from a full-cost base, this basic price is often subject to considerable modifications under a variety of circumstances. Past studies have indicated that even those decision takers in this area who at first describe themselves as adopting a full-cost approach (perhaps because their basic discipline is accountancy) nonetheless admit, for example, that 'that combination of quantity (output) and price which gives the best yield is obviously the combination which we shall adopt';[50] that in respect of the profit mark-up added to the basic full cost 'margins are very sensitive to conditions of the market both over time and between customers';[51] and that considerations such as the need to secure a government contract or to reflect economies of long production runs produce considerable deviation from full-cost prices.[52] Thus, although Skinner in his 1968 survey of Merseyside business men found that 70% of his respondents claimed to use a cost-plus method of pricing, 68% of those (i.e. 68% of the cost-plus pricers) varied the percentage mark-up used on individual products *between* price reviews – which in 96% of all cost-plus cases were annual or more frequent. Of those which varied the percentage mark-up, 81% were influenced by the force of competition, 53% by the strength of demand, and 26% were influenced by other factors such as supply conditions – for example excess capacity in the market.[53]

Among the respondents to some of the smaller-scale questionnaire surveys conducted in the early 1960s there was again little enthusiasm for the use of marginal techniques in business decision taking. Of firms surveyed in the Nottingham area only 12% used marginal costing; and of this number one third did so only occasionally.[54] The results of similar surveys at this time confirm these results;[55] and even among the respondents to the more extensive Hart and Prusmann study only 24% made use of the concept of marginal cost.[56] These findings are also confirmed in the most recent (1974) questionnaire survey, *How British Industry Prices*.[57]

It is probably these modifications to the full-cost approach which account for a false dichotomy between this and the marginalist viewpoint. For example in his account of pricing behaviour P. W. S. Andrews at one point stated that his approach involved quite clearly accepting that 'in particular, prices are thought of as dependent upon costs, and output is not considered to be the result of any balancing of marginal revenue against marginal cost'. On the other hand the reader has been told by Andrews earlier in the same book that 'the gross margin on the basis of which the business man determines his price is very much determined by competition and the threat of potential competition'.[58] What have to be allowed for are the practicalities of the price-setting situation. The business manager determining prices is, at least in the first instance, driven into the hands of the cost accountant for his basic information.[59] But as Hague stresses, 'the fact that pricing *begins* from cost figures certainly does not mean that it will be necessarily cost-plus pricing'.[60] What is significant from the point of view of the economist is the process of adjustment which is undergone in moving from the 'full-cost' figure to the price charged. From the evidence surveyed in this chapter it would appear that although cost conditions exercise a strong influence on pricing decisions, business men do take account of demand factors and competition. Although business decision takers do not have access to the information summarised in the economist's marginal cost and revenue curves, they appear to have the confidence to make adjustments to full-cost prices to reflect these conditions.

F. Conclusions

This examination of pricing practice in business has been partial not only because of space constraint but also because, as has hopefully been made clear in the body of the chapter, business economics is not the only discipline from which those involved in making pricing decisions can learn. Other areas of study must consider the issue of the motivation of business men in setting prices; and a detailed analysis of the information available and its use in pricing decisions must remain primarily the province of the disciplines of marketing and accountancy.

The role of economics and pricing decisions lies in examining the efficiency of a system of pricing so far as the individual business is concerned, and also the implications of such decisions for national resource allocation. It is because of this that the economist is concerned with the relationship between costs and prices, and with the competitive implications of transfer pricing, price discrimination and predatory pricing amongst others.

Pricing behaviour may, therefore, appear to constitute an unsatisfactory area of study for economists. Not only is there a range of other disciplines involved in making the same broad decisions; but for some of these disciplines the actual price of a product may not be the most important variable influencing sales. Then again there are frustrations arising from the apparent disregard by many business people of marginal analysis. This creates a special problem for the economist working at the empirical level. On the one hand economists have been warned that 'we should beware of advocating (pricing) principles based on full-cost simply because it has been found that this is what many businessmen appear to do'.[61] Nonetheless we should be aware of business thinking because this conditions the pricing 'model' which we establish, and the predictive powers of the model given a change in any of the major parameters. A telling example is that of fixed cost changes which are ignored by marginal analysis in the short run. Correspondingly too in respect of demand shifts: 'The suggestion that prices should *rise* in a recession would seem surprising to an economist weaned on simple competitive equilibrium analysis, yet this is the situation that increasingly seems to apply in the real world'.[62] Clearly business pricing decisions are an area with which economists should become more rather than less involved in the future.

References

1. A. M. Alfred, Company Pricing Policy, *Journal of Industrial Economics*, Vol. XXI (1972), 1
2. M. Shubik, A Curmudgeon's Guide to Microeconomics, *Journal of Economic Literature*, Vol. VIII (1970), 406

3. D. V. Harper, *Price Policy and Procedure*, Harcourt, Brace and World, New York (1966), pp. 12–13
4. R. S. Vaile, E. T. Grether and R. Case, *Marketing in the American Economy*, Ronald Press, New York (1952), p. 403
5. R. Shone, *Price and Investment Relationships*, Elek, London (1975), pp. xiv-xv
6. J. F. Pickering, *Industrial Structure and Market Conduct*, Martin Robertson, London (1974), p. 227
7. A. M. Alfred, Ref. 1. As examples of the different economic conditions in which pricing decisions are made the author instances consumer and industrial goods, home and export markets, different degrees of competition, new and existing products, different products showing common costs, and the effect upon costs and price of production capacity variations. *Ibid.*, p. 6
8. See L. Sonkodi, *Business and Prices*, Routledge and Paul, London (1969), Ch. II
9. See A. D. H. Kaplan, J. B. Dirlam and R. F. Lanzillotti, *Pricing in Big Business*, Brookings Institution, Washington (1958), Ch. III
10. See *Nationalised Industries: A Review of Economic and Financial Objectives*, H.M.S.O. (1967), Cmnd. 3437
11. D. C. Hague, *Pricing in Business*, Allen and Unwin, London (1971), pp. 244–5
12. Sir. F. Catherwood, *B.I.M. Bulletin*, Vol. VI (1973), 3
13. For a quick glance at the refinements to this see R. G. Lipsey, *Introduction to Positive Economics*, Weidenfeld and Nicolson London, 4th ed. (1975), pp. 244–6
14. M. Howe, Marginal Analysis in Accounting, *Manchester School*, Vol. XIV (1962), 88
15. L. Sonkodi, Ref. 8, p. 28
16. See D. C. Hague, Ref. 11, Ch. VII
17. P. W. S. Andrews, *Manufacturing Business*, Macmillan, London (1949), pp. 158–9
18. R. H. Barback, *The Pricing of Manufactures*, Macmillan, London (1964), p. viii
19. See generally J. Dean, Pricing a New Product, in B. Taylor and G. Wills (eds.), *Pricing Strategy*, Staples, London (1969), Ch. 47
20. Motorcycle output per man-year (1974) was 10 at N.V.T's Small Heath, Birmingham, plant with a capacity of 10,500 units. At Yamaha the corresponding figures were 200 and 1m. See J. Dodsworth, How British motorbikes went backing down the wrong road, *Financial Times* (2nd August, 1975)
21. J. F. Wright, Some Reflections on the Place of Discrimination in the Theory of Monopolistic Competition, *Oxford Economic Papers*, Vol. XVII (1965), 176

22. See Monopolies Commission, *Electrical Equipment for Mechanically Propelled Land Vehicles*, H.M.S.O. (1963), H.C.P. 21, for example paras. 710 and 899
23. See Monopolies Commission, *Clutch Mechanisms for Road Vehicles*, H.M.S.O. (1968), H.C.P. 32, paras. 170–191. It is interesting to note that this practice prevailed, presumably as a result of the buying power of the motor assembly firms, despite Automotive Products' 63% share of the market for the reference goods. *Ibid.*, Appendix 1.
24. The Monopolies Commission has more recently criticised the monopoly London Brick Co. for *not* discriminating sufficiently in its delivered-price schedules between adjacent and more distant customers. This resulted in undercharging the latter at the expense of the former, which the Commission considered as leading to resource misallocation. See Monopolies Commission, *Building Bricks*, H.M.S.O. (1976), H.C.P. 474, paras. 183–94 and 264–71
25. This functional basis of awarding discounts appears to be more common than different types of quantity discount. See B. Atkin and R. Skinner, *How British Industry Prices*, Industral Market Research, London (1975), pp. 31–2
26. Monopolies Commission, *Certain Industrial and Medical Gases*, H.M.S.O. (1956), H.C.P. 13, paras. 52, 207 and 251
27. See, for example, W. D. Reekie, *Managerial Economics*, Philip Allan, Deddington (1975), p. 191
28. The best known formal analysis of this is contained in J. Hirschleifer, On the Economics of Transfer Pricing, *Journal of Business*, Vol. XXXIV (1956), 112–84
29. Instead of comparing MC_F and MR_F directly the marginal costs other than those incurred from T are subtracted from both sides of the equation, giving Q_F as $D_T = NMR_F$ where $NMR_F = MR_F$ minus all marginal costs other than those incurred from T.
30. K. J. Blois, A Pricing Model Relating to Sales to a Concentrated Industrial Market, *Loughborough University Management Studies Department*, Working Paper No. 1 (1975), p. 4.
31. M. A. Adelman, The Multinational Corporation in World Petroleum, in C. P. Kindleberger (ed.). *The International Corporation*, M.I.T. Press, Cambridge, Massachusetts (1970), p. 229
32. *Report of the Committee of Enquiry into the Relationship of the Pharmaceutical Industry with the National Health Service*, H.M.S.O. (1967) Cmnd. 3410, para. 301
33. See M. Z. Brooke and H. L. Remmers, *The Strategy of Multinational Enterprise*, Longman, London (1970), pp. 172–76

34. For example it has been pointed out that by the early 1970s nearly 60% of U.S. manufacturing shipments were from U.S. parent companies to overseas subsidiaries, and that almost 25% of U.K. exports were carried out under transfer pricing arrangements. See C. Levinson, *Capital, Inflation and the Multinationals*, Allen and Unwin, London (1971), p. 100
35. See A. D. Bonham-Carter, Centralisation and Decentralisation in Unilever, in R. S. Edwards and H. Townsend (eds.), *Business Enterprise*, Macmillan, London (1958), p. 337
36. I am indebted for information on this to A. Young, *Interdivisional Transfer Pricing in Theory and Practice* (Unpublished Ph.D. Thesis, University of Surrey, 1974). The full references to the studies are: Transfer pricing – A Measure of Management Performance in Multidivisional Companies (B.I.M., 1971); F. Livesey, The Pricing of Internal Transfers, *Accountant*, Vol. CLVII (22nd July 1967), 99–104
37. A. Young, Ref. 36, pp. 159–60
38. See R. H. Barback, Ref. 18, pp. 60–62
39. G. L. S. Shackle, Business Men on Business Decisions, *Scottish Journal of Political Economy*, Vol. II (1955), 4
40. See, for example, D. C. Hague, Ref. 11, pp. 83–4, where the author suggests that as a result of information difficulties in a dynamic situation business men are forced in some degree to become satisficers.
41. R. H. Barback, Ref. 18, p. 73
42. See, for example, the more recent (1968) survey reported in R. C. Skinner, The Determination of Selling Prices, *Journal of Industrial Economics*, Vol. XVIII (1970), 201–17
43. Attention has been drawn to this issue since the early classic empirical study by Hall and Hitch. These authors felt in respect of their questionnaire analysis that 'the most striking feature . . . was the number of firms which apparently do not aim, in their pricing policy, at what appeared to us to be the maximization of profits by the equation of marginal revenue and marginal cost', and concluded by casting great doubt on the general applicability of any theory which placed emphasis upon the influence of short-run changes in demand elasticities on pricing decisions. See R. L. Hall and C. J. Hitch, Price Theory and Business Behaviour, *Oxford Economic Papers*, Vol. II (1939), 18 and 32
44. D. C. Hague, Ref. 11, p. 123
45. See R. H. Barback, Ref. 18, pp. 74–5
46. R. Blackwell, The Pricing of Books, *Journal of Industrial Economics*, Vol. II (1954), 178. Opinion here is not, however, unanimous. The appropriateness of full cost analysis – particularly

in a business environment of high levels of fixed production, etc., costs and of inflation – has been questioned by one practising business man who advocated the adoption of some form of marginal pricing. See D. G. Johnson, The Pricing of Consumer Goods, *Yorkshire Bulletin*, Vol. XIV (1962), esp. 75–6. Mr. Johnson was at the time chairman and managing director of Geo. Bassett. Co. Ltd. the confectionery manufacturers.

47. This cannot, of course, be accepted as a strong conclusion. Business men feel that, within the limits of the information at their disposal, full-cost pricing leads to profit maximisation. Thus although Silberston in his excellent review article suggests that 'Hall and Hitch . . . appeared to many to have mounted a root-and-branch attack on the notion of profit maximisation itself', he does stress later that 'what is by no means clear in the literature, however, is whether the full-cost principle is thought to be adhered to – on account of the fair-profits principle – when it is known to reduce profits below the level that could be attained, or whether it is adhered to because it *is* in fact thought to be the most profitable long-run policy'. A. Silberston, Surveys of Applied Economics: Price Behaviour of Firms, *Economic Journal*, Vol. LXXX (1970), 516 and 530
48. R. H. Barback, Ref. 18, p. 51
49. See *Ibid.*, pp. 60–62
50. R. S. Edwards, The Pricing of Manufactured Products, *Economica*, Vol. XIX (1952), 302
51. I. F. Pearce, A Study in Price Policy, *Economica*, Vol. XXIII (1956), 119
52. See N. Balkin, Prices in the Clothing Industry, *Journal of Industrial Economics*, Vol. V (1956), 1–15
53. See R. C. Skinner, Ref. 42, 205
54. J. B. Goodlad, Management Accounting and Industrial Management, *Management Accounting*, Vol. XLIII (1965), 22
55. See J. Sizer, The Accountant's Contribution to the Pricing Decision, *Journal of Management Studies*, Vol. III (1966), 135–7
56. See H. Hart and D. F. Prusmann, *Report of a Survey of Management Accounting Techniques in the S. E. Hants. Coastal Region* (University of Southampton, 1963). This evidence may be compared with the situation found to prevail among forward-thinking American businesses almost a decade before when there was held to be substantial evidence of strong marginalist tendencies in pricing decision-making. See J. S. Earley, Marginal Policies of 'Excellently Managed' Companies, *American Economic Review*, Vol. XLVI (1956), 44–70, esp. 56–8
57. B. Atkin and R. Skinner, Ref. 25, esp. pp. 42 and 48

58. P. W. S. Andrews, Ref. 17, pp. 82 and 23
59. Interestingly enough, nonetheless, one explanation for the pervasive use of some form of full-cost pricing which cannot be sustained is an undue weight given to the views of accountants. A recent study indicated that in only about 5% of cases did accountants play a primary role in pricing decisions. See B. Atkin and R. Skinner, Ref. 25, pp. 37–8
60. D. C. Hague, Ref. 11, p. 156
61. R. L. Smyth, A Price–Minus Theory of Costs?, *Scottish Journal of Political Economy*, Vol. XIV (1967), 111
62. J. F. Pickering, The Prices and Incomes Board and Private Sector Prices, *Economic Journal*, Vol. LXXXI (1971), 229

Chapter IX

Government and Industrial Economics

Overview

In this final chapter attention is given to the role of the Government as it affects industrial economics issues. In particular we shall examine the approach taken by successive U.K. Governments to industrial structure.

A. Rationale

The British economy is characterised by a mixture of public and private decision taking in its direction. In this it is like most other industrial economies; for in the words of Sir Alec Cairncross, 'every economic system is . . . a mixture of organisation and free enterprise. All that is open to debate is the strength of the mixture; the optimum degree of organisation and centralised control'.[1] It is not proposed to discuss here the issue of the optimal strength of this mixture of private industry decision taking and Government power, but to ask on what basis decisions on the need for State intervention in this field may be judged.

If we accept that the purpose of all State intervention in an economy is to lead to the maximum welfare of the community, then we can envisage Government intervention in the area of industrial economics either on the grounds that management is not making the right decisions in its attempt to maximise shareholder welfare, or on the basis that there is a divergence between the welfare of corporate ordinary shareholders and of the community as a whole. Now much of the thinking on these questions will depend upon the State's view of the efficiency of business management in general in the economy, the desirability of various market structures, the extent to which a Government feels that it should superimpose its decisions on the operation of the market economy, or the degree to which private business itself should be required to be aware of the wider social consequences of its actions.

So far as State intervention in restructuring industry is concerned, business men may feel that this is one of the worst manifestations of the 'Whitehall knows best' philosophy. There appears to be an assumption, albeit implicit, on the part of Governments that management alone will not create the newer, more compact industrial structure which Britain may be held to require to compete effectively against America, Japan or our Common Market partners. Since business men may be assumed to have as much, or more, *information* about their companies as the Government, then it must be their *interpretation* of this information which is incorrect – either from the business point of view or in the context of wider social considerations. The impatience of those who would in fact accept neither of these premises is shown in one analysis of the working of the Industrial Reorganisation Corporation – the body established by a Labour Government in 1966 largely to offer industry financial inducements to amalgamation, but which was subsequently wound up in 1971 by a Conservative Government. Hindley has argued that if there were, for example, gains to be achieved from economies of scale as a result of a merger then management would act to obtain them. If there were no such gains to be achieved then, in Hindley's view, there could be no case for such a merger, and State encouragement of amalgamation would be inappropriate.

> 'If they (the two firms) will not merge unless they are offered special inducements to do so, they cannot be obtaining the largest possible returns for their owners. *The*

> *existence of the IRC must therefore be predicated on the belief that firms will not be operated in their owners' interests.*'[2] (Emphasis added.)

Now although we have suggested in our consideration of the theory of the firm that there are many reasons for doubting, where the management of a firm are not significant shareholders, whether businesses are operated in their owners' interests, those who support Government intervention in restructuring British industry appear to base their case on a wider consideration of the imperfections of economic markets rather than on the writings of Cyert and March or Oliver Williamson. Capital markets and the market for corporate control are imperfect. Even in the absence of wider social considerations State intervention could be justified if in its absence desirable changes in industrial structure would not take place.

> 'The second proposition on which the case for IRC rests is that market forces would not have cured these structural inadequacies quickly enough. In theory, where there are economies of scale to be exploited or where one company's management is inadequate, the stock exchange provides a mechanism whereby a take-over bid will occur. In practice, the mechanism is often ineffective. Shareholders are inadequately informed, directors have vested interests; having regard to the risks for any particular party, finance may not be forthcoming. There is no theoretical or empirical justification for believing that the market in company shares will do the reorganisation job that needs to be done; will do it at all, or quickly enough, or achieving the optimum pattern of partnerships, or with due regard to domestic economic interests as distinct from overseas commercial ones.'[3]

A further case where Government action may be called for is, of course, that of monopoly. Here it may be feared that a particular market structure may protect or encourage incompetent management, high consumer prices or poor technological performance. Thus,

> 'The trouble with British industry today is not that managements are so ruthless in their determination to score over their competitors that any less immediate objectives, values and amenities, are forgotten; the risk is rather that both management and organised labour should become complacent and, as a result, sluggish and inefficient. It would be misleading to identify this attitude with the large single-company monopolies, as the most efficient managements may well be found amongst their number. But this attitude is nevertheless clearly related to monopoly.'[4]

Here the question of the appropriate policy to be adopted is complicated by the recognition on the part of most economists and politicians that in some industries a degree of monopoly may be desirable insofar as firm size or market concentration may be positively correlated with technological progress, or to the extent that national monopolies may have to be tolerated if we are to have U.K. firms which remain internationally competitive. The dilemma faced by those responsible for policy formulation was admitted in the same document quoted from above:

> 'By interfering with and retarding normal business activity, an over-rigid monopoly policy might do more harm than good. The danger in an over-rigid policy, is, paradoxically, the same as the danger presented by monopoly itself. Both can act as obstacles to the flexibility of industry and serve to preserve outdated structures. Sound policy lies between the two extremes.'[5]

As will be seen in a separate discussion of the I.R.C. below, its existence was based almost wholly on the assumption that the forces of the private market could not be expected to bring about an industrial structure appropriate to U.K. national, or indeed international, requirements. Some external force operating in the national interest was felt to be required.

The one further area in which it may be argued that State intervention in industrial affairs is legitimate, even in a largely free market economy, relates to the case of externalities. Business decisions affect many more people than may be involved in the initial decision taking. Decisions on whether or not to engage in new investment, and if so whether this should be in the south-east of England or the west-central belt of Scotland, affect the livelihood of many. Decisions on export markets, methods of production and the use of natural resources will have an impact upon our international economic performance, and the welfare of both present and future generations. Even those who are economic liberals – who believe that in general individuals should be left to make their own economic decisions, and that Governments should be bound by clear principles in any intervention – recognise the legitimacy of such specific areas of State activity in the business world.

> 'As a matter of practice, the economic liberal believes that these principles can best be furthered by harnessing the motive of private gain (of which the profit motive is a special case) to the public good. Often, but by no means always, the best way of doing this is by free competitive markets. Competition will not, of course, produce the right result unaided where there are important neighbourhood or 'spillover' costs and benefits. The most obvious contemporary examples are in the environmental sphere. Chemical products discharged into a river impose costs on communities downstream which the factory responsible does not take into account in its profit and loss calculations. An extra car coming into London imposes costs on all other cars, and on the passenger transport system, while the driver does not have to pay. Even here, however, while markets cannot be left to themselves, the economic liberal believes that wherever possible official intervention should make use of the price mechanism to equate private with social costs – for example by a congestion tax on cars in London – rather than by prohibition, rationing or licensing.
>
> *To create an environment in which private enterprise will be truly competitive and responsive to consumer desires clearly requires considerable government activity.* Even the earliest and much maligned classical economists spent a good deal of time discussing the monetary and legal framework, the principles of taxation and public

> expenditure, 'the condition of the people' (welfare policy) and other activities necessary if self-interest is to be socially productive; and today the list has lengthened.'[6] (Emphasis added.)

This debate is essentially concerned with the wider social responsibility of business: with how far business ought to be concerned with the national wellbeing or social issues. Some writers would even go so far as to suggest that business firms should now fill the gap in the patronage of the arts brought about by the disappearance of the private patrons of the 18th and 19th centuries.[7]

Government 'intervention' in industrial economics aspects of the economy may be undertaken in a number of different ways. These will vary between Governments according to their social and political philosophy; and this will cause differences in the legal form of such intervention. In addition to this there will be differences in the degree of 'directness' of intervention: this can vary from complete national control of the economic resources involved, and their utilisation to achieve certain social and economic obligations as well as a minimum commercial performance (i.e. nationalisation), to a strengthening of the power of the private consumer through increasing the information available to him and controlling certain promotional activities on the part of private industry (e.g. the work of the Consumer Protection Advisory Commission established under the 1973 Fair Trading Act).

The Government may also involve itself with a number of different areas of business activity, e.g. pricing, investment, location, advertising, market structure or behaviour. It is, in fact, only with questions of market structure that this chapter deals: with the intervention of successive Governments in influencing market structure in a number of industries.

B. The Industrial Reorganisation Corporation

The I.R.C. was an example of the policy of increased intervention in industry adopted by the Labour Government which came into office in the autumn of 1964. The White

Paper which announced the formation of the I.R.C. with its £150m of capital stressed the need to improve U.K. international competitiveness, and the contribution which 'concentration and rationalisation' could make to this. It was emphasised that British industry needed increased concentration in order to benefit from production economies of scale and to sustain increased research and development expenditures. Reflecting some of the views which were discussed above, the White Paper stressed:

> *There is no evidence that we can rely on market forces alone to produce the necessary structural changes at the pace required.* Some of the industries most in need of rationalisation have an in-built tendency to stay as they are. Either there are a few large firms which are tempted to live and let live; or there are a number of small ones, none of which alone is strong enough to achieve the scale of operations needed for international competition. Moreover, *some mergers simply lead to a concentration of ownership without securing a more effective deployment of the assets of the merged companies* and result in loosely-knit groups of comparatively small production units ranging over a wide variety of manufacturing activities.'[8] (Emphasis added.)

To meet the national requirement of a change in the economic structure of some industries, and in the light of the defects in the market system, the I.R.C. was put forward as an 'organisation whose special function is to search for opportunities to promote rationalisation schemes which could yield substantial benefits to the national economy'.

In practice the I.R.C. operated in a number of distinct ways; playing different roles and using different techniques in order to achieves its broad aims. First, in some cases it acted as a merchant banker to the Government by commissioning or carrying out detailed studies of individual industries: for example, the study of the bacon curing industry in 1969. Second, the Corporation acted as a merger broker; and it is perhaps for this role that it is most remembered. Some of the mergers which were brought about involved the Corporation in playing only a minor catalytic role, as in the case of Rowntree and Mackintosh in the confectionery industry in 1969. On other occasions, as will be seen below, the I.R.C. played a much more active, and sometimes controversial, role in this area. Third, the I.R.C. contributed to 'rescue' situations such as the Rootes/Chrysler affair early in 1967. Finally, the Corporation was responsible for providing finance for individual schemes on an *ad hoc* basis outside a merger context – as in the case of the finance for the de-inking and printed paper reconstituting process for the Reed Paper Group in 1968.[9]

The I.R.C.'s own view of its function and of the means of achieving its goals can be seen from a reading of the Annual Reports issued over its relatively short life. These indicate that the I.R.C. recognised that it was attempting to bring about changes in the structure of U.K. industry which were necessary to improve its international performance but which would otherwise have remained undone.

> 'It is said that I.R.C. causes some managements to take action they would otherwise avoid or postpone. This is true and, if it were not so, I.R.C. would not be making any contribution. Much of I.R.C.'s work is in areas of potential difficulty, which can be turned to profit and benefit through effective action by management. Hence, following initial I.R.C. action, rationalisation or investment or changes in management and techniques are needed. It is these things that management has been avoiding or postponing.'[10]

The main change with which I.R.C. is associated is industrial concentration; and the Corporation is most remembered for its contribution to the significant mergers and takeovers of the period: English Electric and Elliott Automation in electronics, and G.E.C. and A.E.I. in electrical engineering, both in 1967; Leyland and British Motor Holdings, G.E.C. and English Electric, and George Kent and Cambridge Instruments in control equipment the following year; Reyrolle Parsons and Bruce Peebles in heavy electricals, the trawling interests of Ross Group and Associated Fisheries, and the formation of Ransome, Hoffman and Pollard in ball and roller bearings in 1969.

But I.R.C. itself accepted that increased company size alone would not lead automatically to improved efficiency, and this was highlighted in a later Report.

> 'Over the last three years the bulk of I.R.C.'s work has been devoted to effecting reorganisation through company mergers. Public attention has naturally concentrated in particular on the far-reaching re-organisation to which I.R.C. has contributed in such major industries as motor vehicles, computers, electrical and electronic goods, scientific instruments, ball bearings. In these and other areas the purpose was to establish units that could compete successfully in world markets. Mergers in themselves do not create such units, but they provide the basis on which they can be built through better plant utilisation, concentrated effort in export markets, financial strength, and through economies of scale in R & D and new investment programmes.
>
> I.R.C. does not pursue a policy of size for size's sake. Size has no absolute merit; indeed, size has absolute disadvantages where it increases managerial problems and lengthens lines of communication. The spur of competition can also be blunted. Size must be gauged in each case in relation to the competing concerns at home and overseas, and in relation to the products and markets concerned.'[11]

The Corporation was in fact more concerned about the quality of management in many of the large firms which it helped to create. Indeed the poor quality of much U.K. business management was a theme to which I.R.C. frequently returned in its Reports. Thus:

> 'The experience of the I.R.C.'s first full year of operations has confirmed its Members' view that there are considerable opportunities for improving the structure of British industry, and that remedial action has tended to be too slow. Some progress has been made in the past year,

> but there is still timidity and unwillingness to change in several important industries. Too often local prejudices and family and personal interests stand in the way of effective reorganisation. There are still many companies which recognize the need for structural change in their industries, but which continue to prefer the things they know, to opt for the comfortable, familiar *status quo*, and to put the blame for poor results on the Government, the trade unions or mischance. Short-term reverses are often unavoidable, but the responsibility for prolonged stagnation rests upon the shoulders of managements who are unable or unwilling to face up to the need for change, and of shareholders who accept the situation without complaint.'[12]

In subsequent Reports the Corporation continued to speak of 'the need to improve the quality of management in wide sectors of industry, and this need can hardly be over-emphasized'; and that 'above all, reorganisation imposes severe strains on management, which in Britain in particular is still in scarce supply'.[13] Thus, in I.R.C.'s view,

> 'Whilst there is a continuing need for an active policy to promote reorganisation, poor performance in many sectors of industry is not necessarily the effect of fragmentation. Low productivity, late delivery, slow switch of markets, mediocre products and a lack of management control characterise many companies more than large enough to be viable units.'[14]

The I.R.C. had only been in official existence for about nine months when it became involved in what has since come to be regarded as its most significant intervention: the clear-cut support of G.E.C. in its contested takeover of A.E.I. – the sick man of the U.K. electrical engineering industry. The I.R.C. was intervening in the industry at a time when a cutback in C.E.G.B. orders and increased U.S., European and Japanese competition were making the need for rationalisation imperative. The I.R.C.'s subsequent justification for its support of the merger was based upon this need for rationalisation.

> 'The significance of the merger between G.E.C. and A.E.I., which was encouraged by the I.R.C., was its strategic impact in opening the way to rationalisation on a number of fronts where progress had been slow. It is already apparent that this merger will have wide-ranging effects in the electrical industry, not merely by eliminating duplication between G.E.C. and A.E.I. but by facilitating the creation of stronger groupings involving other companies in the industry.'[15]

In fact the subsequent action of I.R.C. was based upon an internal research paper which had also been discussed with the D.E.A. and the Ministry of Technology. In the middle of 1967 I.R.C. informally sounded out the possibility of an agreed merger between G.E.C. and A.E.I. Nothing came of this scheme, however, and it has been suggested that it was the September announcement of A.E.I.'s poor half-year figures which finally encouraged Sir Arnold Weinstock of G.E.C. to make an outright bid for A.E.I. In fact G.E.C. was in a strong financial position to bid for A.E.I. in terms of their relative share prices. Furthermore, the I.R.C. was not the only body which Weinstock consulted in his move: he discussed the matter with a number of Government ministries and the C.E.G.B., and also contacted Lord Nelson, the chairman of English Electric. The role of I.R.C. in G.E.C.'s final acquisition is hard to quantify. No I.R.C. cash was involved. Some writers have suggested, nonetheless, that 'it is doubtful . . . whether G.E.C. would have won the battle for A.E.I. without I.R.C. backing';[16] and the ousted chief executive of A.E.I. subsequently wrote that 'the part played by the Industrial Reorganisation Corporation was the most curious aspect of the G.E.C. bid for A.E.I.' – a comment which should perhaps be placed in the context of his perception of 'the strong anti-A.E.I. feelings of some I.R.C. Board members'.[17] Others by contrast, appear to have cast the I.R.C. in a relatively minor role in the whole affair.[18] However, I.R.C.'s role in highlighting the need for speedy rationalisation in this sector, its failure to place confidence in A.E.I.'s plans for its new future development as an independent business, and its public support for G.E.C.'s acquisition could well justify the subsequent comment by an I.R.C. Board member at the time that the Corporation 'may well have tipped the balance'.[19]

On subsequent occasions, however, the I.R.C.'s role was not so passive. In 1968 the Rank Organisation made a bid to acquire Cambridge Instrument – a relatively small firm in the scientific instruments field. The I.R.C., however, preferred the link up of Cambridge with George Kent – the largest U.K. process control business – and supported the latter's bid for Cambridge. This support took the form of I.R.C. purchase of Cambridge shares in order to enable the Corporation to vote directly in favour of the Kent bid. The I.R.C. also bought Kent shares to force the price of these up and so increase the attractiveness to other Cambridge equity holders of a Kent acquisition involving share exchange. As a result of this strategy I.R.C. acquired 25% of the enlarged Kent equity, agreed to make further funds available to Kent, and appointed a director to the Kent board. The I.R.C.'s rationale was explained in a subsequent press release.

> 'The I.R.C. intervention in connection with Cambridge was made after detailed study of the likely future prospects of much of the instrument industry. Kent was already established as the largest independent British owned company making industrial and process control instruments. To enable it to expand at least as fast as its international competitors it needed to gain access to the latest technologies emerging from academic and other laboratories and to develop a scientific instrument capability. This will be achieved by the merger with Cambridge. In addition Cambridge make a number of industrial instruments which will increase Kent's systems capability and give rise to rationalisation opportunities in both companies in production, marketing and R & D.

> Finally, the establishment of the new group creates a nucleus for further rationalisation and for the continued development of Kent's successful policy of logical acquisitions.'[20]

The I.R.C. action on this occasion was a clear example of the Corporation using its financial strength (£6.5m in this case) to alter the structure of a technologically significant market in a way which would not have occurred had 'free market forces' been allowed to operate unhindered. Cambridge would undoubtedly have fallen to Rank in the absence of I.R.C. intervention.[21]

A much later project supported by I.R.C. funds was the rationalisation of the U.K. ball and roller bearing market through the creation in the middle of 1969 of Ransome Hoffman Pollard as a result of the bringing together of three formerly separate businesses. The I.R.C.'s main objective in promoting this merger was to create a U.K. ball and roller bearing business which would offer strong competition, at least in the domestic market, to the Swedish S.K.F. subsidiary Skefko. In fact I.R.C. activity was directly precipitated by the possible acquisition of Ransome & Marles by Skefko. The I.R.C. was convinced that the U.K. market was too fragmented to be able to achieve the full economies of scale stemming from long production runs of a limited range of bearings. U.K. export performance in this field was also worsening. The I.R.C. saw the situation as follows:

> 'There was an identity of view in the industry that with the possible exception of tapered bearings, where production is shared by Skefko and Timken alone, there were too many companies producing in sub-optimum manufacturing units an excessive range of bearings in too short runs. The fragmentation in the industry was one major factor causing low productivity which international comparisons made clear: output per employee in Europe is on average approximately £3,000 per annum; in the U.K. owned companies the comparable figure averages only just over £2,000 per annum. The performance of the U.K.

industry has reflected these limitations. In 1963 the value of our exports was over 75% more than the value of our imports; in 1968 exports were only 36% more than imports and the U.K. had increasingly heavy deficits in our balance of trade with the advanced economies of Western Europe and North America.'[22]

The I.R.C. thus went ahead and, having persuaded Skefko not to proceed with its planned acquisition of Ransome & Marles, itself acquired a majority equity holding in Hoffman, and supported Ransome & Marles in its acquisition of Pollard. Thus almost £9.5m was spent by I.R.C. in creating a powerful domestic bearings firm: Ransome, Hoffman & Pollard had about 35% of U.K. domestic consumption between them.

What can we conclude about the value of the work carried out by I.R.C. during its own relatively short life? What contribution did the Corporation make towards improving the performance of British industry or the U.K. balance of payments? As in most areas of industrial economics a good deal of the answers to these questions depends upon what 'might have been' in the absence of a body like I.R.C. A full assessment of I.R.C. would also require detailed follow-up studies of all those firms affected by I.R.C. policy; although here again one must bear in mind what would have taken place had no I.R.C. intervention occurred. It has been suggested, for example, that many of the largest mergers in which I.R.C. was involved would have taken place sooner or later in its absence.

'In fact, the giant combinations hardly represented original thinking on I.R.C.'s part. The force of circumstances was so powerful in most cases that many people in industry, the Press and Government had recognized what should be done; and most, if not all, of the I.R.C.-sponsored mergers would probably have materialised if the I.R.C. had never been invented. The British computer industry, for example, had to be welded into one company to stand a fair chance against International Business Machines and the latter's hard-running American rivals. A badly organized

> British Motor Holdings was in danger of financial breakdown under the onslaught of America's Big Three car manufacturers. Over-capacity among the makers of electric power equipment, brought on by overoptimistic demand forecasts from the Central Electricity Generating Board, threatened to wreck an already faltering A.E.I. and to add further burdens to a profits-short English Electric. The nuclear power companies needed stream-lining if they were to sell in the export market. But while there was a great deal of talk on all these points, little corrective action followed. At times, it seemed that the problems were so big, and the inertia so great, that perhaps nothing would be done . . . This, in fact was I.R.C.'s chief contribution. It accelerated, sometimes greatly, the processes already under way.'[23]

Other assessments concur in emphasising the passive or catalytic role of I.R.C.[24] In the light of this and the other methodological problems highlighted above can one blame I.R.C. for the relative failure of the Leyland–B.M.C. or Kent–Cambridge mergers? These factors should certainly be borne in mind in forecasting the likely impact upon U.K. industrial structure of any successor to the I.R.C.

Interest in the activities of the I.R.C. stems not only from its actions during its own relatively short life, or comparisons with the activities of similar bodies in other economies, but also because of its role as an explicit forerunner of the National Enterprise Board (N.E.B.). This is the Government body now charged with restructuring the private sector of the economy. Indeed the N.E.B. has as one of its functions 'to build on and enlarge the activities previously discharged by the I.R.C.'; and was planned to have 'the former I.R.C.'s entrepreneurial role in promoting industrial efficiency and profitability'.[25] In fact the N.E.B. is merely a further extension of a general trend of greater participation by Governments in the private sector of the economy. The Industrial Expansion Act of 1968 gave the Government powers to subscribe to equity capital in those companies which it wished to assist – usually to less than 50% of the total equity, but not requiring the consent of the remainder of the shareholders.[26] It was envisaged at the time that assistance under this Act would be concentrated in three main areas: (a) where restructuring of an industry was involved, e.g. shipbuilding, (b) where an industry was vulnerable but of national importance, e.g. machine tools, (c) where large amounts of research and development expenditure were necessary for long-term development but did not generate short-term profits, e.g. aircraft.[27] This type of assistance to industry and Government participation in the private sector of the economy was continued through the provisions of Sec. 7 and 8 of the 1972 Industry Act dealing with selective financial assistance for industry. Here again the purpose of the assistance was to encourage modernisation, efficiency and expansion; and reconstruction, reorganisation and redistribution were seen as being likely to be necessary. Provision was made for Government acquisition of equity capital in the businesses concerned, although in this case the consent of the company was required for Government subscription to equity capital.[28]

The 1975 Industry Act has somewhat expanded upon these powers and formally brought into existence the N.E.B. and the making of Planning Agreements between companies and the Government.[29]

Some idea of the increase in this form of assistance and of the current situation can be gained from the following data.

Payments Under Sec. 7 of the 1972 Industry Act

(£'000)

Financial year	Loans/Equity	Interest relief	Grants	Total
1972/73	358	47	20	425
1973/74	20,445	2,858	1,652	24,955
1974/75	21,134	9,640	5,619	36,393
1975/76	42,597	16,629	6,474	65,700

Source: Industry Act 1972 Annual Report to 31.3.76 (H.M.S.O., 1976, Cmnd. 619) Appendix F Table 17.

National Enterprise Board
Investments as at 30th September, 1976

	Equity shareholding (%)
Agemaspark	30.0
Anglo Venezuelan Railway Corporation	35.0
British Leyland	95.1
Brown Boveri Kent	17.6
Cambridge Instruments	28.3
Data Recording Instrument Company	53.9
Dunford & Elliott	2.6
Ferranti	50.0*
Herbert	100.0
International Computer (Holdings)	24.4
Rolls-Royce (1971)	100.0
Twinlock	33.3

* plus 100% of non-voting ordinary shares.
Source: National Enterprise Board.

A number of problems enter into this area of economic behaviour. On the one hand some of those concerned with running the nation's economic affairs and who are dissatisfied with its rate of economic progress or level of investment feel that more State intervention of a type which falls short of outright nationalisation is the only remedy. They reject the previously remote relationship between Government policy and industrial behaviour.[30] As regards the role of economics, however, there is a considerable problem of specifying the objectives of such a policy. There is, additionally, the difficulty of what one author has described as 'an unduly neglected aspect of economics: namely, the translation of the recommendations deriving from formal analysis into actual decisions by way of a political process'.[31] Some writers appear to have given up hope, however, of being able to apply a consistent set of principles in this area; and one of them quotes Sir Alec Cairncross as saying in the context of discussion of Government subsidies to industry, 'you can justify, by reference to some principle, help in almost any circumstances you like'.[32]

What Governments of the day now want to achieve, both in respect of the much-publicised 'rescue operations' such as Ferranti and Alfred Herbert in 1975 and 1976 and also longer-term restructuring in, for example, ferrous foundries and transformers, is a much closer and more direct relationship with the firms concerned. General management of the economy and indicative planning are no longer sufficient. Active restructuring and rationalisation are now considered to be necessary. More specific aid to individual businesses, as opposed to general regional assistance to reduce unemployment, or advice or exhortation or research and development assistance to increase productivity, do represent greater direct Government involvement in industry. The fact that the 1975 Industry Act now permits equity acquisition of more than 50% means, however, that aid of any kind may be seen by some managements as a prelude to State control: 'backdoor nationalisation'. It has been suggested that this may be one reason for the relative failure of previous aid schemes in ferrous foundries and machine tools.[33]

C. Competition Policy

Antitrust or competition policy is a weapon which the State can use to correct abuses of market structure or market behaviour which are held to be inconsistent with the achievement of certain general economic performance goals. In the U.K. this has involved the outright prohibition of certain forms of business conduct (e.g. collective enforcement of resale price maintenance agreements) and the reference of other forms of business behaviour (e.g. common trade pricing agreements) to the Restrictive Practices Court for a judgement on their desirability or otherwise. So far as market structure is concerned the Monopolies Commission may investigate and make recommendations where a 'statutory monopoly' exists, or in respect of certain size classes of merger.[34]

Competition policy, then, is a form of intervention in the operation of market forces in the economy; and although it is often seen as a means of 'correcting' departures from the norm of more perfectly competitive market structures, it should not be seen as a naive attempt to recreate a *laissez-faire* economy. Effective antitrust, on the contrary, demands positive State intervention in private-sector decision taking.[35] The objectives of competition policy are normally seen as being to encourage economic efficiency at the market and firm level; wider economic objectives such as balance of payments performance or income distribution normally being left to other more appropriate policy weapons.[36] Monopolies Commission enquiries, however, have been concerned with the balance of payments implications of proposed mergers; and the 1973 Fair Trading Act (Sec. 84) directs the Commission to give consideration to the regional distribution of employment in its enquiries.[37]

It is the purpose of this section to look at one aspect of U.K. competition policy: the control of mergers. This should complement the earlier section's analysis of the work of the I.R.C. and its successor, the N.E.B. The emphasis here should be on the complementary nature of these policies, and not upon any direct contradiction in their goals. The Government thus has it in its power to rationalise and reconstruct certain industrial markets through the N.E.B., while limiting in other markets concentration which, while promoting private gain, might through a reduction in competition lead to inefficiency and a national loss of welfare. Historically Britain was well behind America in introducing competition policy legislation. There the Sherman Act of 1890 had heralded the outlawing of monopoly. By contrast British courts were loath to interpret the laws of monopoly, conspiracy or restraint of trade as preventing business men from acting so as to restrain competition. National committees of enquiry followed a similar course; and although the Committee on Trusts which reported in 1919 did consider that 'it is obvious that a system which creates virtual monopolies and controls prices is always in danger of abuse', the economic climate between the two World Wars was obviously not one in which competition policy attracted a high priority. Thus in general terms Hunter points to enquiries during this period as being characterised by 'hesitancy and disinclination to reach definite conclusions'.[38]

Opinion appeared to change considerably with the prospect of a return to peace and more normal economic conditions. The 1944 White Paper on Employment Policy recognised that Government objectives in this and other areas might be frustrated by restrictive trading agreements, and pledged the Government 'to take appropriate action to check practices which may bring advantages to sectional producing interests but work to the detriment of the country as a whole'.[39] The outcome of this mood was the Monopolies and Restrictive Practices (Enquiry and Control) Act of 1948, which established the Monopolies and Restrictive Practices Commission. The Commission was empowered, on a reference by the then Board of Trade, to enquire into and report on any market where a statutory monopoly existed: basically where one firm, or a group of firms operating together, controlled one-third or more of a market. The Commission, expanded in 1953, investigated 20 industries between 1948 and 1956; and although not all of its reports embodied adverse conclusions, these individual industry Reports plus the general Report on Collective Discrimination published in 1955, persuaded the Conservative Government to take much more positive action. The 1956 Restrictive Trade Practices Act declared a number of trade practices to be 'deemed to be contrary to the public interest' unless the participants to the agreements could prove to the contrary. This proof had to be couched in terms of specific benefits, known as 'gateways', considered to flow from the agreements. Unless such proof were established the agreements became illegal. The result of this procedure was that the great majority of the vast number of agreements (there were 2,240 of them on the public register by 1959) were abandoned without a contest in the Restrictive Practices Court. By 1972 only 37 agreements had been so contested, and 26 had been struck down by the Court.[40]

Monopoly and restrictive practices legislation had been in operation, and by most accounts successful operation, for some time before there was consideration of legislative control over the potential formation of monopolies – namely mergers. Merger activity had been going on in the economy more noticably since the early 1950s. Charles Clore's Sears Holdings, the late Lord Fraser of Allander's House of Fraser, and other colourful personalities such as Wolfson and Jack Cotton provided plenty of material for City editors in the 1950s. Mergers of the time were often characterised by very low prices paid for potentially very profitable companies (for reasons explained in Chapter VII); and often the most important asset of the acquired company was freehold property. Furthermore these mergers and takeovers often occurred after public battles for shareholder's rights, preceded by the surreptitious building up of nominee shareholdings by bidders; and the successful acquirer was often able to replenish his cash funds for further activities by disposing of the property to a financial institution on a 'sale and leaseback' arrangement. But the motion in the House of Commons by Mr. Roy Jenkins early in 1954 deploring 'recent manifestations of take-over bids in so far as they have put large, untaxed capital profits into the hands of certain individuals' was premature.

By the late 1950s, however, attitudes began to change. At the end of 1958 there was an open battle by Tube Investments for British Aluminium. The B.A. case for an alternative linking with Alcoa (Aluminium Company of America) was supported by the incumbent directors and by significant City interests. Nonetheless T.I. won; although the B.A. chairman and managing director left with a tax-free £88,000 (in 1959!) between them. Then late in 1961 I.C.I. made a bid for Courtaulds which, although eventually unsuccessful, made the Government appear uniquely impotent in the face of major potential changes in industrial structure and market competitiveness.[41]

The Conservative approach to the problem was outlined in a White Paper in 1964. The bulk of mergers were to be welcomed as leading to more efficient use of national resources. There was, however, a case for the Monopolies Commission enquiring into the potentially harmful minority. Proposed or recently completed monopoly mergers would, therefore, be investigated by the Commission; and if the final Report were adverse, proposed mergers might be prohibited. Completed mergers would be dealt with under existing monopoly legislation.[42]

The succeeding Labour Government's Monopolies and Mergers Act of 1965, however, went somewhat further. The appropriate Government minister could refer 'qualifying' mergers to the Commission, i.e. monopoly mergers, or cases where the acquired assets exceeded £5m. The Act specifically gave the Government powers to delay prospective mergers pending investigation, to prohibit such mergers, or to 'unscramble' mergers completed up to six months prior to the Commission's reference.

The data in the Appendix to this chapter give some idea of the work of the Commission in this area and of the impact of its decisions. These mergers are, however, a very small part of the number which fall within the criteria established by the 1965 Act and expanded by the 1973 Fair Trading Act's wider definition of a statutory monopoly as 25% of the market. Indeed figures published by the Office of Fair Trading showed that from 1965 until mid-1973, while there were 833 qualifying (non-newspaper) mergers, only 20 (2.4%) were referred to the Commission. Of these 20 only four actually took place; although one has to take account of two cases where the proposed merger was sanctioned but did not take place at the time, and eight cases where the reference of the proposal to the Commission caused a potential merger to be abandoned.[43]

The main concern of the Commission in its investigations has been to balance the increased benefits put to it by the parties as likely to accrue from a merger against any reduction in competition in the industry. The benefits may come from the achievement of economies of scale, the availability of increased funds for research and development, injection of superior management into the acquired firm, or the more 'orderly' contraction of a declining industry. These effects should all lead to more efficient resource use in the economy. The potential detriments from mergers are largely those of reduced competition resulting from increased concentration: increased prices (and perhaps costs), a possible tendency to oligopolistic price leadership and an emphasis on non-price competition.

In its first Report, the Commission was dealing with a case of vertical integration between a motor car assembly firm (B.M.C.) and a component supplier (Pressed Steel).[44] Here it was persuaded that the gains from rationalisation would be significant, and that there would be no loss of competitiveness in the supply of components to the market. So far as horizontal mergers are concerned, however, the Commission has in general taken a tougher line. In the case of commercial banking, for example, the Commission was examining a situation in which (following the merger of the National Provincial and Westminster banks in January 1968 to give the new National Westminster about 25% of London clearing bank deposits) Barclays, Lloyds, and Martins were proposing to bring together a further 47% of such deposits.[45] Here, the Commission, while recognising the potential benefits from the proposed merger in terms of rationalisation of the branch banking network and more efficient use of computers, was by no means happy with either the existing or likely future degree of competition between banks. It was also clearly worried about the likely future tendency towards a banking duopoly of National Westminster–Midland, and Barclays, Lloyds and Martins. A potential loss of competition was also a major deciding factor in the cases of United Drapery Stores and Montague Burton (where the Commission was in any case sceptical of resource savings),[46] and the Ross Group and Associated Fisheries in the trawling and fish merchanting market.[47] Again the Commission in this latter Report felt that the rationalisation economies from the merger would not compensate for the very real market power which would accrue to the combined business in some important markets. To this extent the Commission's sanction of the merger of Thorn and Radio Rentals in 1968 is perhaps a little surprising. Both of these firms had significant interests in the manufacture, distribution and rental of television sets. So far as manufacture was concerned Thorn had 25–28% of the home sales market and Radio Rentals 6–8%. But in the rental market the combined firm would have had 32% of total rented sets: although this figure rose to 45% if one considered rentals from specialist rental outlets only. The Commission, although doubtful of some of the merger rationalisation gains put forward by the two firms, did not consider that there would be any real reduction in competition in manufacturing or retailing from the merger.[48] In the case of the proposed takeovers of Glaxo by Beecham and by Boots, the Commission's principal concern centred on the possible reduction in the number of independent U.K.

centres of pharmaceutical research. The Commission clearly thought that any reduction in the number of such centres would, by diminishing the competitive spur to devote resources to pharmaceutical research and development, reduce the U.K. industry's prospects of success in finding and developing new products.[49]

The Commission does not, however, appear to have come down against size or market concentration as such. Where there was the possibility of countervailing power through customers manufacturing their own requirements – as in the G.K.N. acquisition of Birfield in the market for motor propeller shafts sold to motor car assembly firms – the Commission was prepared to sanction a merger.[50] Similarly, in the case of the proposed link-up of Unilever and Allied Breweries – respectively the 5th and 16th largest British industrial companies – the Commission was satisfied that there would be no loss of competition from the amalgamation of their largely complementary interests.[51] Indeed in the case of the conglomerate interests of British Match and Wilkinson Sword the Commission saw an enlarged 'presence' as being one of the most significant advantages of the merger for the combined group – particularly in respect of overseas markets.[52]

One area in which the Commission has felt able to exercise a degree of pragmatic judgement has been where a takeover bid was contested by the potential victim company. The Commission has doubted, on such occasions, whether the prospective benefits of a merger could in practice be realised. In the case of the attempted acquisition by Rank of De La Rue, for instance, the Commission not only appeared sceptical of the Rank management's ability to handle the rather confidential security printing side of De La Rue's interests, but was also swayed by the threat of the vast majority of De La Rue's senior management to resign if the proposed takeover went ahead.[53]

The case of Boots and House of Fraser was one of the bidding company (Boots) subsequently wishing to withdraw its offer in the light of changed circumstances, but being unable to do so because of legal and procedural technicalities. Here again the largest part of the reason for the Commission's rejection of the proposed merger lay in its view that 'this would be a merger of two very large enterprises accompanied apparently by strong feelings of resentment within Fraser, and by a lack of enthusiasm on the part of the Boots management'.[54] Most recently the Commission has protected the board of Herbert Morris, the Loughborough crane manufacturers, from control by Amalgamated Industrials. Amalgamated Industrials had built up a minority shareholding of about 33%, and sought in 1975 to gain a controlling interest. The Commission was sceptical of the benefits of such control by a company (Amalgamated Industrials) which, in the Commission's words, 'appears to have bought and sold subsidiaries with regard mainly to the immediate financial interests of the group'.[55] The Commission therefore came to the conclusion that not only should Amalgamated Industrials not seek complete control of Morris, but that its Morris shareholding should be reduced to 10%, and the remainder disposed of in an orderly manner over a period of time.[56]

Academic economists have not, by and large, given the Monopolies Commission much credit for its work; and most would like to see the adoption of a much 'tougher' policy on mergers. The following comments by Professor George are representative of the general view:

> 'In the United Kingdom, legislation has not so far been a factor which has had any significant effect in controlling the upward trend in concentration levels. Indeed the probability is that legislation has had a significant net effect of *increasing* concentration. The success of the 1956 Restrictive Trade Practices Act probably contributed in some degree towards the increasing concentration of industry, *and the permissive attitude of the Government towards mergers, especially during the second half of the 1960s*, has been even more important. As far as mergers are concerned, there is need for a reversal of policy. This does not mean that all mergers should be prohibited but rather that there should be a tight control over mergers and acquisitions with the emphasis instead on encouraging firms to concentrate on internal growth.'[57] (Emphasis added.)

As regards a change in philosophy, one author has suggested that 'for a start requiring that positive benefit to the public be shown by any challenged increase in market power rather than simply the absence of public detriment seems a better approach'.[58] It has even been suggested that there should be an almost total prohibition of merger or takeover activity on the part of the top twenty-five firms in the economy.[59] Such proposals would indeed represent a considerable 'tightening up' of Government policy, and a significant increase in the degree of intervention in private decision taking on industrial structure. But such a policy may be unavoidable if the present trend towards (for many economists) unacceptably high levels of aggregate and market concentration is to be halted.

Given that the Commission itself is making an acceptable job of the individual references given to it (a view not accepted by all economists),[60] the solution to the present limitations appears to involve: (1) the development of a more coherent 'economic model' for choosing references and assessing individual cases; (2) greater use of the present 'qualifying' criteria of monopoly and asset size as compared with the small number of qualifying cases actually going to the Commission;[61] and (3) greater resources being devoted to investigating merger references and monitoring approved mergers. Those who argue for a 'structural' approach to merger policy – for the consistent application of formal rules as opposed to the current pragmatic approach – would submit that the case against high levels of market concentration is already proved. Monopoly does not appear to be associated with high levels of efficiency. Although there are problems of defining markets (or rather obtaining data which correspond with the economist's concept of a market) and of identifying the appropriate dimensions of market structure, a merger policy based upon such criteria might generate increased confidence in the work of the Commission. The Commission itself, however, appears to favour a pragmatic approach, arguing that precise guidelines for reference of mergers to the Commission (and thus, by implication, for the Commission itself) are not appropriate in the U.K.[62] This approach by the Commission is, however, largely dictated by the circumstances of U.K. antitrust policy. The Commission is expected, within a relatively short period of time, to come to conclusions as to whether the conditions for a 'qualifying' merger do in fact exist, whether market power is thereby significantly increased, *and* whether this market power is likely to be operated against a vaguely-defined public interest. There is no automatic assumption in British monopoly policy that monopoly as such is against the public interest. To this extent it may be that it is Parliament itself which has forced the Commission to rely upon 'intuition and presentiment as a substitute for scientific analysis' in merger inquiries.[63]

D. Conclusions

This chapter has examined the operation of two Government bodies concerned with intervention in the structure of the U.K. economy. Any appraisal of the benefits of such organisations is bound to be complex insofar as one cannot compare what was brought about with what would otherwise have happened. Furthermore, and particularly so far as the I.R.C. was concerned, the general view appears to be that many of the changes in structure brought about by the Corporation would *in time* have taken place as a result of free market forces.

One of the most immediate criticisms of the two bodies is that their aims, and possibly on one occasion their actions, were contradictory. The I.R.C. was concerned with promoting concentration; the Monopolies Commission with preventing it. Witness, say the critics, the prohibition by the Commission of the merger of the Ross Group and Associated Fisheries in 1966, and the I.R.C.'s formation of British United Trawlers from the trawling interests of the two companies in 1969.[64] In general terms, however, there need be no contradiction in the existence of two such bodies with apparently different functions, so long as there is cooperation and liaison between them.[65] Once the need for such intervention is accepted, 'intervention' may imply increased or reduced concentration. Thus,

> 'Where there is a difference between public net benefit and private net benefit it is sensible for Government to do what it can to rectify the situation; and the circumstances of the particular case will determine whether more size is

needed, or less. Given that the workings of the market cannot be invariably relied upon to produce the appropriate solution, it is not in principle inconsistent to "interfere with the actions of those who are prepared to back their personal choices with cash" in different directions in different cases, sometimes encouraging action and sometimes preventing it.'[66]

A further criticism of Government control of private sector market structure is the open-ended nature of the remit to the bodies concerned. This can be seen from the White Paper establishing the I.R.C. and the wide powers given to the N.E.B. through the 1975 Industry Act. Similarly the Commission in examining merger references is required to 'take into account all matters which appear in the particular circumstances to be relevant'.[67] This has led to accusations of the I.R.C. being 'out of control' of its sponsoring Government Department, and of such bodies developing their own logic as they go along: an approach described in the context of the I.R.C. as 'short term controlled intelligent *ad hocery*'.[68]

This line of criticism has extended into comment on the depth of analysis carried out by the investigatory bodies, and of the lack of any underlying 'model' upon which policy can be based. The spirit of the I.R.C.'s approach may be judged from the comment by its deputy managing director to Graham Turner: 'We don't feel the need for economists, and we don't believe in great volumes of analysis. It's not a question of analysing the problem – there are plenty of Little Neddies already and twenty five reports on everything – what is needed is action'.[69] Young too appears to rejoice in the fact that there were no economists on the I.R.C. Board, and explains this by suggesting that 'the Government wanted the I.R.C. to avoid, for example, complex analyses of the optimum capacity for an industry in 1980, in favour of producing practical ideas'.[70] Sutherland's analysis of the first eight of the Monopolies Commission's non-newspaper merger Reports led him to conclude that 'it is not easy to see . . . the underlying logic of the Commission's approach to merger';[71] and more detailed analysis of some of the Commission's Reports by economists has led to comments on the intuitive and arbitrary nature of the treatment of, for example, cost savings.[72]

However, if a Government believes that the market mechanism alone will not produce an 'ideal' industrial structure, in the sense of one which promotes the welfare of the whole community, then some form of intervention in this area is inescapable. Any assessment of the value of the exercise – any cost–benefit analysis – is, however, likely to be complex if not impossible.[73] The Monopolies Commission itself has to deal with imponderables regarding the future: will cost savings be generated by a merger, and if so how will they be used? If the Commission were to permit one merger to go ahead, would this lead to further mergers which the Commission would find it difficult to prevent? In a wider context, does the very existence of the Commission prevent the coming forward of what might prove to be desirable mergers?[74]

But the question cannot be avoided of how far the activities of such bodies as those discussed in this chapter have succeeded in assisting the U.K. economy, promoting industrial efficiency and international competitiveness and providing productive employment. For improvements along these dimensions are the ultimate aim of the restructuring, granting of selective financial assistance, and 'rescue' operations which are the immediate activities of the N.E.B., and the vetting of mergers by the Monopolies Commission. Certainly Britain has not entered an economic Elysium as a result of such policies. 'After five years of ardent intervention and dedicated consultation', wrote one commentator in 1969, 'Britain's growth rate is still precarious and the pound is still a shaking currency'.[75] The only correction required to bring the statement up to date is that such planning has now been with us for more than a decade! Whatever the weaknesses of the present system, however, there would be few who would deny that further changes in Britain's industrial structure are necessary, and that the functioning of the market mechanism alone is unlikely to achieve these. The existence of the Commission allows such intervention to be carried out within a broad economic framework independently of direct Government participation. It remains to be seen how effectively the new N.E.B. will operate in this context.

Appendix: Mergers Referred to the Monopolies Commission (excluding newspapers) (31.12.76)

Year	Proposed or Actual Merger	Criteria	Conclusions	Outcome
1965	B.M.C./Pressed Steel	Assets	Permitted	Occurred
1966	Ross Group/Associated Fisheries	Assets	Prohibited	Did not take place
1966	Dental Manufacturing/Amalgamated Dentist Supply/Amalgamated Dental	Assets	Permitted	Did not take place
1966	G.K.N./Birfield	Monopoly and Assets	Permitted	Occurred
1966	B.I.C.C./Pyrotenax	Monopoly	Permitted	Occurred
1967	U.D.S./Burton	Assets	Prohibited	Did not take place
1968	Barclays/Lloyds/Martins Banks	Assets	Prohibited	Did not take place
1968	Thorn/Radio Rentals	Assets	Permitted	Occurred
1969	Unilever/Allied Breweries	Assets	Permitted	Did not take place
1969	Rank/De La Rue	Assets	Prohibited	Did not take place
1969	Marley Tiles/Redland	Monopoly and Assets	Abandoned	———
1970	Burmah Oil/Laporte	Assets	Abandoned	———
1970	British Sidac/Transparent Paper	Monopoly	Prohibited	Did not take place
1971	Reed International/Bowater	Monopoly and Assets	Abandoned	———
1972	Beecham/Glaxo Boots/Glaxo	Assets	Prohibited	Did not take place
1972	Sears Holdings/Timpson	Assets	Abandoned	———
1973	Tarmac/Wolseley Hughes	Assets	Abandoned	———
1973	Glynwed/Armitage Shanks	Monopoly and Assets	Abandoned	———
1973	Whessoe/Capper-Neill	Monopoly and Assets	Abandoned	———

1973	London & County Securities/Inveresk Group	Assets	Abandoned	———
1973	British Match/Wilkinson Sword	Assets	Permitted	Occurred
1973	Bowater/Hanson Trust	Assets	Abandoned	———
1973	Boots/House of Fraser	Assets	Prohibited	Did not take place
1973	Davy International/British Rollmakers	Monopoly and Assets	Prohibited	Did not take place
1974	Charter Consolidated Investments/Sadia	Monopoly	Permitted	Occurred
1974	Dentsply International Inc./A.D. International	Monopoly and Assets	Permitted	Occurred
1974	Eagle Star Insurance/Bernard Sunley and Grovewood	Assets	Permitted	Occurred (Grovewood only)
1974	N.F.U. Development Trust/F.H.C.	Assets	Permitted	Occurred
1974	Sears Holdings/Nottingham Manufacturing	Assets	Abandoned	———
1975	H. Weidmann A.G./B.S. & W. Whiteley	Monopoly	Permitted	Occurred
1975	Amalgamated Industrials/Herbert Morris	Assets	Prohibited	Did not take place
1975	Eurocanadian Shipholdings/Furness Withy	Assets	Prohibited	Did not take place
1975	Norvic Securities/W. Canning	Assets	Abandoned	———
1976	Pilkington Brothers/U.K. Optical and Industrial Holdings	Assets	Awaiting report	
1976	British Petroleum/Century Oils Group	Assets	Awaiting report	
1976	Fruehauf Corporation/Crane Fruehauf	Assets	Awaiting report	
1976	Babcock & Wilcox/Herbert Morris	Assets	Awaiting report	

Data provided by Office of Fair Trading.

References

1. A. Cairncross, The Managed Economy, in A. Cairncross (ed.), *The Managed Economy*, Blackwell, Oxford (1970), p. 7
2. B. Hindley, *Industrial Merger and Public Policy*, I.E.A., London (1970), p. 10
3. W. G. McClelland, The Industrial Reorganisation Corporation 1966/71: An Experimental Prod, *Three Banks Review*, No. 94 (1972), 27
4. Conservative Political Centre, *Monopoly and the Public Interest*, London (1963), p. 7
5. *Ibid.*, p. 5
6. S. Brittan, *Government and the Market Economy*, I.E.A., London (1971), pp. 2–3
7. See E. Moonman and D. Alexander, *Business and the Arts*, Foundation for Business Responsibilities, London (1974)
8. *Industrial Reorganisation Corporation*, H.M.S.O. (1966), Cmnd. 2889, para. 4
9. See S. Young, *Intervention in the Mixed Economy*, Croom Helm, London (1974), pp. 42–3
10. Industrial Reorganisation Corporation, *1966/70 Report and Accounts*, p. 19
11. *Ibid.*, p. 6
12. *Ibid. 1967/68*, p. 13
13. *Ibid. 1968/69*, p. 6
14. *Ibid. 1969/70*, p. 7
15. *Ibid. 1967/68*, p. 9
16. G. Turner, *Business in Britain*, Eyre and Spottiswoode, London (1969), p. 81
17. J. Latham, *Take-over: The Facts and the Myths of the GEC/AEI Battle*, Iliffe, London (1969), pp. 57 and 63
18. See R. Jones and O. Marriott, *Anatomy of a Merger*, Jonathan Cape, London (1970), Ch. 15
19. W. G. McClelland, Ref. 3, 35
20. I.R.C., *1968–69 Annual Report*, Appendix 2
21. The latest development in this particular field is that Cambridge's successor, Scientific and Medical Instruments (S.M.I.), has been hived off from Kent with Government financial backing. See *Financial Times* (15 November 1975)
22. I.R.C., *1969/70 Annual Report*, p. 42
23. D. Smith, What I.R.C. Wrought, *Management Today* (October 1969), 91–2

24. See, for example, B. R. Cant, The Role of the I.R.C. in Promoting Structural Change, in B. W. Denning (ed.), *Corporate Long Range Planning*, Longman, London (1969), p. 46. Mr. Cant was a director of I.R.C.
25. *The Regeneration of British Industry*, H.M.S.O. (1974), Cmnd. 5710, para. 24
26. A. Samuels, Government Participation in Private Industry, *Journal of Business Law*, Vol. XII (1968), 299
27. *Ibid.*, 297
28. See *Industry Act 1972* Sec. 7(4) and Sec. 8(3). Sec. 7 deals with selective financial assistance for those industrial schemes in assisted areas, i.e. Development Areas and Intermediate Areas. Sec. 8 deals with national selective assistance
29. Under the 1975 Act for example (Sec. 2(2)(c)) the N.E.B. has as one of its functions 'extending public ownership into profitable areas of manufacturing industry', which, taken together with the broad purposes of the Board (e.g. 'the development or assistance of the economy'), gives the new body very wide powers.

    It is interesting to note that this type of legislation has advanced regardless of the political party in power. The I.R.C. and the 1968 Industrial Expansion Act were of course the products of a Labour Government. The 1972 Industry Act was, however, passed by a Conservative Government, and the 1975 Act by a Labour Government. The only major difference in the legislation was the greater reluctance of the Conservatives to see unlimited State acquisition of equity capital, especially if financial assistance could be given in another way.
30. This is essentially the argument of the opening paras. of *The Regeneration of British Industry*.
31. J. Wiseman, in A. Whiting (ed.), *The Economics of Industrial Subsidies*, H.M.S.O., London (1975), p. 77
32. T. E. Chester, Public Money in the Private Sector, *National Westminster Bank Quarterly Review* (May 1973), 25
33. See K. Gooding, Industry Aid: A Tale of Two Sectors, *Financial Times* (11th August 1976)
34. For a good general introduction to this topic see P. H. Guénault and J. H. Jackson, *The Control of Monopoly in the United Kingdom*, Longman, London, 2nd ed. (1974)
35. This point is emphasised in C. K. Rowley, *Antitrust and Economic Efficiency*, Macmillan, London (1973), p. 11
36. See J. P. Cairns, Competition Policy and Economic Objectives, in J. B. Heath (ed.), *International Conference on Monopoly, Mergers and Restrictive Practices*, C.U.P., Cambridge (1969), p. 44

37. What this implies is that in traditional antitrust the authorities have adopted a simple social welfare function which ignores distributional consequences between or within groups of producers or consumers. Policy is thus concerned with efficiency and not equity. See Sec. 14 of the 1948 Act. For a fuller discussion of this see M. A. Crew and C. K. Rowley, Anti-Trust Policy: Economics Versus Management Science, *Moorgate and Wall Street* (Autumn 1970), 21–22
38. A. Hunter, *Competition and the Law*, Allen and Unwin, London (1966), p. 76
39. *Employment Policy*, H.M.S.O. (1944), Cmnd. 6527
40. A good review of the work of the Court is J. D. Gribbin, Recent Antitrust Developments in the United Kingdom, *Antitrust Bulletin*, Vol. XX (1975), 377–410
41. An interesting account of this period is given in W. Davis, *Merger Mania*, Constable, London (1970), Chs. 2–4
42. See *Monopolies, Mergers and Restrictive Practices*, H.M.S.O. (1964), Cmnd. 2299, paras. 21–27
43. See J. D. Gribbin, The Operation of the Mergers Panel Since 1965, *Trade and Industry* (17th January 1974), 72–3. There have, however, been cases where a decision *not* to refer a proposed merger to the Commission has been conditional upon assurances on their future behaviour by the companies concerned. To this extent some merger policy is conducted behind the scenes. See M. E. Beesley and G. M. White, The Control of Mergers in the U.K., in J. M. Samuels (ed.), *Readings on Mergers and Takeovers*, Elek, London (1972), p. 131
44. Monopolies Commission, *British Motor Corporation Ltd. and Pressed Steel Co. Ltd.*, H.M.S.O. (1969), H.C.P. 46
45. Monopolies Commission, *Barclays Bank Ltd., Lloyds Bank Ltd. and Martins Bank Ltd.*, H.M.S.O. (1968), H.C.P. 319, para. 13
46. Monopolies Commission, *United Drapery Stores Ltd. and Montague Burton Ltd.*, H.M.S.O. (1967), Cmnd. 3397
47. Monopolies Commission, *Ross Group Ltd. and Associated Fisheries Ltd.*, H.M.S.O. (1966), H.C.P. 42. In the case of B.I.C.C.'s acquisition of Pyrotenax in the mineral insulated cable field (giving the two firms a total of 90% of U.K. manufacturers' sales, with no import competition) the Commission was forced to accept a virtual monopoly situation resulting from the sale by I.C.I. to B.I.C.C. of about 20% of the Pyrotenax equity. There was also some competition from other types of cable in most use areas. See Monopolies Commission, *British Insulated Callender's Cables Ltd. and Pyrotenax Ltd.*, H.M.S.O. (1967), H.C.P. 490

48. Monopolies Commission, *Thorn Electrical Industries Ltd. and Radio Rentals Ltd.*, H.M.S.O. (1968), H.C.P. 318
49. See Monopolies Commission, *Beecham Group Ltd., Boots Co. Ltd., and Glaxo Group Ltd.*, H.M.S.O. (1972), H.C.P. 341, para. 252
50. Monopolies Commission, *Guest, Keen & Nettlefolds Ltd. and Birfield Ltd.*, H.M.S.O. (1967), Cmnd. 3186
51. Monopolies Commission, *Unilever Ltd. and Allied Breweries Ltd.*, H.M.S.O. (1969), H.C.P. 297
52. Monopolies Commission, *British Match Corporation Ltd. and Wilkinson Sword Ltd.*, H.M.S.O. (1973), Cmnd. 5442
53. See Monopolies Commission, *Rank Organisation Ltd. and De La Rue Co. Ltd.*, H.M.S.O. (1969), H.C.P. 298
54. See Monopolies Commission, *Boots Co. Ltd. and House of Fraser Ltd.*, H.M.S.O. (1974), H.C.P. 174, para. 140
55. See Monopolies Commission, *Amalgamated Industrials Ltd. and Herbert Morris Ltd.*, H.M.S.O. (1976), H.C.P. 434, para. 127. The Commission was hardly comforted in the knowledge at the time that the affairs of Amalgamated Industrials' parent were being looked into by Department of Trade Inspectors!
56. *Ibid.*, paras. 133–4. In fact Amalgamated Industrials, ignoring the Commission's recommendation, disposed of its entire 38% shareholding to Babcock & Wilcox, whose own attempt to gain complete control of Morris, again in opposition to the incumbent management, was referred to the Commission. See *Financial Times* (22nd September 1976)
57. K. D. George, The Changing Structure of Competitive Industry, *Economic Journal*, Vol. LXXXII (1972), 367
58. M. Howe, Anti-Trust Policy: Rules or Discretionary Intervention?, *Moorgate and Wall Street* (Spring 1971), 68
59. A. Sutherland, The Management of Mergers Policy, in A. Cairncross, Ref. 1, p. 132
60. For a discussion of some apparent inconsistency in the Commission's analyses see J. F. Pickering, The Monopolies Commission and High Street Mergers, *Scottish Journal of Political Economy*, Vol. XVIII (1971), 69–82. Also for a critical analysis of some of the early merger Reports see C. K. Rowley, Mergers and Public Policy in Great Britain, *Journal of Law and Economics*, Vol. XI (1968), 75–132
61. Although in terms of the 1973 Fair Trading Act the Director General of Fair Trading has the power to initiate monopoly references to the Commission (subject to Ministerial veto), the power of reference on mergers lies entirely with the Minister (sec. 64).

62. See *Mergers: A Guide to Board of Trade Practice*, H.M.S.O. (1969), para. 4
63. C. K. Rowley, Ref. 60 (1968), 85–6
64. The 1969 merger was of course only between the fishing interests of the two firms. The land-based operations remain separate.
65. A particular case where this is said to have occurred was in respect of the Thorn/Radio Rentals merger sanctioned by the Commission in 1968, where the I.R.C. withheld action until the Commission had reported. See S. Young, Ref. 9, p. 108. There is no doubt, however, that the I.R.C. gave much less weight to considerations of domestic competition as opposed to international market performance than the Monopolies Commission: consider particularly the G.E.C.–English Electric merger's likely reception by the Commission. See M. E. Beesley and G. M. White, The I.R.C.: A Study of Choice in Public Management, *Public Administration*, Vol. LI (1973), 83
66. A. Sutherland, *The Monopolies Commission in Action*, C.U.P., Cambridge (1970), p. 10
67. *Monopolies and Mergers Act*, 1965 Sec. 7(10)
68. S. Young, Ref. 9, p. 87
69. G. Turner, Ref. 16, p. 83
70. S. Young, Ref. 9, p. 48
71. A. Sutherland, Ref. 59, p. 69
72. J. F. Pickering, Ref. 60, 75. As most writers would agree, some part of this apparent lack of depth of analysis may be due to the speed with which the Commission's Reports are prepared. They must be presented within six months (with a possible extension of a further three) of the reference being made; though in practice the period for the first 15 references varied from 13 to 22 weeks. See G. Howe, Government Policy on Mergers, *Trade and Industry* (1st November 1973), 234
73. One major factor which frustrates this exercise is the absence of follow-up studies in respect of changes in market structure brought about by Government intervention. So far as explicit costs are concerned figures have been quoted which put the annual cost of the Monopolies Commission itself at about £170,000. This, of course, covers the work of the Commission on dominant-firm enquiries as well as merger references. For the firms themselves involved in dominant-firm investigations the direct money costs are said to have varied between £60,000 and £320,000. For shorter merger enquiries these costs might well be somewhat less. See M. A. Crew and C. K. Rowley, Anti-Trust Policy: The Application of Rules, *Moorgate and Wall Street* (Autumn 1971), 45

74. There was a period, for example, between November 1972 and October 1973 when, of six mergers actually referred to the Commission, five were subsequently abandoned by the parties concerned in the light of the reference. See G. Howe, Ref. 72, 232. In addition some proposed mergers have been abandoned following Government discussion of the matter but prior to a formal reference to the Commission. These include Imperial Tobacco and Smiths Crisps, and Chloride and Oldam. See J. F. Pickering, *Industrial Structure and Market Conduct*, Martin Robertson, London (1973), p. 147
75. G. Turner, Ref. 16, p. 73

Index